Variable Annuities

Variable Annuities
A Global Perspective

Edited by Tigran Kalberer and Kannoo Ravindran

Riskbooks

Published by Risk Books, a Division of Incisive Financial Publishing Ltd

Haymarket House
28–29 Haymarket
London SW1Y 4RX
Tel: + 44 (0)20 7484 9700
Fax: + 44 (0)20 7484 9797
E-mail: books@incisivemedia.com
Sites: www.riskbooks.com
      www.incisivemedia.com

© 2009 Incisive Media

ISBN 978-1-906348-21-2

British Library Cataloguing in Publication Data
A catalogue record for this book is available from the British Library

Publisher: Nick Carver
Managing Editor: Jennifer Gibb
Designer: Lisa Ling

Copy-edited and typeset by T&T Productions Ltd, London

Printed and bound in the UK by PrintonDemand-Worldwide

Dedicated to the Memory of Hubert Mueller
(November 22, 1960–November 18, 2009)

It is our sad duty to note to the readers of this book that our good friend and colleague, Hubert Mueller (author of Chapter 2, *North American Variable Annuities*), died unexpectedly just prior to publication of this book. Hubert was a principal of Towers Perrin and was a consummate professional.

The editors of this book knew Hubert as a very energetic, friendly and deeply committed individual and he was a pleasure to work with. He was a recognised actuarial thought leader in Germany and the US, a tireless supporter of the advancement and development of the variable annuities industry and practice. We will most certainly miss him, his ongoing participations, honest opinion and valuable contributions.

Contents

List of Figures

List of Tables

About the Editors

Tigran Kalberer pioneered the application of market-consistent valuation and risk-based capital techniques in life insurance during the past 20 years. He has applied risk management and, notably, asset-liability management techniques for life insurance companies in a wide variety of situations. He has supported several companies in developing VA products, ensuring that the policyholder behaviour risks, volatility risks and basis risks are well under control. Tigran is a partner in the actuarial practice of KPMG.

Kannoo Ravindran pioneered the use of derivatives to manage market risks embedded in variable annuities at a time when writers of such risks used only traditional reinsurance or retrocession or took on the risks naked. Since then, Ravi has been working on all aspects of variable annuity risk management (including managing such risks on a total account value exceeding US$100 billion) and product development. He chairs the Equity Based Insurance Guarantee Conference Series held annually by the Society of Actuaries. Ravi is also a visiting professor at Háskólinn í Reykjavík.

About the Authors

Darin Arita is an analyst for Deutsche Bank Securities Inc, equity research in New York.

Jay Blumenstein received a Bachelor's degree in mathematics from Brown University in 1994 and a PhD in mathematics from Columbia University in 1999. He then joined the derivatives research group at JP Morgan, where he spent six years as an equity derivatives desk quantitative analyst. He joined Swiss Re in 2005 and, with Vinay Kalro, built an in-house grid computing solution for the pricing, hedging and risk management of variable annuities to help launch their multi-billion-dollar reinsurance effort in that space.

Tze Ping Chng is senior manager of actuarial services at Ernst & Young. Based in Hong Kong, he has spoken at various events on the topic of variable annuities.

Naveed Choudri is a marketer on the Equity Derivatives desk at Credit Suisse, covering insurance companies. Prior to joining Credit Suisse, Naveed worked in various positions at BNP Paribas, Goldman Sachs and KPMG. Naveed holds a BSc from the University of Birmingham and is a fellow of the Institute of Chartered Accountants in England and Wales.

Pin Chung is a vice president with Allianz Investment Management LLC in the firm's Minneapolis office. Since joining Allianz Investment Management in May 2008, Pin has been the leader of the Asset-Liability Management (ALM) and Strategic Asset Allocation (SAA) team, which provides ALM/SAA services for the North American Life and P&C insurance subsidiaries of Allianz, SE. Pin has more than 10 years of experience in a variety of areas including asset liability management, hedging, financial modelling and investment management for a variety of life and annuity products. He is an Associate of the Society of Actuaries (ASA) and a member of American Academy of Actuaries (MAAA). He is also certified as a financial risk manager (FRM) by the Global Association of Risk Managers (GARP). Pin earned a BSc in mathematics from Tung-Hai University in Taichung, Taiwan, and a Master's degree in mathematics and a second Master's degree in actuarial science and statistics, both from the University of Iowa. He obtained his PhD in economics from Iowa State University. Pin has written several articles about financial time-series econometrics which have appeared in *Quarterly Review of Economics and Finance* and *Applied Economics*. He has also written two instructors' manuals.

Rajeev Dutt has 20 years' experience implementing risk management strategies for a range of financial institutions and currently helps lead a team responsible for the development of retirement savings products and guarantees for North American 401(k)-type plans. Rajeev currently manages a large financial risk management programme at Milliman with account value in excess of US$50 billion. He has a wealth of experience with large-scale, multinational, risk management enterprise installations. Rajeev is a Fellow of the Society of Actuaries and the Canadian Institute of Actuaries, and has the Chartered Enterprise Risk Analyst designation. He is a regular speaker at industry events and has chaired a past SOA Enterprise Risk Management task force.

Stefan Engeländer works for KPMG as senior manager in the Center of Competence Insurance and in the actuarial department of the German practice. Within that role he is responsible for actuarial issues of national and international accounting and supervision of insurance companies. Before joining KPMG in 2000, he worked for 13 years at several life insurers in the reporting area, as well as working as a Responsible Actuary. He is the German representative in the IAA International Actuarial Standards Subcommittee and a member of the IAA Actuarial Standard Drafting Group. Within the DAV, he is member of the International Accounting Committee, the International Committee and the Professionalism Committee. He is a lecturer on international accounting and US-GAAP and German life insurance law at the German Actuarial Academy. Stefan has published various articles and given lectures on the above-mentioned topics.

Kirk Evans has 20 years' experience working in various aspects of the life insurance industry. Over the last 10 years he has focused on the variable annuity business from product development and pricing to hedging variable annuity guarantees. He is a Fellow of the Society of Actuaries (FSA), CFA Institute's CFA Charter holder, and a Member of the American Academy of Actuaries (MAAA). Kirk is currently a vice president at Samsung Life Insurance Company.

Mark Evans is vice president and actuary at AEGON USA Investment Management, Inc. He has 30 years of actuarial experience at the FSA level. He currently works in the derivatives department, where his primary responsibilities are hedging equity index annuities and minimum guarantees in variable annuities. Previously, he worked in life and annuity product development, which included developing equity index annuities. Mark has extensive experience with the development of actuarial-related software, including that used for stochastic and historical modelling of equity and interest derivatives, as well as hedging software. He has written papers and articles appearing in actuarial publications and is a frequent speaker at SOA meetings. Mark has a BSc from the University of Nebraska-Lincoln. He majored in mathematics with a minor in actuarial science.

Sam Gutterman has provided actuarial advice to and analysis of the life and health and property and casualty insurance industries and government agencies for more than 35 years, primarily in the area of financial reporting, in the Chicago office of Pricewaterhouse-Coopers. Sam has been actively involved in the actuarial profession, including service as a former president of the Society of Actuaries. Sam has been active in international accounting and auditing discussions relating to insurance for the past dozen years. As chair of the International Actuarial Association (IAA)'s Committee on Insurance Accounting, he serves as the IAA representative on the International Accounting Standards Board's Insurance Working Group and on the Consultative Advisory Group to the International Auditing and Assurance Standards Board.

Daniel Heyer is vice president of quantitative risk management at Nationwide Financial. He received his Bachelor's degree in mechanical engineering from The Ohio State University in 1991, his Master's degree in statistics from Rochester Institute of Technology in 1993 and his Certificate in quantitative finance in 2005. He is a Fellow of the Casualty Actuarial Society and has been recognised by the society for his innovative research in both reserve valuation and reinsurance decision-making. Daniel's professional career includes appointments as controls engineer, statistician, P&C actuary and credit derivative analyst. Daniel joined Nationwide Financial Services in 2002 and is responsible for hedging financial guarantees embedded in variable annuity and other insurance contracts.

Vinay Kalro received a Bachelor's degree in aerospace engineering from the Indian Institute of Technology, Kanpur in 1991 and a PhD in aerospace engineering with a focus on high performance computing from the University of Minnesota in 1996. He spent several years at Citigroup Alternative Investments managing fixed income strategies prior to being employed at Swiss Re. There, together with Jay Blumenstein, he designed and built a scalable analysis and hedging platform for the Variable Annuity Reinsurance programme.

Michael L. Kaster is an independent consultant, with experience covering such roles such as chief actuary, as well as in product development, valuation, financial reporting and corporate finance. Michael has over 25 years of experience working for life insurance organisations in the US as both a consultant and a part of the internal management. He has extensive experience in both actuarial/financial analysis and product development for life, annuity and health products. He has spoken on various topics including IUL, securitisation, EV reporting and product development, and is a Member of the American Academy of Actuaries (MAAA) and a Fellow of Society of Actuaries (FSA). Michael has a MBA in marketing and finance from the University of Illinois Chicago, and a BA in maths and economics from Wabash College.

Mun Kurup is currently regional head of products for ING Asia Pacific and is based in Hong Kong. His responsibilities include providing leadership and support for developing products including variable annuity products for ING business units in the region. He has a strong background in product development and risk management with work experience in the US, Canada, the UK and Asia. His recent accomplishments include the launch of ING's "de-risked" and first variable annuity product in Australia in October 2009. Before joining ING, he lead the pricing and development process for rolling out first of its kind variable annuity products in three markets in Asia for Manulife Financial. Mun has a postgraduate diploma in actuarial science from Heriot-Watt University, Edinburgh and an MBA from the University of Edinburgh.

Yves Lehmann joined Société Générale (SG) in 1995. In his career with SG, he first developed structured products in Japan, then started the Lyxor alternative investment platform, the bank's alternative risk transfer (ART) programme and the ALM advisory practice. Since 2004, Yves has been focusing on variable annuity schemes. Before joining Société Générale, Yves worked with France Telecom and EGIS, a specialised consultancy. Yves is a graduate from École Polytechnique and Telecom ParisTech.

Warren Manners is the head of actuarial and market risk management in the retirement and investment solutions division at ING Australia. He earned a Bachelor's degree in mathematics and a Master's degree in economics from Albany University in New York and a Master's degree in actuarial science from Georgia State University. Warren attained his Fellowship in the Society of Actuaries in 2001, and became a Chartered Financial Analyst in 2005.

James Masserio is a managing director of Credit Suisse within the Investment Banking division, based in New York. James is co-head of the US Equity Derivatives Trading desk. He joined Credit Suisse First Boston in 2000 and has been a trader in equity derivatives throughout his career with the bank. James holds a degree in finance from the Wharton School of the University of Pennsylvania.

Hubert Mueller was a senior consultant with the Risk & Financial Services consulting practice of Towers Perrin, having joined the practice in 1986. He was a member of the firm's Global Enterprise Risk Management Team and managed the firm's quarterly CFO Survey. His consulting experience included developing and implementing a framework for economic capital, assisting companies with the implementation of principles-based regulation for capital and reserves, actuarial valuations with particular focus on embedded/appraisal values and the implementation of economic value added as a performance measurement system, the design, implementation and review of ALM, capital management and ERM strategies and providing assistance in developing and implementing strategies for the risk management of guarantees on equity-based products (including reinsurance and hedging). Hubert was a Fellow of the Society of Actuaries, a Chartered Enterprise Risk Analyst and a member of the American Academy of Actuaries' Life Capital Adequacy Subcommittee and its Annuity Capital Working Group. He was also a qualified German Actuary (Aktuar DAV). He was a frequent speaker at industry seminars in the US, Europe and Asia, and co-authored several articles on insurance topics in US and European trade publications. Born and educated in Germany, Hubert received an MS in mathematics and economics from the Albert Einstein University at Ulm, Germany, and an MS in probability and statistics from Syracuse University.

Marianne Purushotham is a consultant in the Hartford practice of Watson Wyatt Insurance and Financial Services. Prior to joining Watson Wyatt, Marianne worked for LIMRA International, where she was responsible for the individual life insurance research programme as well as industry-level experience studies focusing on lapse and policyholder behaviour for life, disability and long-term care insurance products. With over 15 years' experience in the financial services industry, Marianne's previous responsibilities have included pricing of fixed and variable annuity products as well as financial reporting and valuation for both the individual life and annuity product lines. Marianne holds a Master's degree in applied mathematics from Virginia Polytechnic Institute, is a Fellow of the Society of Actuaries and a Member of the American Academy of Actuaries.

Scott Robinson is a senior vice president in the Life Insurance Group at Moody's Investors Service. He is a frequent speaker at life insurance industry events and has written extensively about variable annuities. At Moody's, his primary focus is coverage of a portfolio of life insurance companies. Prior to joining Moody's in 1999, Scott worked in the Investment Policy and Strategy Group of the Trust Company of the West. Previously he had been with AXA Financial. He holds a degree in economics from Duke University and a Master's degree in actuarial science from Georgia State University.

Jorg Sauren leads the market risk team within corporate insurance risk at ING, with a focus on economic capital modelling, Solvency II, market-consistent pricing and valuation and hedging of guarantees embedded in insurance products. He has experience with financial derivatives products in various asset classes such as equity, fixed income, foreign exchange and credit, as well as in model validation and risk management methodologies. Jorg has been in various risk management roles at ING since 1997 and has worked in Amsterdam, London, Hong Kong and Singapore.

Adam Stolz is an actuary who has worked at AXA since 2003. He was head of new product risks in the Group Risk Management department until early 2009, when he moved to a new product development role with AXA's US subsidiary. He has extensive experience in developing and managing variable annuities and other guaranteed products from a global insurance perspective. Adam qualified as an actuary in Australia, where he grew up and spent his first working years as an actuarial consultant with Trowbridge Deloitte.

Edward K. Tom is the head of equity derivatives strategy at Credit Suisse, where he is responsible for the development of derivatives research and strategies for hedge funds and major financial institutions. Prior to joining Credit Suisse in 2001, he worked in the quantitative research, derivatives structuring and portfolio trading groups at JP Morgan, Salomon Brothers and Donaldson, Lufkin & Jenrette. Edward has a BS in management information systems, a BS in accountancy and a MA in mathematical economics from New York University.

Michael Winkler is head of life and financial solutions life/health at New Re. He is based in Switzerland.

Matthew Wion is a senior actuarial advisor at Ernst & Young LLP in New York. He began his career at Prudential Insurance Company, and since 1999 he has been a consultant with the Insurance and Actuarial Advisory Services practice at Ernst & Young, where he has contributed to a variety of risk- and investment-related projects and leads the life insurance hedging practice area. Matthew has spoken at industry forums on topics including asset modelling, asset liability management and variable annuity risk management.

Joe (Zhenwei) Zhao works for Deutsche Bank. Previously he was a quantitative strategist at Swiss Re. He has a PhD in mechanical and aerospace engineering from Princeton University.

Lukas Ziewer leads the finance and risk management practice of Oliver Wyman's European Insurance division. He advises senior executives of major global and regional insurance groups, regulators and industry associations in a wide range of topics, including the design of hedging operations for financial guarantees in life insurance. A main area of his work is managing the dependencies between strategy and the choice of operational set-up for companies offering variable annuities in Europe. Lukas is based in Dublin and manages the firm's relationships in the insurance sector of the Republic of Ireland, in particular the International Financial Services Centre (IFSC). He is a member of the Society of Actuaries in Ireland, the German Actuarial Association (DAV) and the CFA Institute.

The editors support United Nations Children's Fund, an agency of the United Nations responsible for programmes to aid education and the health of children and mothers in developing countries.

The editors and authors of this book have kindly donated all royalties from the sale of this book to Unicef.

http://www.unicef.org/

Preface

Variable annuities (VAs) are life-insurance products with investment guarantees. Basically, they combine the advantages of traditional life-insurance products (long-term savings with a high degree of security and guaranteed benefits) with the advantages of unit-linked products (upside potential). Thus, from a policyholder standpoint, with VAs, it is possible finally to purchase an investment product that

- has rich and transparent benefits,
- is segregated from the other assets of an insurance company and hence is protected in the event of an insurance company going bankrupt,
- is linked to actively managed funds, as a consequence making it easier to "invest in" mutual funds,
- has personal tax benefits, and
- is sheltered from the policyholder's creditors.

While this may sound very attractive from a consumer standpoint, the drawback is that it is by no means easy to produce prudently risk managed VAs, since producing VAs generates high risks for the insurance company. These risks, unfortunately, can only be managed with a highly disciplined approach, since they are typically exposed to equity market risk, interest-rate risk, currency risk, mortality risk and policyholder behaviour risk.

THE NEED FOR VARIABLE ANNUITIES

The modern life-insurance industry has been successfully offering a tremendous variety of life-insurance products for several hundred years. Some of these life-insurance products (eg, with-profits endowments and annuity products) are aimed at providing investment possibilities.

These products typically provide substantial investment guarantees, which is one of their main advantages, along with tax privileges and prudently managed assets.

There are some clear disadvantages, which may be relevant to some, but not all, customers, and the forces of competition led to the development of new products which addressed these disadvantages. Examples of these disadvantages are the opaqueness of the investment process, a lack of customer control over the investment process, insufficient profit sharing of returns above the investment guarantee and the opaqueness of this profit-sharing mechanism.

Over time it became apparent that there is an additional disadvantage from a company perspective, which is the substantial required risk capital these products generate due to the guarantees they provide.

VA products first appeared in the US after the initial launch in the late 1950s of the Teachers' Insurance and Annuities Association College Retirement Equities Fund. Changes in regulations during subsequent years helped with the boom of the VA product sales, which started increasing exponentially as soon as death benefits were embedded in VAs during the early 1990s. Since the introduction of the death benefits, the VA markets in the US have seen a huge proliferation of riders. As a consequence of the US success, in light of some of the concerns with traditional products in Europe and Asia, many of the multinational insurers started introducing the VA feature philosophy to their respective local markets.

In Europe and Asia, the problems associated with the traditional insurance and investment products were addressed by the so-called unit-linked products, which did not provide investment guarantees.

Unit-linked products invested the savings part of the policyholder's premiums transparently in investment vehicles (which could be either internally or externally managed funds) and let the policyholder participate fully in the investment returns of these funds.

While these products clearly address the issues mentioned above, they typically do not provide any investment guarantees.

The obvious solution was to build investment guarantees into unit-linked products, which is basically what variable annuities did. This development was further fuelled by the fact that the multinational insurers who were already offering VAs in the US were now interested in repeating their success in the Asian and European markets.

VAs combined the advantages of traditional life-insurance products with long-term investment guarantees, while providing the advantages of unit-linked products (transparency of the investment and full upside participation). This of course came with a price, which must be borne by the policyholder. As a consequence, the company has to manage the substantial risks generated by such products using the premium generated from the sale of these guarantees.

Following on the heels of the tremendous success in the US and Asia, in the past few years VAs have also been offered in the European markets (including Switzerland, where such products have generated a lot of interest due to the weaknesses of the traditional life products).

VAs allowed the insurance industry to offer products that cannot be found elsewhere, and this helped the industry to defend or enlarge their market share against competing providers from the financial services industry, notably banks.

The challenges the industry is facing, however, are new and there is much to learn about the substantial risk management requirements these products create; this book aims to address these challenges.

Variable Annuities

While the use of the term "variable annuity" is understood in the US (where these products were invented), this term sometimes tends to cause confusion in other parts of the world. VAs are sometimes also known as unit-linked product with investment guarantees, segregated funds, equity linked guarantees, etc, outside the US. VAs allow the allocation of premiums into a range of investment options, which usually contain stocks, bonds, money market instruments or some combination of the three that in many cases include mutual funds.

The benefits to the policyholder will then depend on the performance of this investment option. Typically, the benefit for a defined event (eg, death, maturity) is the higher of the value of the policyholder investment and the guaranteed amount. This implies that the policyholder is protected against the insured event (eg, death) and poor investment performance.

Of course the insurance companies will charge a premium (fee) for issuing these guarantees, as well as for administering the contract (and paying its sales channel).

There are four major types of VA-guarantees:

(i) **Guaranteed Minimum Death Benefits (GMDBs)**, the proto-typical VA product. These products offer a guarantee in case of death. The death benefit will be the asset value of the contract or, if higher, the guarantee, which typically is the invested amount, sometimes rolled up with a notional interest rate.

(ii) **Guaranteed Minimum Accumulation Benefits (GMABs)**, which offer a similar guarantee at maturity.

(iii) **Guaranteed Minimum Income Benefits (GMIBs)**, which offer a guaranteed annuity income.

(iv) **Guaranteed Minimum Withdrawal Benefits (GMWBs)**, which allow the policyholder to withdraw a certain amount of assets at certain dates and to receive minimum payments.

THE NEED FOR THE BOOK

Given the current state of the global VA market and onerousness of the guarantees associated with these products, it is not surprising to see the attention that writers of these risks have been receiving from regulators, shareholders, rating agencies and analysts. Although there have been numerous conferences, courses and articles on various aspects of the VA business globally, there is no single source of reference to which any practitioner can go pertaining to these products. Since the quantification and management of risks underlying these products span disciplines ranging from financial economics to actuarial science and information technology, as well as computer science to mathematics (pure, applied, combinatorics, probability, optimisation, statistics, etc), any good reference book on this topic would need to cover all the various aspects of the VA business. To ensure that the material we have put together was done so in a quality fashion, we approached leading experts around the globe for contributions. As a consequence, within the book we have an "industry driven initiative" to educate and increase the knowledge of all practitioners in this area so as to give relevant stakeholders of the business (including regulators, rating agencies and analysts) the comfort that VA related risks, if properly understood, quantified and managed, can be both a great product for the policyholder and a profitable product for the insurance company.

When we first embarked on this project in late 2008, we had the vision of creating a book in which all topics associated with VA would be covered. However, due to the practicality of trying to get this book to print in a timely fashion, we had to make the executive decision to omit certain topics. Despite this, it was our intent to ensure that the book in its current form does contain the core ideas that any practitioner can easily use for their day-to-day needs. In addition, it is also our intent to include specialised topics in the future editions, so that this book can be a "living document", paralleling the development of initiatives in this area. In the spirit of trying to make future editions of this book better, we do welcome readers contacting either of us at kravindran@annuitysystems.com or tigran@kalberer.com with suggestions on new topics to cover or even contributions in future editions.

THE STRUCTURE OF THIS BOOK

This book looks at VAs from different angles and tries to give the big picture. Since a large number of different topics are covered, different subject matter experts provide their views on these topics, which are summarised accordingly in the introductions to the respective sections.

In Section 1, we give an introduction to the history and development of the VA market, concentrating on the following three main economic areas:

- North America, where these products were invented and hence have a long history,

- Australasia, where these products have been tremendously successful in recent years, and

- Europe, where these products have been introduced only within the past decade and have met keen interest.

Section 2 describes how companies address the issue of identifying and quantifying VA risks. We give an overview of the risks associated with VAs, describe the popular approaches for determining the value of VA contracts and their guarantees and discuss the different models used to value these guarantees. We also focus on the important subject of quantifying actuarial and policyholder behavioural risks in VA guarantees.

Risks associated with VAs are typically not eliminated but rather are transformed into other risks (which insurance companies are better at managing).

VA guarantees can be estimated by making reference to observed market prices of financial instruments that have similar characteristics to the VA guarantees. This estimation, however, may end up not being accurate enough.

Section 3 presents insights into how these risks can be managed. There are three popular ways of managing the remaining capital market risks for VAs: reinsurance, acquiring cover from the capital markets and dynamic hedging; typically, these approaches are applied together.

After giving an overview over typical risk management strategies for VAs, the important role of product management in managing VA risks is described. The three prototypical risk mitigation strategies are then described in more detail.

As VAs are life-insurance products with a considerable duration, the risks must be monitored and reported continuously over a potentially long period of time. In Section 4 we explain how this task is typically performed. We describe not only how the risks are measured, monitored and reported, but also how the effectiveness of a hedging strategy can be measured and which issues are related to running a hedging programme. We also try to answer the question of whether hedging really works.

The production of VAs does not happen in a vacuum; companies must account for VAs in their balance sheet and profit and loss accounts and they are supervised. Section 5 focuses on issues related to these topics.

Section 6 discusses quantifying and managing basis risks. It also addresses the numerical challenges of a dynamic-hedging programme. In addition, perspectives from a financial analyst and a rating agency are also given. This section concludes with a discussion on the impact of a major financial crisis (such as that in 2008–9) on the risk management of VAs.

October 2009

Section 1

Variable-Annuity Products

Introduction

Kannoo Ravindran

Annuity Systems Inc and Háskólinn í Reykjavík

The first variable annuity (VA) contract was issued by the Teachers Insurance and Annuities Association–College Retirement Equity Fund in 1952 (Poterba 1997). For about 40 years following this issue, the growth of the VA market was gradual. Since the early 1990s, however, there has been an exponential growth of the market in terms of market size and complexity of the VA products.[1] It was also during this time that death benefit guarantees[2] were first offered to policyholders in the form of a return of premium for the purposes of estate planning. These death benefit guarantees quickly grew in complexity and severity over the years; features of the death benefits now include at least one of the following.[3]

- **Roll-ups.**[4] This feature rolls-up the deposit at some pre-specified annual roll-up rate. The roll-up rates tend to be as low as 0% (which is trivially the same as the return of principal guarantee) and as high as 7%. Assuming that r refers to a simple annual roll-up rate and the policyholder makes a deposit of $AV_{15/7/2008}$ on July 15, 2008, Table 1 illustrates how the death guarantee due to the roll-up feature is computed for the first few years.[5]

- **Ratchets.**[6] This feature allows the death benefit to be ratcheted up at certain times. Although the frequency of ratcheting ranges from once a day to once every five years, this is typically done once a year on policy anniversary dates. Assuming that the policyholder makes a deposit of $AV_{15/7/2008}$ on July 15, 2008, on an annually ratcheted policy, Table 2 illustrates how the ratcheting feature is computed for the first few years.[7]

- **Resets.**[8] This feature allows the death benefit to be reset at certain times of the year. Although the frequency of resetting ranges from once a year to once every five years, this is typically done once every five years (on policy anniversary dates).

Table 1 Computation of death guarantee due to the roll-up feature

Dates	Roll-up values
15/7/2008–14/7/2009	$AV_{15/7/2008}$
15/7/2009–14/7/2010	$AV_{15/7/2008} \times (1 + r)$
15/7/2010–14/7/2011	$AV_{15/7/2008} \times (1 + r)^2$
15/7/2011–14/7/2012	$AV_{15/7/2008} \times (1 + r)^3$

Table 2 Computation of death guarantee due to the ratcheting feature

Dates	Ratchet values
15/7/2008–14/7/2009	$AV_{15/7/2008}$
15/7/2009–14/7/2010	$\max(AV_{15/7/2008}, AV_{15/7/2009})$
15/7/2010–14/7/2011	$\max(AV_{15/7/2008}, AV_{15/7/2009}, AV_{15/7/2010})$
15/7/2011–14/7/2012	$\max(AV_{15/7/2008}, AV_{15/7/2009}, AV_{15/7/2010}, AV_{15/7/2011})$

Table 3 Computation of death guarantee due to the resetting feature

Dates	Reset values
15/7/2008–14/7/2009	$AV_{15/7/2008}$
15/7/2009–14/7/2010	$\max(AV_{15/7/2008}, AV_{15/7/2009})$
15/7/2010–14/7/2011	$\max(AV_{15/7/2008}, AV_{15/7/2010})$
15/7/2011–14/7/2012	$\max(AV_{15/7/2008}, AV_{15/7/2011})$

Assuming that the policyholder makes a deposit of $AV_{15/7/2008}$ on July 15, 2008, on an annually resetting policy, Table 3 illustrates how the death guarantee due to the resetting feature is computed for the first few years.[9]

- **Bonus.**[10] This feature pays an upfront bonus so that the account value (ie, deposit) at the time of deposit automatically gets credited with a certain percentage. Although this can range from 0% to 7%, typically this tends to be either 3% or 5%.

The above-mentioned death benefit guarantees are typically offered in a manner whereby policyholders can add-on these guarantees as riders to a base death benefit (which only contains the return of the premium feature) by paying an extra premium for the rider(s) chosen.

In the late 1990s, insurance companies introduced the concept of Guaranteed Minimum Income Benefits (GMIBs) to the VA marketplace as a living benefit rider. By purchasing this rider,[11] the policyholder is allowed to convert the account value after a certain period of time (typically any time after the tenth policy anniversary) to an annuity using conversion rates[12] that were pre-specified at the inception of the contract.

In 2000, a few years after the introduction of the GMIB, another living benefit, called the Guaranteed Minimum Accumulation Benefit (GMAB), was introduced to the market as a rider. Unlike the GMDB and GMIB riders, this rider has the concept of a maturity benefit embedded within it. Thus, on the rider maturity date (which is typically the seventh policy anniversary date), the policyholder is guaranteed to get back at the minimum all the deposits.[13] Assuming that the policyholder makes a deposit of $AV_{15/7/2008}$ on July 15, 2008, in purchasing the GMAB rider that matures on the seventh policy anniversary date (ie, July 15, 2015), the policyholder would receive an amount of $\max(AV_{15/7/2008}, AV_{15/7/2015})$. [14]

In 2003, another living benefit, called the Guaranteed Withdrawal Benefit (GMWB), was issued by insurance companies. The purchaser of this rider was allowed to withdraw up to a pre-specified annual amount (also called the guaranteed withdrawal base amount).[15] In practice, this percentage ranged from 3% to 7%. Furthermore, the policyholder could only withdraw this amount as long as the guaranteed withdrawal base amount was not exhausted (ie, did not vanish to zero).[16] Assuming that a policyholder makes a deposit of $AV_{15/7/2008}$ on July 15, 2008, on a GMWB rider with a 5% maximum allowable annual withdrawal rate when the guaranteed withdrawal base is only ratcheted once every third policy anniversary date, the scenarios given in Table 4 illustrate the mechanics underlying this product.

Given the backdrop of the VA market development in US, it is also interesting to note that, during this period, multinational insurers started to export these concepts to other parts of the world (eg, UK, Germany, France, Japan, Korea). Some of the reasons for the successful adaptation of these products into the local markets with local flavours are

- lack of transparency in the investment products that were being sold to the policyholders (eg, the bonus payment schedule associated with profits products),

Table 4 GMWB computations

Dates	Guaranteed withdrawal base*	Maximum allowable annual withdrawal amount**	Amount withdrawn***
15/7/2008–31/12/2008	$G_0 = AV_{15/7/2008}$	$A_0 = 0.05 G_0$	$W_0 = A_0$
1/1/2009–31/12/2009	$G_1 = G_0 - W_0$	$A_1 = \max(0.05 G_1, A_0) = A_0$	$W_1 = 0$
1/1/2010–31/12/2010	$G_2 = G_1 - W_1$	$A_2 = \max(0.05 G_2, A_1) = A_0$	$W_2 = 0.25 A_0$
1/1/2011–31/12/2011	$G_3 = \max(AV_{15/7/2011}, G_2 - W_2)^{\dagger}$	$A_3 = \max(0.05 G_3, A_2) = \max(0.05 G_3, A_0)$	$W_3 = A_3$
1/1/2012–31/12/2012	$G_4 = G_3 - W_3^{\ddagger}$	$A_4 = \max(0.05 G_4, A_3) = A_3$	$W_4 = 0.5 A_4$

*Each item in this column is computed at the commencement of the time period and applied for the period. For example, the first entry in this column is computed on July 15, 2008 and applied over July 15, 2008 – July 31, 2008. **This column highlights the maximum allowable amount that the policyholder can withdraw. More precisely, while the first entry in this column corresponds to the maximum allowable withdrawal amount computed on July 15, 2008 for the time period July 15, 2008 – December 31, 2008, the second entry refers to the amount computed on December 31, 2008 corresponding to the time period January 1, 2009 – December 31, 2009, the third entry refers to the amount computed on December 31, 2009, corresponding to the time period January 1, 2010 – December 31, 2010, etc. In practice the policyholder is not obliged to withdraw any fraction of this amount. Furthermore, the policyholder is also allowed to exceed the annual maximum amount, which in turn would "penalise" the policyholder when calculating the guaranteed minimum base. ***This column describes the total amount actually withdrawn during the time period given by the left-most column (since the withdrawal does not have to be done in single transaction). Furthermore, we have assumed that the amount actually withdrawn does not exceed the allowable withdrawal amount for that period given by the column on the left. †This is due to the ratchet that takes place on the third policy anniversary (ie, July 15, 2011). Furthermore, it is important to note that $AV_{15/7/2011}$ has been appropriately reduced due to the units of the fund that were redeemed to pay for the rider fees. ‡This contract ceases to exist the moment this amount reduces to 0. As mentioned in note 16, later variations of the contract came with a lifetime withdrawal benefit (ie, even if this number reduced to zero, the numbers in the column to the right would be continued to be computed and the policyholder would be allowed to continue to withdraw a maximum annual amount that was equal to this computed amount).

- bankruptcy of insurance companies resulting in policyholders losing their investments,

- transparency underlying the VA products and the segregation of the investment assets from the general account of the insurance companies,

- changes in tax and pension regulations introduced in the marketplace for consumers,

- low interest rates and a volatile equity market environment,

- changes in insurance regulations in regards to product filing (eg, "Freedom of Service" in the European Economic Area).

Many of these are discussed in greater depth in subsequent chapters.

SUMMARY OF SECTION 1

This section comprises four chapters, starting with a history of the development of the global VA market by Michael Kaster and Marianne Purushotham (Chapter 1). The section then continues with Hubert Mueller's discussion (Chapter 2) on the US VA market as it pertains to the product, risk management and regulatory landscape. Michael Winkler contributes the next chapter of this section (Chapter 3), in which he discusses the Asia-Pacific VA market. Yves Lehmann and Lukas Ziewer (Chapter 4) conclude this section with an analysis of the European VA market.

1 The reasons behind this exponential growth have ranged from changes in tax regulations to ageing population to consumer sophistication to aggressive pricing to availability of reinsurance covers.

2 Also known as Guaranteed Minimum Death Benefits (GMDBs).

3 If more than one feature is included in the death benefit, the payout to the policyholder's beneficiary becomes the highest (maximum) of all the values obtained from each individual feature that is embedded in the contract.

4 The rolling-up of the death benefit is stopped once the policyholder reaches a certain age (which is usually anywhere past 80 and tends to deviate across companies).

5 In this example, the roll-up values are set on the inception of contract (July 15, 2008) and on each policy anniversary date thereafter (eg, July 15, 2009, July 15, 2010, July 15, 2011, etc). Furthermore, as can be seen from Table 1, these roll-up values remain unchanged during periods between the roll-ups (eg, July 15, 2008 to July 14, 2009, July 15, 2009 to July 14, 2010, etc).

6 Like the roll-up benefits, these also stop once the policyholder reaches a certain age.

7 In this example, the ratcheted values are set at only the contract-inception (July 15, 2008) and policy-anniversary dates (July 15, 2009; July 15, 2010; July 15, 2011, etc). Furthermore, as can be seen from Table 2, the ratcheted values remain unchanged for the entire policy year once they have been set.

8 Like the roll-up and ratchet benefits, these also stop once the policyholder reaches a certain age (which deviates across companies).

9 In this example, the reset values are set only at contract-inception (July 15, 2008) and policy-anniversary dates (July 15, 2009; July 15, 2010; July 15, 2011; etc). Furthermore, as can be seen from Table 3, the reset values remain unchanged for the entire policy year once they have been set.

10 For paying this bonus, the surrender charge period (for example) tends to be more prolonged or the product charges could be higher. Furthermore, this bonus affects the death benefit guarantees since they are linked to the bonused deposit.

11 Unlike those for a death benefit rider, where the premium paid was a function of the underlying account value, fees for this rider are calculated using the benefit base (which, for example, is based on a 5% annual roll-up rate and an annual ratchet) as opposed to the account value.

12 An example of this conversion rate would be the use of a 2.5% interest rate and an Annuity 2000 mortality table with a five-year setback.

13 In certain riders, these guarantees may include roll-ups and ratchets.

14 On the maturity date, should the account value ($AV_{15/7/2015}$) be less than the initial deposit ($AV_{15/7/2008}$), the account value is automatically topped up with units of funds in a manner such that the value topped up is equal to $AV_{15/7/2008} - AV_{15/7/2015}$.

15 This amount is typically a function of the roll-ups and ratchets. Furthermore, the maximum annual withdrawal amount gets computed on December 31 of each year and applies to the following calendar year. Additionally, in the first year of deposit, this amount is typically the percentage of the deposit.

16 This was relaxed for later generations of the GMWB design, in that shortly after 2003 insurance companies started offering lifetime withdrawal benefits (ie, the ability to keep withdrawing until the policyholder dies).

REFERENCES

Poterba, J., 1997, "The History of Annuities in the US", Working Paper 6001, National Bureau of Economic Research.

1

History and Development of the Variable-Annuity Market

Marianne Purushotham; Michael L. Kaster

Watson Wyatt; Kaster Actuarial Resources, LLC

How do we know where we are going if we do not know where we have been? If we do not study the past, we are doomed to repeat our mistakes. With that thought in mind, this section focuses on the history of variable annuities (VAs).

We first provide some general background on the structure of the VA contract and key factors that have contributed to the growth in VA sales over the past few decades. Next, we review the history of the product and its introduction in the US as well as details regarding the evolution of the product's design over time. We also discuss the increased popularity of the VA on a global scale. Finally, we outline some of the product's significant risk management issues and recent events that have significantly impacted on the VA market.

BACKGROUND

At a basic level, an annuity is an insurance contract that provides for regular payments for a specified period of time. These payments can be made for a certain period (eg, 10, 20 or 30 years) or for the annuitant's lifetime. The annuity contract usually provides for both an accumulation and an income-payment phase, so the policy has both a savings component and an insurance component. Having said that, there are "immediate" annuities available that offer only the income phase.

With a variable immediate annuity, the contract holder purchases the policy with a single premium, which is then allocated among a selection of funds underlying the contract. In addition to this, an assumed rate of return on the selected funds of eg, 0%, 3.5% or 5% is chosen by the policyholder. Based on this assumed interest rate, an

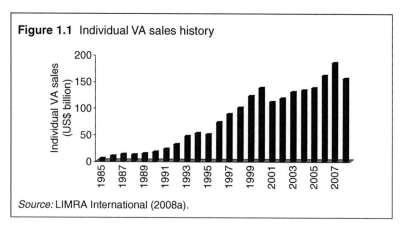

Figure 1.1 Individual VA sales history

Source: LIMRA International (2008a).

initial monthly payment to the policyholder is determined. In each subsequent month, the payment is determined as follows.

- If the actual return is equal to the assumed return at the start of payment, then the payment level for the second month equals the payment made in the first month.
- If the actual return is less than the assumed return, then the payment level for the second month is reduced (for the second month and for all future assumed payment months) based on the difference in the associated policy "account" balance.
- If the actual return is greater than the assumed return, then the payment level for the second month is increased (for the second month and for all future assumed payment months) based on the difference in the associated policy "account" balance.

VAs began to gain popularity in the late 1970s, but sales have grown most significantly over the past decade (Figure 1.1) (mostly in the deferred annuity arena). Immediate annuities sales were approximately US$8 billion in 2008 (excluding structured settlements) and represented less than 5% of total individual annuities sales, whereas variable immediate annuities sales during the same period of time were approximately US$100 million.

With a variable deferred annuity, US buyers typically purchase the contract with a single premium deposit at issue and then select the funds into which the deposit (net of charges) will be allocated. In the 1980s, it was common for VAs to offer only a handful of investment options (eg, a stock fund, bond fund, fixed account or stable value fund). As the popularity of VAs grew, insurers began

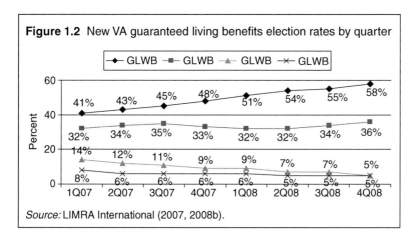

Figure 1.2 New VA guaranteed living benefits election rates by quarter

Source: LIMRA International (2007, 2008b).

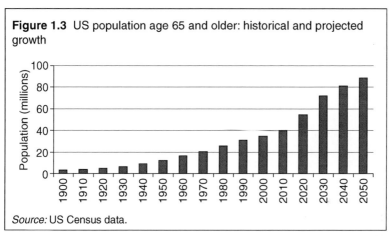

Figure 1.3 US population age 65 and older: historical and projected growth

Source: US Census data.

adding a variety of funds to their VA product line-up. As a result, it is quite common to see current VA products with 70 or more different investment options, including diversified funds like international and emerging markets, energy, target date and "green" funds. In addition to increased investment options, a strong catalyst for VA growth in recent years has been the introduction of stronger VA savings and income guarantees (eg, guaranteed living benefits). The real advantage of such guarantees to the customer became more apparent during the economic downturns in 2000–2 and 2008–9. Today, election rates for these benefits continue to be high (Figure 1.2).

Almost 80% of individual VAs sold in 2007 had one or more guaranteed living benefit elections.

From the time the first VA contract was introduced in 1952 through to the mid 1980s, sales grew slowly, mostly due to strong regulatory restrictions governing the sale of separate account-based products in many states. However, beginning in 1982, with the passage of the Tax Equity and Fiscal Responsibility Act, the Deficit Reduction Act and the Tax Reform Act of 1986, VAs began to be viewed as viable long-term retirement and savings instruments with strong tax advantages. From a tax perspective, annuities now had the following key features that were not available with other investment products:

- tax deferability of investment earnings until the commencement of withdrawals;

- favourable tax treatment of annuity income payments through the determination of an exclusion ratio to allow for a portion of each payment to be considered return of principal and a portion to be considered return of taxable investment earnings;

- tax-free transfer of funds between VA investment options;

- protection of VA assets from the insurance company's creditors in the event of an insurer bankruptcy.

In addition to tax law changes that provided new impetus for investment in VA contracts, the low-interest environment of the 1970s, followed by equity market growth starting in the late 1980s, provided additional consumer and producer incentives to look to VAs as an attractive retirement-planning tool. Today, with the ageing of the baby-boomer generation, the primary market for this product is projected to continue growing over the next 40 to 50 years (Figure 1.3).

US VA HISTORY

In the early part of the 20th Century, insurance companies and pension programmes viewed the fixed deferred annuity as a vehicle to help accumulate assets during working years, so as to provide income during retirement. However, over time, it became evident that earning a conservative, low-risk, long-term rate resulted in the need for larger principal payments in order to offset the declining purchasing power of these savings due to inflation. During the early

1950s, it was recognised that the single largest flaw of any retirement plan was the inability to create a fixed-income retirement programme that was protected from the adverse affects of inflation. By adding an element of equity return to the retirement vehicle, assets accumulated in a VA could be somewhat insulated from the effects of inflation.

In 1952, Teachers Insurance and Annuities Association (TIAA) created the College Retirement Equities Fund (TIAA-CREF). This special fund was established to provide VA coverage within the retirement income programme of TIAA. While it was not an individual annuity contract, the development of this first VA concept by TIAA-CREF paved the way for future variable contracts.

Until 1952, regulatory restrictions had prohibited pension funds from investing in contracts that were based on stock returns. However, as more pension programmes sought solutions to mitigate the risk that an individual's retirement income would not keep pace with cost-of-living increases, regulators began to loosen these restrictions. In 1956, the first VA programme was approved for use in a Canadian pension plan. However, the concept did not take off as quickly in Canada as it did in the US. Although no VA contracts were offered by the life-insurance industry at this time, the environment began to change in the US in 1959, when the US Supreme Court ruled that VAs came under the jurisdiction of the Securities Act of 1933. With this ruling, VAs were placed under the dual regulatory authority of the individual state insurance departments and the Securities and Exchange Commission (SEC), and state regulators began to modify their laws to allow for individual annuity contracts on a variable basis.

During the 1960s, as the regulatory environment for VAs became more clearly defined, the insurance industry began to consider VAs as a potential means to obtaining a larger market share of the retirement savings dollars being invested. However, insurance organisations had a long-standing aversion to customer savings programmes that had little or no "insurance" element and, in the case of the early VA contracts, there was no concept of guarantees or insurance. Additionally, insurance companies had always viewed their primary role as providing a safe and secure alternative for customers' premiums and considerations. VAs, and the potential for loss of principal, were a clear divergence from this philosophy.

In 1957, during a hearing in Massachusetts regarding the appropriateness of the insurance industry participating in business with segregated funds, Metropolitan Life, arguing against, made the following statement:

> The public, over the years, has come to look upon life insurance contracts as being safe and certain. When they buy shares in mutual funds, or when they buy stock through a broker, they know that they are taking some risk. But when they buy a life insurance contract they feel that no risk is involved. That reputation… is thoroughly justified…. You just cannot change the nature of common stocks. They are bound to go down as well as up, and when they go down some people are bound to be hurt. It is then that the great reputation of the life insurance business will suffer.
>
> (Campbell 1969, p. 16)

With the dynamics of recent market changes, and the change in consumer attitude towards the insurance industry, it is interesting that a statement made over 50 years ago is so "on point". Despite the industry's long-standing aversion to risk, insurance companies today are well suited to offer consumers access to equity growth through VA products. Over time, these contracts, while continuing to evolve, have been subject to stronger regulatory oversight; more importantly, insurance companies continue to explore sophisticated risk management strategies to help manage the risks inherent in these products.

VARIABLE-ANNUITY PRODUCT DESIGN EVOLUTION

The base VA contract provides the policy holder with a tax-favoured retirement savings vehicle that allows for investment choice and optional protection from the impact of market downturns. A VA typically includes some combination of the following structure of charges.

- Upfront sales charge: typically expressed as a percentage of the purchase premium.

- Surrender charge: typically expressed as a percentage of the account value at the time of contract surrender. These "back-end" charges decline over time and run from three to seven years, depending on the form of annuity purchased.

- Mortality and expense charge: typically expressed as a percentage of assets under management and deducted from the fund value on a daily basis.

- Individual fund expense charges: also expressed as a percentage of assets under management.

- Administrative charges: typically a flat (US dollar) amount deducted from the account value monthly.

During the 1990s, VA writers began offering additional contract benefits in the form of guaranteed minimum death benefits (GMDBs) to help VA policyholders with estate planning concerns. The early GMDBs provided for a death benefit equal to the greater of the premium paid into the contract or the current account value at the time of the policyholder's death. Over time, this benefit was enhanced to provide for an increasing minimum death benefit equal to the maximum of the "guaranteed amount" and the current account value, where the "guaranteed amount" was reset every few years to equal the greater of the previous guaranteed amount and the then current account value. For example, a contract might provide that, on each fifth contract anniversary, the guaranteed amount would be reset. This design was called the "five-year ratchet" structure. So if the policy experienced strong fund performance, the GMDB could increase significantly over time.

The next generation of VA product enhancements expanded on the concept of guarantees with the development of various "living benefit guarantees" including the following.

- **Guaranteed Minimum Income Benefit (GMIB).** This optional benefit provides a guaranteed minimum level of income for the policyholder regardless of fund performance. A typical GMIB would provide for an account value "roll-up rate" (6% was not uncommon before 2009) along with a relatively conservative guaranteed purchase-rate basis (eg, 3% interest and a specified mortality table). When the policyholder is ready to annuitise and begin drawing income from the contract, they have the option to determine the income-payment level based on the account value determined under the application of the 6% roll-up rate each year or the actual account value based on underlying fund performance. If the policyholder elects to apply the account value determined using the roll-up rate, then the income payments are determined using the more conservative guaranteed purchase rates. Otherwise, the policyholder can withdraw the actual account value and shop for more favourable purchase rates to determine income payments. There is no option to withdraw the account value determined using the roll-up rate and there is typically a waiting period before commencing income payments.

- **Guaranteed Minimum Accumulation Benefit (GMAB).** This optional benefit offers the policyholder an account value guarantee regardless of fund performance. Typically, these riders provide that at the end of a specified period (typically 7–10 years) after the purchase of the benefit, the account value will be no less than the total premiums made during the first year of the contract even if the actual investment performance has been poor. These riders also typically offer a step-up option at the fifth contract anniversary that allows the policyholder to lock-in a guarantee of the fifth-year-contract-anniversary value.

- **Guaranteed Minimum Withdrawal Benefit (GMWB).** This optional benefit offers the policyholder a guaranteed minimum monthly withdrawal amount regardless of actual account value at the time the policyholder elects to begin making withdrawals from the contract. The guaranteed minimum withdrawal amount is equal to a stated percentage of the policy's "guaranteed amount". Similar to the original guaranteed income benefits, the guaranteed amount is equal to the greater of the actual account value and the account value determined using the contract's annual roll-up rate (commonly 6–7% prior to 2009) applied over the roll-up period (eg, 10 years). The cost of these guarantees varies with the contract holder's age at time of first withdrawal, whether the GMWB applies to a single life or joint lives and the length of the minimum withdrawal guarantee (lifetime is the most common).

VARIABLE-ANNUITY MARKET GROWTH AROUND THE GLOBE

As mentioned earlier, the VA market in the US has undergone a period of significant growth over the past five years, due in large part to the development of strong living benefit guarantees that allow policyholders to participate in equity market growth with significant downside protection. Following on the heels of this success, both multinational companies and domestic companies overseas have begun to take a closer look at these products. Today, VAs are sold in Asia (Japan, Taiwan, Singapore, Hong Kong, South Korea) and Europe.

In Japan, annual VA sales reached US$40 billion during 2004 and 2005 and, prior to the economic crisis of 2008–9, product sales were expected to reach or exceed levels seen in the US. In contrast to the US, VAs experienced very low lapse rates in Japan and therefore net flows (defined as new money coming into VA products exclusive of roll-overs of existing policies from one company to another) were already very close to US levels.

The success of VA products in Japan stemmed from several sources:

- deregulation of banks in 2002, which opened the way for VA sales through banks and stockbrokers;
- the expiration of the government's unlimited guarantees on bank savings deposits;
- the fact that Japan has a generally older population (the average issue age for VAs in Japan is 65);
- the prolonged low-interest-rate environment;
- the conservative nature of Japanese investors, resulting in a significant interest in guarantees;
- the higher savings rates experienced in Japan compared with the US and other wealthy countries.

The development of the Japanese market followed a path similar to the US market in that guaranteed death benefits emerged first, followed by guaranteed minimum income benefits and guaranteed minimum accumulation benefits, and finally guaranteed minimum withdrawals benefits. Typical product charges included a 4–5% premium charge as well as asset charges (including mortality and expense as well as fees for the guarantee) in the range of 300 basis points.

The top sellers of VAs in Japan were affiliates of foreign companies including MetLife, ING, AIG and Hartford Life. These companies entered the market with bank and stockbroker distribution channels that they developed from the ground up. Japanese domestic insurers attempted to sell through their existing structures and found themselves dealing with channel conflict as well as less product experience and lower compensation. Further discussion on the Asian VA market is given in Chapter 3.

VAs have also made inroads to Europe over the past few years. Like the Japanese market, customers tend to be more conservative and the age 50+ population continues to increase. Generally, VAs offer lower roll-up rates (2–3% is common) and, while guarantees cost approximately 50–100bp, they can be significantly greater for riskier fund offerings.

However, there can be significant differences in market by country and carriers have found that they often need to customise their product and distribution approaches for these different markets. For example, in the UK, changes to pension regulation over the past few years have increased the need for flexibility in investment choice within VA products offered. The European VA market is discussed in greater depth in Chapter 4.

VA RISK MANAGEMENT

Risk management is an important consideration for companies heavily marketing VA products. Although the base VA policy shifts the risk of poor investment performance to the policyholder, the complex living benefit guarantees that have been developed over the past decade have increased the insurer's risk considerably. As a result, the risks that arise from policyholder options to lapse, shifting their underlying asset mix or locking in guaranteed living benefits are now the focus of insurer risk management programmes.

The primary areas of risk management for today's VAs include some combination of the following:

- product design;
- reinsurance;
- hedging strategies.

From a product-design perspective, in 2009, with the crisis in the financial markets and the ensuing volatility, the VA marketplace has undergone a "de-risking" process, whereby more liberal VA designs have been pulled from the shelf and replaced by contracts with more conservative provisions.

Another risk management strategy has been to use professional reinsurers to diversify VA risks. In 1999, over 85% of the top 25 VA writers in the US used reinsurance as a form of risk management. Today, in terms of traditional reinsurance programmes, although several reinsurers had offered coverage for VA guarantees, the financial crisis of 2008–9 precipitated a significant withdrawal of those services and/or increased costs of coverage.

In terms of hedging strategies, most large VA writers maintain some form of hedging programme. Some more complex hedging programmes involve the execution of trades on a daily basis, while others simply perform hedging through the purchase of over-the-counter instruments that offset the risk profile to the insurer. These and other hedging strategies will be discussed in more depth in Sections 4 and 5.

REFERENCES

Campbell, P. A., 1969, *The Variable Annuity: Its Development, Its Environment, and Its Future* (Hartford, CT: Connecticut General Life Insurance Company).

LIMRA International, 2007, "Variable Annuity Guaranteed Living Benefit Election Tracking, Fourth Quarter 2007", Report, URL: http://www.limra.com.

LIMRA International, 2008a, "Individual Annuity Sales Survey", URL: http://www.limra.com.

LIMRA International, 2008b, "Variable Annuity Guaranteed Living Benefit Election Tracking, Fourth Quarter 2008", Report, URL: http://www.limra.com.

2

North American Variable Annuities

Hubert Mueller

Towers Perrin

In the last chapter, we discussed the history and the development of the global variable annuity (VA) market. In this section, we will continue our discussion on the VA market in North America. In particular, we look at market size, distribution channels, product trends, key VA providers, drivers of demand, risk management and regulatory developments and the outlook for these products in North America.

SIZE OF THE MARKET

VAs have been sold in North America since the initial launching of the product in 1952 by TIAA-CREF. They generally lagged the sales of fixed annuities (FAs) until the mid 1990s, when the equity market boom drove up VA sales significantly. By 2000, annual VA sales had reached a peak of US$138 billion, more than twice the level of FA sales, as shown in Figure 2.1 and Table 2.1.

The stock market decline during 2000–2 led to a drop in the annual VA sales by about 20%, until the introduction of Guaranteed Minimum Withdrawal Benefits (GMWBs) in late 2002, and the recovery of the equity markets in 2003–7 led to a dramatic increase in VA sales, to a peak of US$186 billion in 2007. Most recently, the financial turbulence of 2008 caused VA sales to drop by 17% to US$155 billion in 2008, back to about the level of 2006 sales. For 2009, VA sales were expected to drop further to approximately US$130 billion, while FA sales were expected to make up for the shortfall, by increasing to about US$130 billion. In the fourth quarter of 2008, for the first time since the mid 1990s, FA sales were at the level of VA sales in North America.

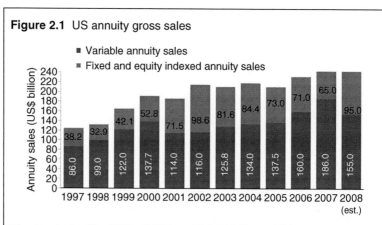

Figure 2.1 US annuity gross sales

- Variable annuity sales
- Fixed and equity indexed annuity sales

VA sales declined by 17% in 2008 from US$186 billion to US$155 billion.
Source: Variable sales data from Towers Perrin VALUE Survey includes all non-pension VA premiums (first-year and renewal, separate account and fixed account). Fixed sales from LIMRA data includes deferred and immediate annuities, equity-indexed annuities and market value adjusted annuities (excludes structured settlements) and Towers Perrin estimates.

Table 2.1 US annuity gross sales

| | Compound annual growth rate (%) | | |
	1995–2000	2000–7	1995–2007
VA	23	4	11
FA	1	3	2
Total	14	3	8

VA ASSETS

As of September 30, 2008, total VA assets under management were approximately US$1.3 trillion, down almost 13% from US$1.49 trillion on September 30, 2007 (Figure 2.2). This number dropped another 24% to US$1.12 trillion at the year-end of 2008. Of the total assets under management reported as of September 30, 2008, 76% were held in a separate account as compared to 82% on September 30, 2007.

This shift towards the more conservative fixed account assets with guarantees reflects the drop in the equity markets, as well as the general policyholder sentiment of moving to guarantees, and "safer" funds, when equity markets are more volatile.

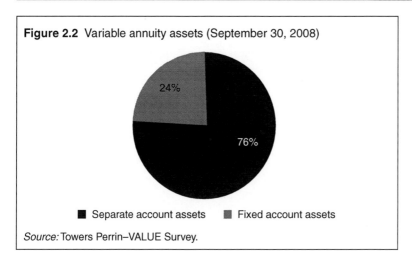

Figure 2.2 Variable annuity assets (September 30, 2008)

24%

76%

■ Separate account assets   ▨ Fixed account assets

Source: Towers Perrin–VALUE Survey.

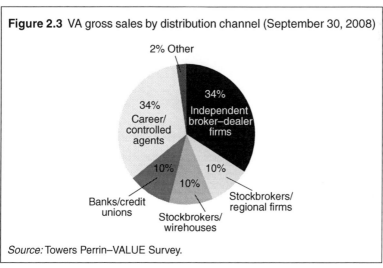

Figure 2.3 VA gross sales by distribution channel (September 30, 2008)

2% Other

34%
Independent
broker–dealer
firms

34%
Career/
controlled
agents

10%   10%

10%

Banks/credit
unions

Stockbrokers/
wirehouses

Stockbrokers/
regional firms

Source: Towers Perrin–VALUE Survey.

DISTRIBUTION CHANNELS

VA distribution channels in North America include the following.

- **Career/controlled agents** (includes Branch Managerial, General Agents and Controlled 403(b)). Historically focused on life-insurance sales, this category includes producers who primarily and exclusively sell for one company. Included in this category is the TIAA-CREF sales force, which sells mainly into the 403(b) market.

- **Financial advisors.** Included in this category are channels like

  - wirehouses (for example, Merrill Lynch, Wachovia Securities, Citi Smith Barney),
  - regional brokerage firms (for example, A. G. Edwards, E. D. Jones),
  - independent broker–dealer firms (for example, Linsco Private Ledger).

  Financial advisors, often referred to as stockbrokers, have historically focused on the sale of investment-oriented products such as stocks, bonds and mutual funds. The distinction between the three channels is very much a function of the geographical focus of the firm and the nature of the relationship between the selling firm and the individual advisor.

- **Banks/credit unions** (for example, JP Morgan, Wells Fargo). This category includes sales made through commercial banks and credit unions, using one of their sales channels, which would typically take the form of either a platform or investment brokers.

- **Direct response** (includes fee-only and fee-based financial planners). This category includes business sold direct to consumers via the telephone or Internet or in a branch office.

Among the four distribution categories, the independent broker–dealer firms and career agents[1] dominated channels for VA sales, with each capturing 34% of the market during the first nine months of 2008 (see Figure 2.3). During the same period of time, banks, wirehouses and regional brokerage firms each captured 10% of the market.

PRODUCT VARIATIONS

VAs are offered in both tax-qualified and non-qualified versions. In 2008, 68% of total VA premiums were tax-qualified, which was up from 63% in 2007. The reason for this is due to contributions into roll-over individual retirement arrangements and 403(b) plans.

The following list summarises the definitions and the product types that are currently offered in the US marketplace.

- **A-Share.** Annuities with front-end loads.

- **B-Share.**[2] Annuities with traditional back-end loads (surrender charge period is typically 7–8 years or longer).

- **C-Share.** Annuities with no back-end loads (no surrender charges).

- **L-Share.**[3] Annuities with a short surrender charge period of three or four years.

- **Bonus.** Annuities that credit a bonus (typically 3–5% of premium) to the policyholder's account value at contract issue. Presence of the bonus may come with a lengthened surrender charge period, higher product charges, a lower gross dealer concession, reduced profit margins or some combination thereof.

- **VIAs.**[4] Variable immediate (payout) annuities.

Guarantees play a big role in the success of VAs in North America as a vehicle for retirement security. They are offered as death benefits and living benefits. In contrast to Europe, guarantees are offered directly by the insurers, rather than by the underlying investment funds. Typical guarantees currently offered include the following.

- **GMDB.**[5] The Guaranteed Minimum Death Benefit is offered as a lump sum upon death. Typically, the payout to the policyholder is a function of the higher of premium paid and account value (eg, annual reset, highest anniversary value, roll-up value[6]). The typical charge level is 15–35bp.

- **GMIB.**[7] This Guaranteed Minimum Income Benefit is offered as a guaranteed income payment upon annuitisation. To determine the guaranteed account value to be annuitised, the initial premium minus withdrawals is accumulated at an annual rate of 5–6%, and then translated to an annual income amount. A waiting period of 5–10 years typically applies. The typical charge level is 50–75bp.

- **GMAB.**[8] This Guaranteed Minimum Accumulation Benefit is offered as a one time "top up" of account value at a specified time, eg, after 10 years. This guaranteed amount typically equals the initial premium or a roll-up thereof. The typical charge level is 25–60bp.

- **GMWB.**[9] This Guaranteed Minimum Withdrawal Benefit is offered as guaranteed amounts via optional annual withdrawals. Annual withdrawals are generally limited to 5% or 6% of the initial premium or a ratchet/roll-up amount and are typically offered for life. Higher guaranteed amounts are offered if the policyholder defers the initial withdrawal. Also, guaranteed amounts may increase upon attaining certain age thresholds. The typical charge level was 60–90bp (until 2008).

The financial market meltdown of 2008–9 resulted in a number of significant challenges for VA providers, including

- significant drop-off in VA sales, to an annual run-rate of approximately US$130 billion in 2009,
- write-downs in deferred acquisition cost, due to reduced profitability,
- lower levels of hedge effectiveness, and increased losses from hedge breakage,
- increased levels of required VA risk-based capital (C-3 Phase II) and asset adequacy reserves (AG 39) at year-end 2008.

In response, companies are currently implementing a number of product design changes:

- repricing their guarantees, charging higher fee levels and restricting certain aggressive product features or asset allocation options,
- introducing lower-cost fund options, like index funds,
- introducing simpler, low-cost products without significant guarantees.

As a result of the repricing, GMWB rider fees had increased to 90–150bp by mid-2009, with guaranteed fee levels in the 100–250bp range.

DRIVERS OF DEMAND

Despite the current financial crisis, the outlook for VA sales globally and in the US is still good, due to a variety of factors:

- a growing number of individuals are reaching retirement age in the US;

- there is a growing pool of retirement assets and roll-over assets;

- product charges are only rising modestly;

- only life insurers can offer lifetime guarantees; banks and mutual funds cannot provide such guarantees;

- a shift in the retirement savings responsibility from employers to employees.

Hence, VAs are expected to continue to be a key product for providing retirement income. In addition, US life insurers can leverage their product expertise internationally. Already, US-style VA products are offered in most major insurance markets in Asia and Europe, generally by multinationals (Figure 2.4).

Despite the current market volatility, there continues to be a significant interest in introducing VA-style products in many markets in Asia and Europe, so this global expansion of VA is likely to continue.

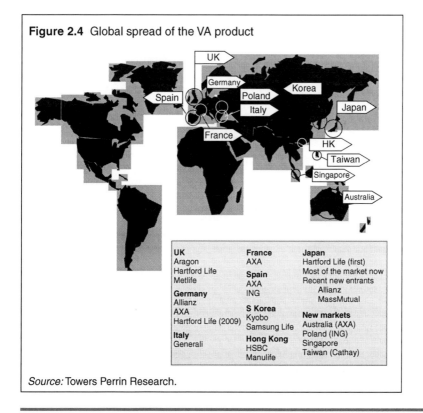

Figure 2.4 Global spread of the VA product

UK	France	Japan
Aragon	AXA	Hartford Life (first)
Hartford Life	**Spain**	Most of the market now
Metlife	AXA	Recent new entrants
Germany	ING	Allianz
Allianz		MassMutual
AXA	**S Korea**	
Hartford Life (2009)	Kyobo	**New markets**
	Samsung Life	Australia (AXA)
Italy		Poland (ING)
Generali	**Hong Kong**	Singapore
	HSBC	Taiwan (Cathay)
	Manulife	

Source: Towers Perrin Research.

RISK MANAGEMENT

As mentioned in Chapter 1, risk management for VAs generally consists of three pillars:

- product design/pricing;
- reinsurance;
- hedging.

In response to the financial crisis in autumn 2008, VA providers have been proactively de-risking their VA products, resulting in higher product charges and more restrictive guarantee designs.

Aside from product changes companies are now taking the following actions:

- increasing the number of risk factors analysed when evaluating the effectiveness of their hedging programmes,
- attempting to utilise external reinsurance (which is now, at the end of 2009, even less available than in the beginning of 2008),
- exploring the use of off-shore captives for reinsurance,
- improving their risk management practices, including the use of efficient modelling methods like replicating portfolios and representative scenarios,
- halting the sale of living benefits (temporarily or permanently),
- selling or running-off the VA business.

Given the lack of availability of reinsurance and other structured solutions in 2008–9, hedging remains the key risk-mitigation tool. Most large VA providers have implemented dynamic-hedging programmes in order to hedge delta (equity market), vega (volatility) and rho (interest rate) risks. As of October 2009, most companies only hedge the GMWB and GMAB risks, because of a disconnect between the economic risks and the accounting treatment under US Generally Accepted Accounting Principles (GAAP).

REGULATORY AND ACCOUNTING TRENDS

The introduction of principles-based regulation (PBR) in the US resulted in a new model for VA risk-based capital (RBC) called C-3 Phase II in 2005. Under this approach, RBC is based on the tail risk of the underlying business, using the greater of a real-world stochastic model and a deterministic scenario. Partial hedging credit is available if certain conditions are met. The rating agencies have picked up this approach and will determine rating agency capital for VAs using a similar methodology, with higher confidence levels applied for companies rated above BBB.

Similarly, a new reserve model (VA commissioners annuity reserve valuation method (CARVM)) will be introduced for VAs at year-end 2009, replacing the existing combination of base reserves plus additional reserves (AG 34, AG 39) for the various guarantees offered. It is expected that for most companies the new VACARVM reserve will be at or above current reserve levels.

The introduction of PBR has led some companies to implement captive reinsurance solutions, to reduce the volatility of statutory capital and reserves. In late 2008, the SEC published a proposed roadmap for the introduction of International Financial Reporting Standards (IFRS) in the US by 2014. This, in turn, could lead to a better alignment of economic and accounting risk.

OUTLOOK

The long-term outlook for VA products in North America is good, despite the upheaval in the financial markets. VA products should remain a key product for providing retirement income. The proliferation of VA guaranteed living benefits is expected to continue (although perhaps at a slightly less frantic pace), which will lead to further market consolidation in the near term. While short-term growth rates are likely to be slow, the growing US retirement population should drive up demand in the medium to long term. Thus, VAs are expected to continue their market success.

---

1 This also includes sales from TIAA-CREF, which accounts for a significant portion of the total share.

2 Along with the L-share, this is one of the two popular versions that are purchased by policyholders. In 2008, 38% of the new premiums were of this type.

3 Along with the B-share, this is one of the two popular versions that are purchased by policyholders. In 2008, 29% of the new premiums were of this type.

4 Less than 1% of the new premiums in 2008 were from VIAs. Almost all VAs were sold as single premium deferred annuities.

5 Guaranteed Minimum Death Benefits (GMDBs) have been available in VAs since 1990s.

6 This typically used to be based on an annual roll-up rate of 5%.

7   The proliferation of VA Guaranteed Living Benefits (GLBs) began in the late 1990s with the introduction of Guaranteed Minimum Income Benefits (GMIBs).

8   This followed in 2000 after the introduction of GMIBs in late 1990.

9   This was introduced in 2002.

3

Asia-Pacific Variable Annuities

Michael Winkler

New Re

Before we look into the development of variable annuity (VA) products in Asia-Pacific, we must first define the term "variable annuity". As in the US, the term should include accumulation and life cover products and not be restricted only to products with periodic "annuity" payments. The benefits are defined by reference to both the value of an investment in funds (as in a unit-linked or fund-linked product) and a guarantee.

As a differentiating factor from many unit-linked products, VAs are also assumed to have a guarantee charge (the total charges for the product are fixed at the start of the policy and will not change during its lifetime). The charges will explicitly cover the cost of the guarantees.

In many Asian markets, there have been unit-linked life contracts with implicit guarantees in case of death but without any explicit charge for those guarantees. These contracts showed up decades ago and could be seen as the very first VA products.

However, "true" VAs (including explicit charges for guarantees) have a much shorter history in Asia. The first products were launched in the late 1990s, following the development of similar products in the US. At first, they had rather limited success.

The success story for VAs in Asia began in Japan (Ino 2006) and was largely driven by bancassurance. In the second wave of deregulation in October 2002, banks and security houses were given permission to sell a restricted range of life-insurance products: annuities and nothing else. Until then, VA sales in Japan had not been very promising and it is possible that this led regulators to view them as a suitably niche product to control the impact of deregulation. If this was the intention, the results were far different from planned.

There were various factors contributing to the Japanese banc-assurance success story. Examples of these are given in the following list.

- Japanese people (in particular, older generations) are in the habit of saving considerable amounts of money for their old age or to pass on to the next generation.

- As conservative investors, many savers make extensive use of bank deposits for some or all of their capital. However, due to the low interest rates in Japan, there is almost no return left after charges. In spite of this, there are trillions of US dollars invested in Japanese bank deposits (of which only a very small percentage has been invested in variable annuities so far).

- Equity investments did not perform well in Japan during the past decades, so most savers are concerned about the risk of losing money. As a consequence, while savers are interested in investments with higher potential upside, they are also looking for a product with guarantees to help protect their principal. With a guarantee and exposure to upside potential, VAs appear to be a good fit for this need. Distribution through bancassurance provides a natural connection between the money held in bank deposits and the VA product.

- While in some cases banks may be protective of their deposits, VA sales provided some strong benefits in Japan. As well as saving solvency capital by removing deposits from their balance sheets, banks also earned some commission income in place of the small spread possible on deposits.

- Many banks also offered investment management for the underlying funds of the VA product. This brings two benefits for the banks: not only do they have new fund management income but the VA sales do not even reduce their assets under management.

Looking at all these factors, the success story for VAs in Japan now seems almost inevitable. So it proved. Sales rocketed from practically nothing in 2001 to a record high of over ¥4 trillion in 2005 (see Figure 3.1). This development was almost entirely driven by bancassurance; the contribution of agency forces and brokers remained at a very low level (around 1%).

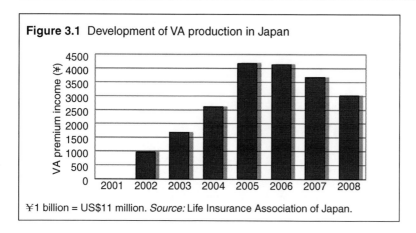

Figure 3.1 Development of VA production in Japan

¥1 billion = US$11 million. *Source:* Life Insurance Association of Japan.

In 2007, a new regulation for the sales process was introduced. This regulation required a customer to be led through a detailed questionnaire. The consequence of this was that each policy sale took longer and so new production dropped significantly. In the following year, the financial market crisis had a significant impact on production. It may be expected that market conditions made investment sales more difficult in general, but the VA market also suffered from some specific issues. In particular, bad news about some foreign companies raised doubts about the financial stability of their Japanese operations and discouraged clients from buying long-term investment products from them. In some cases, there was an even more direct effect on production, as providers withdrew VA products or ceased operations in Japan. Consistent with the current market conditions, new products are less attractive for customers than those that were available in the recent past. The effect of these product developments on sales is not yet known.

It is very difficult to obtain transparent statistics on VA-type products in South Korea. Statistics for several different variable products (VAs, variable universal life and variable whole life) are recorded under one heading. Thus, it is not easy to determine the amounts that have been invested into "true" VA products. However, it is clear that growth in the Korean life-insurance market since 2002 has been mainly driven by variable products. The main guarantees offered are Guaranteed Accumulation Benefits (GMABs) and Guaranteed Minimum Death Benefits (GMDBs), sometimes with additional benefits such as Guaranteed Minimum Withdrawal Benefits (GMWBs) or loyalty bonuses. In general, the guarantees offered are very onerous

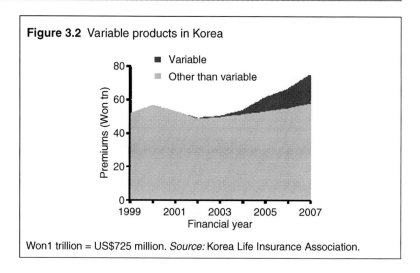

Figure 3.2 Variable products in Korea

Won1 trillion = US$725 million. *Source:* Korea Life Insurance Association.

after taking account of all the product features such as fund selection and policyholder options. As a consequence, the guarantees appear to be very difficult to manage effectively.

In other Asian markets (Hong Kong, Taiwan, Singapore, Malaysia), there were a few VA product launches from 2007 onwards. However, the VA market did not reach a significant share of the overall life business. In Hong Kong, the launch of one product with very rich guarantees was highly successful, attracting large volumes of business. While this product has now been withdrawn, its success has made the launch of less onerous but prudently designed products very difficult. In Taiwan, structured notes represent a significant share of the life-insurance market and may be seen to offer a more interesting upside than the "boring" (but much more transparent) investment of a VA. However, structured notes are under regulatory scrutiny in that there has been some mis-selling of structured notes and there are additional concerns about the counterparty risk of the issuers. With more scrutiny and controls on structured note sales, it seems likely that VA products may have a strong future in Taiwan.

Australia has significant volumes invested for retirement saving in "superannuation funds". During the first boom of GMDBs in the US, attaching similar guarantees to superannuation funds was discussed, but the idea did not really take off. In 2008, a true VA product was launched and the old discussions started again. As retirement funds have become more material for individuals, recent market falls have personalised investment risks for a large group of people. Attention is also turning to what can be done for people in the income phase, after the earlier focus on the savings phase. In this environment, there appears to be a strong case for VA guarantees which protect accumulated wealth or income. On the other hand, customers have to be prepared to pay the price for the guarantees. With charge levels being generally low, the answer to this question is not yet clear (even if interest rates are still relatively high in Australia and the guarantees are therefore cheaper than in many other places).

REGULATION
Japan

Japan has by far the most developed regulation in Asia for VAs. This is not surprising given the huge amounts invested in VA products and the underlying risks which could easily jeopardise the solvency of the issuing insurance company. Noticing the fast growth in the VA market, the Financial Services Agency (FSA) became concerned about the increasing industry exposure to the product guarantees. In 2004, the FSA published a new regulation which became effective in the fiscal year ending March 2006. It requires reserves for minimum guarantee risk and an additional solvency risk item (denoted by "R_7") for variable products with minimum guarantees.

Reserving requirement

While there are two methods for calculating reserves (the "standard method" and the "alternative method"), all companies essentially follow the standard method because companies have to demonstrate that the results from the alternative method can provide at least the same level of protection as the standard method.

Under the standard method, the reserve requirement is calculated as the present value of future loss from the guarantee (ie, paid benefit in excess of account value) minus the present value of future income related to the guarantee (ie, the portion of the mortality and expense (M&E) fee attributable to the guarantee). Future benefits are calculated using the Black–Scholes put-option formula. The alternative method is used if a straight formula is not applicable (eg, for more complex guarantees or policyholder options). In this case, future results are projected by using a Monte Carlo simulation with at least 1,000 scenarios.

The valuation assumptions are specified by the regulator. The expected return is assumed to be the same as the valuation interest rate (which is based on the historical average of the treasury yield) and the volatility assumption is specified for each asset class.

Capital requirement (risk-based capital)

Insurance companies have to hold at least 100%[1] of the risk capital which is calculated according to the following formula

$$\sqrt{(R_1 + R_8)^2 + (R_2 + R_3 + R_7)^2} + R_4$$

where R_7 is the term for minimum guarantee risk (R_1 is insurance risk, R_2 is interest rate risk, R_3 is assets risk, R_4 is operational risk and R_8 is the third-sector insurance risk). This component is required for insurance companies writing any minimum guarantees. The requirement is 2% of the guaranteed amount when the account value is 110% of the guaranteed amount or less and 0% when the account value is larger than 110% of the guaranteed amount.

In February 2008, the FSA published its plan to revise the solvency margin. Under the new regulation, R_7 is calculated as the increase in the reserve for minimum guarantee risk when the account value drops suddenly. The drop rate is determined by asset class in line with the factor of price fluctuation risk. For each asset class, expected return, volatility and correlation with other asset classes are also specified by the regulation.

Compared with the previous method, the 2008 regulation has aligned the value of R_7 more closely with the actual guarantee risk.

Allowance for risk management

The R_7 term for minimum guarantee risk can be reduced for hedging, provided that the hedging has been demonstrated to be effective. This approach is consistent with a hedge protecting the company against a change in conditions and an increase in its future liabilities. However, the reserve represents a "snapshot" of the current liability value for the minimum guarantee. For the reserve, therefore, the use of hedging does not affect the current liability of the company (though it may provide some asset value with which to meet the liability). So, using hedging does not allow the company to reduce the reserve requirement.

Before the market crisis in 2008–9, both the reserve and the solvency risk requirement could be reduced for risks transferred through reinsurance (co-insurance of the guarantees). Balancing this, insurance companies had to include a counterparty-risk component in the capital requirement equal to 1% of the ceded reserve if reinsurance is used. However, it did not take into account the actual financial health of the reinsurance company.

After the financial crisis, the regulators have raised concerns towards the counterparty risks of reinsurers of VA business. In June 2009 the FSA issued a new supervisory guideline which included the following recommendations.

- While an insurance company can obtain reserve credit on the ceded proportion, the insurance company has to demonstrate that the risks have been transferred. They also have to evaluate the chance of having the reinsurance claims paid.

- Insurance companies are responsible for ensuring the collected information about the financial conditions of the reinsurers is as detailed as possible.

- Counterparty risks of reinsurers must be considered when setting up scenarios for stress testing.

South Korea

The current Korean regulations relating to VAs focus on policyholder protection. The regulator (the Financial Supervisory Commission) even obliges companies to provide some form of guarantee (GMDB and GMAB) in order for a product to be classified as a "variable annuity". If a company offers a life annuity after the accumulation period, the annuity rate applied at maturity has to be set at the start of the original policy.

Apparently prompted by the financial market crisis, a new regulation will limit the acquisition expense loading and thus the corresponding surrender penalty in order to increase payments to policyholders in case of lapse. From a risk management perspective, this increases the sensitivity to policyholder behaviour significantly.

Hong Kong

Regulations in Hong Kong are principles based. The reserving requirements for VAs follow general "Guidance Note 7", which requires that there must be a provision for any investment guarantees at a 99% confidence level. To calculate the reserve under this requirement, insurance companies can use stochastic, deterministic or factor-based approaches. However, for the last two approaches, a stochastic adequacy test has to be performed at least once a year. If significant changes have occurred, the factors need to be revised based on stochastic analysis.

Any risk management strategies (use of derivatives or structured investments as well as reinsurance) must be reflected in the valuation.

Other countries, in particular those with a more rules-based regulatory approach, are still investigating how to establish adequate rules for VA business. A starting point is to analyse the corresponding regulations in more advanced regulatory frameworks (for VA at least) such as the ones in the US, Canada and Japan.

TYPICAL PRODUCTS

The first VA products in Japan allowed access to a wide variety of mutual funds, causing several challenges for effective risk management. Over the years, an informal market standard fund investment has been developed which is the basis for most products. The standard is a basket consisting of four components: Japanese equity (index tracker fund linked to Topix); foreign equity (linked to MSCI Kokusai), Japanese bonds (linked to Nomura BPI Composite) and foreign bonds (linked to Citigroup WGBI). Foreign investments may be yen hedged in order to reduce the hedging (or reinsurance) cost. Furthermore, the equity and foreign bond components tend to be smaller in times of high volatility.

As a reaction to the financial market crisis, some fund rebalancing concepts have been introduced in order to manage (a part of) the guarantee risks in the fund. There have been some products based on the "constant proportion of portfolio insurance" technique, where the part of the fund above the discounted value of the maturity guarantee after annual costs (the "bond floor") determines the equity investment. More recent products adjust the equity proportion depending on the current value of the fund compared to the original investment, which leads to a similar type of rebalancing. Some rebalancing concepts are quite opaque and leave a lot of discretion to the fund provider or insurance company.

The guarantee features normally combine a maturity benefit (expressed as a GMIB or GMAB) with a death benefit. In times of low interest rates, where it is not possible to support a lump sum guarantee of 100% of the single premium, the premium refund is spread out as an annuity certain over a period of up to 15 years. If the client wants a lump sum, they get the present value of the annuity certain which is less than 100% of the initial investment.

A very common feature in Japanese products is "target setting": at policy inception, the client chooses a target level they would like to achieve for their investment, eg, 120% of premium. As soon as the fund reaches this level, the policy is immediately transferred to the General Account and the fund investment is lapsed (a "knockout"). This feature has proved to be a very powerful marketing tool. Additionally, it also helps to control the lapse risk for out-of-the-money (OTM) guarantees, since the lapse is automatic as soon as a certain OTM level has been reached.

A similar control for lapse risk can be achieved by offering a "ratchet" feature. This feature will increase the guarantee, depending on fund performance. The increase may either partially or fully reflect the fund increase or operate in a series of steps when certain predefined levels (a "ladder") are reached.

In Korea, the main guarantees offered are GMAB and GMDB. The GMDB guarantee may apply in the case of both death and disability of more than 80% (first-grade disability). In most cases, single and regular premiums are accepted. There is a cap for the equity proportion, with a wide range of funds available. Fund choices are seen to include some from emerging markets, which are difficult to hedge. The charge for the guarantees is normally around 50bp and does not always depend on the riskiness of the fund mix. The policyholder can choose to switch between funds at any time, with some restrictions on the maximum equity proportion and possibly the switch frequency. In general, the guarantees provided are onerous compared with the charge level after considering the various product features (eg, fund choice, regular premiums). The products are apparently much more focused on customer attractiveness than the effectiveness of the risk management.

In Hong Kong, the first VA products launched immediately created a very competitive environment. They are all US dollar products with single premiums and no initial loading. The guarantees were "roll-up" guarantees that become difficult or impossible to support in a low-interest-rate environment. The most successful product made available a wide range of funds with full freedom to invest into exotic funds such as Greater China funds or other Asian emerging-market funds. Policyholders also had some freedom to choose even more specialist funds such as mining or emerging markets funds. While this product has been withdrawn from the market, its success has set strong expectations about what future products will look like.

1   Note that this is a minimum requirement. Companies operating in Japan generally maintain a capital and surplus ratio of at least 600%.

REFERENCES

Ino, R., 2006, "Variable Annuity Market in Japan. The Sun also Rises", Milliman *Perspective Magazine*, August, URL: http://www.milliman.com/perspective/.

4

European Variable Annuities

Lukas Ziewer; Yves Lehmann

Oliver Wyman; Société Générale/Catalyst Re

The recorded history of American-style variable annuities (VAs) as a strategic innovation in Europe began in 2006, when AXA launched its first "TwinStar" product in Germany and AEGON, Royal London and Lincoln started their respective VAs in the UK (which were then quickly followed by Hartford Life and MetLife with VA launches in the UK).

Before that, there had been isolated product launches that combined the benefits of unit-linked life-insurance and investment guarantees, in particular with Guaranteed Minimum Death Benefit (GMDBs) and Guaranteed Minimum Accumulation Benefits (GMABs) (such as Generali's "Investment Plan Plus" in Switzerland). However, such initiatives had limited visibility and were not positioned to shift the market.

The initial strategic innovative push in Europe was dominated by international insurance groups, who were able to import the capabilities, infrastructure and experience required to design and manage VAs from substantial businesses in North America. Furthermore, while companies in the UK stayed close to the product designs known in established VA markets, AXA departed significantly from known designs by trying to replicate to a great extent the features of the traditional domestic with-profits products in Germany, by offering regular premiums and deferral periods beyond 20 years.

During 2007, it was mainly AXA that pushed aggressively to expand its VAs business platform across Europe, with launches in Spain, Italy, France, Belgium and Portugal. More recently, Allianz (which has organised their European VA business in a separate new division "Allianz Global Life"), AEGON and ING all have started to enter additional markets more aggressively with a potential to catch up quickly with AXA in terms of covering of European markets.

Table 4.1 VAs in Europe

Market	Company	Product	Type
Belgium	Allianz	Invest4Life	GMWB
Belgium	ING	LifeLong Income	GMWB
Belgium	MetLife	CitiVA	GMWB
France	AEGON/ La Mondiale	Terre d'avenir	GMWB, DB
France	Allianz	Invest4Life	GMWB
France	AXA	Capital Ressource	GMWB
Germany	Allianz	Invest4Life	GMWB
Germany	AXA	Twinstar	GMIB
Germany	Canada Life	Garantie Investment Rente	GMWB
Germany	ERGO	Global Top Return	GMAB, IB
Germany	Friends Provident	FriendsPlanPrivate	GMAB
Germany	R+V	Premium-Rente Garant	GMWB
Germany	Swiss Life	Swiss Life Champion	GMAB
Hungary	ING	Europerspektiva	GMAB
Italy	Allianz	Invest4Life	GMWB
Italy	AXA	Accumulator	GMWB, AB
Italy	Generali	Risparmio	GMWB, AB
Luxembourg	Old Mutual	Beacon Navigator	GMIB, DB, WB

September 1, 2009, data, based on the author's independent research.
Sources: company websites; Société Générale Monitor; Milliman; business press.

At the other end of the spectrum, a few local insurers have created their own VA products. An example of this is in Germany, where the more regionally focused companies R+V, ERGO and Swiss Life have taken the initiative to launch VA products, when other large insurers decided to wait until the second half of 2008 for Allianz to take its typical market lead. Additionally, Canada Life, which has an existing product platform in Dublin, has added VAs to its existing product offering in Germany. Similarly, in most European markets a combination of pan-European groups and local insurers now offer a wide range of VA products. Within the past few years, VAs have become a widely spread and strategically positioned product line in Europe (see Table 4.1).

Table 4.1 VAs in Europe (*cont.*)

Market	Company	Product	Type
Netherlands	ING	RVS Guarantee Perspective	GMAB, DB
Netherlands	SNS Reaal	Principal Protection 3	GMAB
Poland	ING	Europerspectiva	GMAB, DB
Poland	MetLife	Citi VA Orchidea	GMWB
Portugal	AXA	Accumulator	GMAB
Spain	AXA	Accumulator Futuro	GMAB, DB, WB
Spain	ING	Generacion F unico	GMAB
Spain	MetLife	Citi VA (Avida)	GMWB
Switzerland	AXA	Twinstar	GMAB
Switzerland	Baloise	RentaSafe	GMWB
Switzerland	Generali	Investment PlanPlus	GMAB
Switzerland	Swiss Life	Champion	GMIB
UK	AEGON	5 for life	GMWB
UK	AIG	Living Time 75	GMWB, AB, DB
UK	Hartford	Platinum	GMWB, IB
UK	Hartford	SafetyNet	GMDB
UK	MetLife	Trustee Investment Plan	GMWB
UK	MetLife	MetLife Guaranteed Bond	GMWB
UK	Prudential	Pru Flexible Retirement	GMAB

September 1, 2009, data, based on the author's independent research. *Sources:* company websites; Société Générale Monitor; Milliman; business press.

VAs in Europe do not fill as much of a void as they did in North America or Japan, since in most European markets there is still significant supply of traditional participating businesses that offer their policyholders both long-term guarantees and the opportunity to participate in higher realised investment returns through profit participation. Also, many European markets are much more dominated by longer wealth-accumulation and dissaving contracts, rather than the short-term single-premium contracts typical in North America that support wealth management during the transition into retirement. In addition to this, distribution is typically through traditional channels (eg, financial advisors and tied agents), who are often sceptical about the VA proposition and require a combination of support, incentives and direction.

On the other hand, insurers have become sceptical of the economics associated with traditional with-profits businesses, and customers have become increasingly unhappy about the lack of transparency and choice associated with these products. Therefore, VAs appear to be a product class that meets the need of important customer segments and which can be profitably manufactured. This appears to be an important driver behind the particular activity, for instance, in Germany.

One of the success factors explaining the rapid growth of VAs in Europe has been the ability to write the product in a single legal entity and sell it in different European markets under the "Freedom of Service" rule of the European Economic Area (EEA), which excludes only Switzerland as a major insurance market in Europe. By invoking this rule, insurers can choose a jurisdiction that provides suitable regulation for VAs. This is particularly important as, in some European jurisdictions, insurers cannot legally write VAs. For instance, in Germany there are strict rules around reserve accounting and the admissibility of assets that do not allow for the investment guarantees of VAs, and recently proposed legislature that would have changed this situation failed in parliament. The jurisdiction where most VA writers are domiciled to do pan-European business is Ireland, where the International Financial Services Centre (IFSC) has offered an attractive environment for cross-border business since 1987, and where the large companies now have their VA businesses. Luxembourg, which is considered as having particularly attractive regulation, has attracted only a few companies so far, including Swiss Life. Finally, the Principality of Liechtenstein has some relevance as a jurisdiction that uniquely offers the ability to sell into both the EEA and Switzerland, which is what attracted Swiss insurer Baloise to establish their VA business there. Apart from these pan-European domiciles, some insurers write VAs domestically (eg, AXA in France sells VAs underwritten by the local entity and not AXA Life Europe in Dublin).

Apart from regulation, an important consideration in the selection of a domicile is the availability of the intellectual resources, expertise and experience, as well as the availability of services such as appointed actuaries, third-party administration and legal advice. Dublin, in particular, is seen as leading in these areas.

The majority of the leading international groups have built their business on in-house risk management capabilities, with the ambition to set up hedging operations that would be ultimately suitable for managing all the market risks to which the insurer is exposed through the options and guarantees embedded in the products sold. In contrast, smaller, regional groups typically tend to "outsource" the risk management by getting the support of a reinsurer or investment bank, and transacting into solutions that allow them to retain only limited market risk. However, this "outsourcing" is usually done with the intent of freeing up capacity during an initial build phase and subsequently developing the in-house capabilities.

SOME CLOUDS OVER THE HORIZON

Despite their initial commercial success, VAs are not without problems. Because the European VA market is still young, the impact has so far been more limited than in North America and Asia.

In 2007 and 2008, many VA writers blamed the market environment for the volatility in their financial statements, the need for extra capital and slippages in their hedging programmes. As a consequence, in early 2009 several insurers had to reassess their strategy (including exiting the market altogether).

The crisis highlighted some of the following issues.

- **For the insurer:** proper quantification of basis risks, volatility risks, lapse and switch risks (which are correlated to market risks) and operational/compliance costs linked to dynamic replication (Ziewer 2009a).

- **For the distributor and the policyholder:** poor investment returns and high cost of guarantees given the backdrop of low rates and high-volatility market environment.

- **For the regulator:** although most issuance is concentrated in three countries (Ireland, Luxembourg and Liechtenstein), the losses flow back to the parent companies, which are regulated in the rest of Europe. For instance, the Irish Financial Regulator has recently issued a discussion paper that indicates a tightening of the current regulatory practice, which is based on the responsibilities of the appointed actuary for an appropriate valuation and risk assessment (Irish Financial Regulator 2009).

What does the future hold for VAs? Most of the recent issuance has been in long-dated VAs, especially Guaranteed Lifetime Withdrawal Benefits, so the actual losses might not show up in the near future.

A CONTINENTAL VARIATION IN EUROPE: DYNAMIC VARIABLE ANNUITIES

In parallel to traditional VAs, similar products began to emerge in Europe as early as 2001. Like VAs, these involve unit-linked insurance contracts with individual guarantees, but with a caveat that these guarantees are a dynamic hybrid of protected investment funds and traditional with-profits funds.

Starting from Germany, this product was driven by two constraints:

- from the fiscal side, an incentive for offering regular-premium products that help to accumulate savings for retirement over a longer time;
- from the regulatory side, a cost-accounting approach to setting up technical provisions that does not allow insurers to assume and manage the risk of marked-to-market options.

The first generation of dynamic VAs (see Table 4.2) was initiated by Skandia Leben, ifa[1] and Lyxor Asset Management in 2002. These contracts were based on a series of protected funds that locked-in the highest monthly net asset value. Such schemes have subsequently been widely reproduced, but provide very limited flexibility.

In 2005, it was HDI Gerling (Talanx group) that issued a second generation of dynamic VAs, again supported by ifa and Lyxor. This concept brought the dynamic allocation down to the individual account level. For each contract, premiums are allocated according to a formula relating the protected investment fund and the insurer's with-profit fund. This allocation is revised only monthly, which reduces the operational burden compared with an American VA or a constant proportion portfolio insurance.

In contrast to the traditional American VA, where the insurance company provides guarantees independently from the funds, the guarantee of such a "dynamic" VA is spread over four "legs":

- the underlying mutual fund provides protection against short-term market risks;

Table 4.2 Dynamic VAs in Germany

Insurer	Product
Alte Leipziger	Alfonds
ARAG Rentenversicherung	FoRte 3D privat
Deutscher Ring	RingStrategiePolice
FinanceLife	FlexProtection
HDI Gerling	Two Trust
LV 1871	RieStar
Nürnberger Versicherung	Doppel-InvestRente
Signal Iduna	Global Garant Invest (SIGGI)
Universa	TopInvest
Volkswohlbund	Safe Invest
VPV	Power-Rente
Zurich Deutschland	Förder Renteinvest

Source: Société Générale Product Monitor.

- the with-profits fund provides long-term duration and pooling of actuarial risks (mortality, longevity and persistency);

- monthly dynamic allocation at the account level reduces the embedded option and therefore its cost;

- insurer retains the tail actuarial risks, operational risks and general business risks.

The immediate appeal of dynamic VAs is that the guarantees are cheaper, regardless of market conditions, and continue to use traditional profit-participation mechanisms to share the risks of long-term duration and actuarial risks between different generations of policyholders, and the "senior tranche" that the insurer retains in the with-profits fund.

Dynamic VAs avoid the most "toxic", and therefore costly, risks of American VAs from the insurers' perspective: lapse, switch and basis risks and exposure to long-term volatility. This is because there is no "embedded option" in the product; instead, the option is replicated at the individual account level.

With this structure, the operational requirements for providing dynamic VAs are much lighter than those required for American VAs, as there is only a straightforward monthly reallocation process to be managed at the account level. That is especially relevant for smaller insurance companies, which often operate only in one country.

On the other hand, American VAs can accommodate almost any range of underlying investments and are not limited to the rather exotic universe of protected funds. Also, they provide the full transparency and upside potential of financial options, and policyholders are fully invested over the whole duration of their policy, so that they benefit from the guarantee even in adverse market conditions. Finally, they do not rely on a with-profits fund that is adequately capitalised with policyholder surplus funds to be profitable.

LOOKING AHEAD: INNOVATIVE PRODUCT DESIGNS FOR VARIABLE ANNUITIES IN EUROPE

While the VA market in Europe is still young, we can anticipate three potential product developments.

(i) **Secondary VA market.** In Europe, VAs are often marketed by banks or independent-advisor networks. A secondary market, which has already started in the UK and Germany for traditional insurance, might develop in the next few years. This should mean more dynamic policyholder behaviour to select against the insurer, and therefore higher lapse risks.

(ii) **Collective pensions.** VAs offer efficient solutions, between defined-benefits (DB) and pure defined-contribution (DC) schemes. The market should develop first with corporate pensions in countries that have an advanced system of pension governance, such as the Netherlands, Switzerland and the UK.

(iii) **Guaranteed Minimum Health Benefits (GMHBs).** After accumulation and withdrawal benefits, we can expect the emergence of a new type of VAs, focusing on disability and health insurance. As of 2006, total health-care expenditures across Europe represented between 6.8% and 11% of GDP. Looking ahead, GMHBs should allow individuals to effectively self-insure for current expenditures, effectively buying protection for major ailments or hospitalisation.

THE INDUSTRY STRUCTURE FOR EUROPEAN VA HAS YET TO EMERGE

Since the beginnings of VAs in Europe, it has been clear that the choice of the right product for the right market is essential for success. While initially many international groups started VAs in Europe by importing product know-how and design from the US and Japan, the market has now reached a stage where insurers compete in specific customer segments for which an attractive and tailored VA offering can be designed, and operationally VA writers in Europe are mostly decoupled from the bases in North America.

As the experience of many VA writers during the months following the 2008–9 financial crisis has confirmed, product design and risk management need to go hand in hand, as some product features such as regular premiums or longer-duration products have proven difficult to hedge when markets become excessively volatile or dry up. In Central and Eastern European markets that are not part of the "Eurozone", the absence of financial instruments for hedging is a limitation for the development of VAs. There will be a greater necessity to design product features and hedging strategies in synchrony, and insurers with superior access to hedging capabilities will be able to offer product features that are essential for European customers, combining elements of established products, such as participating pensions, with innovative features, such as a choice from a range of investment funds (Ziewer 2009b).

Several factors have contributed to the fact that VAs are seen as the ideal product for pan-European platforms. On the one hand, insurers need to be able to spread the significant investment required to build and maintain both the capabilities and the infrastructure for designing a sustainable product offering and operating a professional hedging programme. Also, specialist skills that are not easily replicated in multiple locations are required for insurers, service providers and regulators. On the other hand, VAs as a product class are ideal for delivery on a "Freedom of Services" basis from one location (such as Ireland) into several European markets, as the underlying product logic is the same for each market.

There are several ways of building such a pan-European product platform for VAs: the first group of VA manufacturers in Europe will be the large global insurance groups, such as Allianz and AXA. They are poised to lead the VA markets with their own products in most countries in Europe. A second group of competitors will not rely on an existing pan-European distribution franchise, but rather will become manufacturing specialists for VAs that they sell to or through partners (other insurers, banks and advisor networks) in several European markets. Although no such specialist leader has clearly emerged as yet, there are a number of candidates, such as Swiss Life in Luxembourg.

Finally, reinsurers will be able to support insurers in both product development and hedging of VAs. While there is significant interest in this market from, for instance, Munich Re/New Re, there are also potential specialists such as White Mountain, Catalyst Re or Nexgen Re. Similarly, investment banks will be able to capture some of this market, either by assuming the risks in a captive reinsurer or by offering suitable hedge assets.

Of the many insurance companies in Europe, only a handful have already committed to a VA strategy. Even among these, it is likely that some will exit the market again due to lack of financial resource, product and risk management capability, market size or risk appetite. On the other hand, it has been established that VAs can offer features that important customer segments in Europe require. We will see how the first experimental steps with VAs in Europe and (having established the fundamental competencies) how competition begin to mould the industry's landscape.

1 Institut für Finanz- und Aktuarswissenschaften, a German actuarial consultancy.

REFERENCES

Irish Financial Regulator, 2009, "Capital Requirements for Variable Annuities", Discussion Paper, Irish Financial Regulator Insurance Supervision Department, August, URL: http://www.financialregulator.ie/.

Ziewer, L., 2009a, "Hedging in Turbulent Times", Current Issues in Life Assurance, May.

Ziewer, L., 2009b, "Is There a Future for Variable Annuities in Europe?", Oliver Wyman Insurance Newsletter, Edition 1, October.

Section 2

Identifying and Quantifying Risks

Introduction

Tigran Kalberer
KPMG

Section 2 describes the typical risks of variable annuity (VA) products and approaches to valuing VAs and their guarantees. The first chapter describes the risks implied by VAs.

The risks and the valuation of VAs are tightly interlinked for the following two reasons.

- Risks are events which might change the value of the guarantee such that the insurance company can no longer meet its strategic objectives. In order to identify and quantify risks it is necessary to first value these guarantees. This enables identifying the events which have an impact on the value of the guarantees and thus represent risks.

- The pricing and valuation of VAs involve their own category of "pricing risks". Sometimes these risks are called "model risks" and can be very substantial.

The risks of VAs can be broadly categorised into the following three classes.

- **Shortfall risk:** the risk that, due to insufficient asset performance of the underlying assets or adverse development of insurance risk, the assets are not sufficient to cover the guarantees. This is the direct and obvious risk associated with VA guarantees. The shortfall risks can be split into asset shortfall risks, biometric shortfall risks and combined shortfall risks.

- **Pricing risk:** the risk that the price of the guarantees is inadequate. There are at least two pricing approaches: theoretical pricing, based on financial economic theory, and hedging pricing, based on a specific hedging approach. The main pricing risk is model risk, caused by inadequate pricing models, including inadequate calibration.

- **Hedging risks:** the risks which arise just because a company manages the shortfall risks. These hedging risks include, among others:

  - long-term volatility risk;

  - interest-rate risk;

  - gamma risk, better known as non-linearity risk;

  - foreign exchange risk;

  - basis risk;

  - dividend risk;

  - funds choice risk;

  - other policyholder behaviour risk;

  - liquidity risk;

  - counterparty credit risk;

  - key-person risk;

  - other operational risks;

  - correlation risks;

  - bond credit-spread risk;

  - pricing credit-spread risk;

  - liquidity for collateral risk;

  - transaction cost risk;

  - cost of capital risk;

  - cost of risk management risk;

  - opaqueness premium risk.

All these risks will be explored in Chapter 5.

An important message is that the risks associated with VAs are typically not eliminated but only transformed. One risk is replaced with another, hopefully more easily manageable risk. It is important to bear this in mind when using the term "hedging".

This transformation of risks is the core competency of insurance companies. We will elaborate on this transformation in Chapter 5.

The valuation of VAs can be separated into two categories:

- the valuation of the underlying unit-linked contract, not considering guarantee charges and guarantee costs;
- the valuation of the embedded options, reflecting the guarantees: these options have a financial market and an insurance component.

Chapter 6, by Vinay Kalro, Jay Blumenstein and Joe Zhao, focuses on the valuation of the underlying unit-linked contract and the valuation of the insurance component of the embedded options. The fees, costs and commissions of a typical unit-linked contract are considered in order to value the unit-linked base contract. The valuation approach is based on a deterministic approach, the so-called "certainty-equivalent" approach. This approach allows modelling of the development of the total account value and the fees, costs and commissions involved.

The insurance component of the embedded option is based on market data, actuarial assumptions and policy data, which are combined in a sophisticated algorithm, discussed by Kirk Evans and Daniel Hayer (Chapters 7 and 8).

Apart from a static valuation, additional steps to determine profitability are discussed, notably internal rate-of-return (IRR) cash-flow analysis, shock/sensitivity analysis and other profitability considerations.

The focus of Chapter 7 is on the valuation of the financial-market component of the guarantee elements of a VA product. These embedded options arise due to the asymmetric dependence of the payout of the guarantee on the underlying funds performance.

The risk-neutral valuation concept is discussed as a well-known concept of financial economics. The assumptions for the validity of this concept, notably complete markets and no-arbitrage, are discussed and a simple binomial example explains the theory.

Due to the path dependency of most VA guarantees, there are typically no closed-form solutions available for valuation. As a consequence, the most popular approach to valuation is the Monte Carlo simulation. This, however, depends on the availability of capital-market scenarios consistent with the requirements of market-consistent valuation and calibration to the capital markets.

This pricing approach depends on key assumptions which are not necessarily valid for pricing of VA guarantees. Thus, it is important to use sensitivity testing to assess whether the valuation is robust in regard to these, and other, key assumptions.

It is also necessary to perform a "hedge efficiency test", where the effectiveness of the risk management approach is assessed under a real-world distribution.

Chapter 8 focuses on the production of market-consistent scenarios for valuing VA guarantees. The risks from VAs have become increasingly complex and it is important to identify the risks which must be reflected in scenario generators. Stochastic processes, stochastic calculus, no-arbitrage principles and other mathematical tools are used to produce adequate market-consistent scenarios and these techniques must be well understood for pricing VA guarantees. Otherwise, implicit assumptions of the pricing model are easily overlooked and may lead to unrecognised risk which inevitably will materialise: a phenomenon which has been observed frequently in the financial markets. The discretisation approach used needs proper attention and must be consistent with pricing formulas used. A brief menu of the possible models (eg, Hull–White, Cox–Ingersoll–Ross, Black–Karasinski and Libor market models) is introduced, but it is necessary to develop highly customised models (which typically are not available in standard textbooks), as common models are too simplistic.

Proper robustness checks, typically involving a wide variety of different pricing models, are necessary to ensure a minimal degree of comfort in the valuation.

The scenario generators are based on inputs and assumptions which might be regarded as questionable when valuing VAs. Input parameters like implied volatilities typically do not exist for the long timescales we need to consider for VAs. Also, volatilities may have a time and in-the-moneyness structure which is not properly reflected in the model, or, if reflected, cannot be calibrated to the market due to the lack of financial instruments implying these parameters.

So, in the end, all known approaches interpolate, and to a great extent extrapolate, the value of a VA guarantee from observed prices of instruments traded in a liquid market. And it is a philosophical question as to whether or not this interpolation and extrapolation leads to prices a liquid market would attach to such guarantees.

Chapter 9, by Tze Ping Chng and Matthew Wion, focuses on the impact of assumptions regarding policyholder behaviour on the value of the VA guarantees.

The policyholder has the ability to surrender the policy, vary the timing and amount of withdrawals, vary the timing of annuitisation, change the underlying asset allocation and potentially to change much more decisive features of their insurance contract. These policyholder options impact on product design, pricing, valuation and risk management of VAs.

The "in-the-moneyness" (ITM) of the guarantees is a decisive factor in determining formulas which model policyholder behaviour.

Typically, these formulas cannot be based on a sufficient amount of robust data but rather have to be based on management judgement. Several popular approaches to modelling policyholder behaviour (lapse, annuitisation, withdrawal, asset allocation) for typical VA guarantees (GMDB, GMIB, GMWB) are presented and discussed.

5

Risks Underlying Variable Annuities

Tigran Kalberer
KPMG

This chapter provides an overview of the risks underlying variable annuity (VA) contracts. It is important to note that it cannot give a complete overview of all possible risks, and we thus only focus on the risks which have gained attention so far.

The risks associated with VAs can be classified in two broad areas:

- risks which are typically implied by life-insurance products, but are not specific to VAs, such as mis-selling risks, the risks arising from mis-specified policy conditions or other sales material, regulatory and accounting risks, etc.

- risks which are specific to VAs.

We will elaborate only on the specific risks for VAs in this chapter.

We define a risk as any event which is detrimental to the business strategy of the insurance company. Mostly, but not always, these will be negative financial impacts like losses on the profit and loss (P&L) account or decreasing equity.

It is obvious that issuing guarantees regarding asset performance implies the risk that this asset performance is insufficient to cover the guarantees. In some cases the necessary asset performance to fulfill the guarantees depends on biometric factors, eg, mortality rates. If these develop adversely, then even a good asset performance might be insufficient to ensure that the associated assets cover all guarantees. Also the amount of shortfall in case of insufficient asset performance may be dependent on biometric risks. We will call these risks the "shortfall risks".

Clearly the company will charge a premium for issuing the guarantees. It also may be the case that these premiums may be inadequate; we will call this "pricing risk" – and it has yet to be defined what "inadequate" means in this context.

The guarantee premium will in most cases not cover a potential shortfall if the guarantees bite.

Most companies will manage this risk, but this will give rise to the new risk that the risk management strategies may fail. We will call these "hedging risks".

SHORTFALL RISKS

We want to split the shortfall risks into two categories.

- Risk that the performance of the underlying assets is insufficient to cover the guarantees given a certain expected realisation of biometric (or more general, insurance) risk, eg, a certain pattern of expected deaths or surrenders.

- Risk that the biometric factors insured (eg, death) develop adversely such that even an asset performance sufficient to cover the guarantees in the expected case is insufficient to ensure that the assets are sufficient to cover the guarantees. This could, for example, be the case if longevity exceeds expectations.

These two categories of risk cannot be viewed as separate. The combination of asset performance and biometric risks in a multiplicative way, as is usually the case, results in a combination problem when trying to hedge VAs. Let us consider a Guaranteed Minimum Death Benefit. The payment in case of death is the higher of the value of the underlying funds and the guarantee value. The shortfall for the insurance company in a certain year is

$$\max(G, 0) \times N_D$$

where N_D denotes the number of deaths in that year and G denotes the guarantee-asset value. This is why we talk about a multiplicative risk. The shortfall, S, can be decomposed as follows

$$S = \max(G, 0) \times N_D$$
$$= \max(G, 0) \times E_D$$
$$+ \text{expected value of } \max(G, 0) \times (N_D - E_D)$$
$$+ (\max(G, 0) - \text{expected value of } \max(G, 0)) \times (N_D - E_D)$$

where E_D denotes the expected number of deaths in that year. We call $\max(G,0) \times E_D$ the "asset shortfall", the expected value of $\max(G,0) \times (N_D - E_D)$ the biometric shortfall and $(\max(G,0) - $ expected value of $\max(G,0)) \times (N_D - E_D)$ the "combined shortfall".

This example shows that even if the asset risk is hedged perfectly, the biometric risk will remain. The usual way to manage biometric risk is diversification, which results in a lower volatility of the biometric risk (we understand volatility in a rather general sense here, meaning undesirable dispersion of the distribution under question; this is not the mathematical concept of volatility). The problem is that even if the biometric risk can be minimised, the risk from the asset part in the combined shortfall part stays and is unhedged. The combined risk cannot be hedged if there are no instruments that are dependent on asset developments and the biometric risk in the underlying insured collective in a combined way, and such assets typically do not exist (and are definitely not liquidly traded).

PRICING RISKS

We define pricing risk as the risk that the price of the guarantees may be inadequate; but what exactly do we mean by "inadequate"?

In practice we can identify two opinions about what an adequate price might be.

(a) Theoretical price. The price should cover the theoretical value of the guarantee, consistent with the insights of financial economics – although it is not clear whether these insights are sufficient to determine a unique and unambiguous price.

(b) Hedging price. The price should be just sufficient to cover the costs of hedging – it must be clear, however, which hedging method is chosen to determine the price.

First there is the risk that opinion (a) is chosen and then the guarantee charge is insufficient to hedge the exposure properly, due to the fact that a theoretic price neglects frictional costs which arise in practice, like transaction costs, bid–offer spreads or simply the fact that the requirements of a theoretical model are rarely really fulfilled, eg, continuous re-hedging, complete markets, no cost of capital, etc. The model underlying the pricing might also be inadequate or insufficiently calibrated; we call this risk "model risk".

But even if we stick to pricing opinion (b) there are remaining risks.

- The risk that available hedging instruments used for pricing do not really replicate the exposure: replication risk.

- The risk that in fact very often there will be a "scope creep", as we might identify a hedging programme to determine the price, but not all prices of the hedging instruments are readily available and theoretical models will be used to determine the prices of these hedging instruments, such that in the end we use theoretical models to determine these prices and end up with the same problems presented by using pricing opinion (a).

- The guarantees included in a VA are typically paid by deducting a certain number of basis points of the underlying fund's value from the policyholder's funds account on an annual basis. Very rarely they are charged immediately as a single initial deduction. When determining the right price for the guarantee, a certain amount of policyholder lapsation is expected. If a policyholder lapses, then they lose their guarantees in most cases, such that a certain amount of lapsation results in a lower overall cost for the guarantees. This can be reflected in the pricing, resulting in lower (and thus more competitive) prices. Policyholders, however, will, at least to a certain extent, act financially rationally (we assume that they always will act rationally, but non-financial benefits might prevent purely financially rational behaviour). This implies that when the value of the underlying funds is low the value of the guarantee is high, but guarantee charges will stay fixed (or even decrease in absolute amounts), and policyholders will feel inclined to stay and not to lapse their contract: "in-the-money persistency". Conversely, if the value of the underlying funds is high (in relation to the guarantees), then the value of the guarantees will be low, even vanishing in extreme cases. Policyholders will thus feel inclined to lapse and avoid the now unnecessary guarantee charges: "out-of-the-money lapsation". Thus, the lapsation will be asset dependent. This should be reflected in the pricing assuming a certain policyholder behaviour. But this behaviour has not been explored in depth and can change over time. The resulting risk is called "policyholder behaviour risk" (see also page 65).

HEDGING RISKS

As we will see, there are quite a few methods for hedging the risks arising from VAs. We will focus on the dynamic-hedging approach here, but some of the risks mentioned also arise for other approaches.

A dynamic-hedging programme requires the creation of a hedge portfolio which tightly follows the value of the guarantees. And, as we will see in this chapter, the value of the guarantees is dependent on a whole range of parameters, for example

- features of the guarantee,

- value of the underlying assets,

- volatility of the underlying funds,

- interest rates in the policy currency,

- proportion of surviving policyholders,

and potentially much more. In turn, some of these parameters are dependent on more basic parameters, eg, the value of the underlying funds is dependent on the value of the components of the funds in their denomination currency, the exchange rate between denomination currency and policy currency, the size and timing of dividends of the underlying assets and so on. The volatility of the underlying funds is dependent on the volatility of the underlying assets, the volatility of the exchange rates between denomination currency and policy currency, the correlation between the underlying assets, the correlation between all involved currencies and so on, and of course volatility has a time dimension.

The general risk of a hedging strategy is that the development of the hedging portfolio deviates from the development of the value of the guarantees, determined by the above-mentioned parameters.

This potential deviation could be caused by a deviation in development regarding one or more of the "pricing parameters" mentioned above, eg, the value of the hedging portfolio increases by a certain amount if the value of the underlying funds changes while the value of the guarantees changes by a different amount, thus the interpretation of the development in the underlying funds as cause of the deviation. Of course, this identification of a root cause may be arbitrary, but it is important to categorise these risks, so we use these perceived causes as categorisation tool, as follows.

Long-term volatility risk

The risk that the implied, ie, market, volatility of the underlying funds increases in an unforeseen way over time, resulting in losses when trying to roll over a potential hedge of the product: "long-term volatility risk". There are very few instruments which can be used to hedge this risk and for most terms and markets no hedge will be available to hedge this risk.

Interest rate risk

The risk that the level of interest rates changes, resulting in losses when trying to roll over a potential hedge of the product or losses when trying to purchase hedges for incoming premiums: "interest rate risk". While this is a risk which often is not hedged, there is typically a wide range of instruments available in the market to hedge this risk, such as long-term swaps, and this risk can in most cases be hedged away quite efficiently. It should be noted that for regular premium products, which are quite popular in Europe, this risk, at least during the first few years of the contract, will in most cases be by far the largest risk and we should focus on hedging this risk in such cases.

Gamma risk

The risk that the hedge of the underlying does not work perfectly, ie, the hedge develops differently from the value of the guarantee if the value of the underlying funds changes, eg, due to non-linearity of the value of the guarantee while the hedge is linear, is called "gamma risk". This risk typically arises when the hedging instruments are linear, eg, short futures.

Foreign exchange risk

The risk that the guarantee is denominated in a policy currency, eg, euro, which is different from the currency of the underlying funds, eg, US dollars, such that not only the asset performance of the underlying funds but also the fluctuations between the two currencies must be hedged. If these fluctuations are not hedged properly "foreign exchange risk" arises.

Basis risk

In most cases there exist no hedging instruments on the underlying assets, eg, if these assets are mutual funds which cannot be shorted.

The typical approach then is to map the funds to a (potentially time-varying) portfolio of assets which can be hedged, typically consisting of stock market indexes, often called the "benchmark portfolio". And of course this implies that the value of the hedging assets can develop differently from the value of the guarantees, causing so-called "basis risk".

Dividend risk

A special case of this basis risk is the "dividend risk". Typically, the assets of the benchmark portfolio are stock indexes, some of which are purely price indexes, which do not reflect dividend payments. In addition, the dividend payments of the funds are typically not synchronised with the dividend payments of the underlying assets, and there are fund management fees (that could be regarded as a negative dividend) which should also be considered. As the exact amount of dividend payments on the benchmark assets fluctuates, this can cause hedging deviations, resulting in a risk we would like to call "dividend risk". In most cases of which the author is aware, this risk is not substantial if dividend expectations and fund management fees are properly reflected in pricing and determining hedging ratios.

Funds choice risk

In some cases the underlying funds are not fixed, but rather the policyholder has the contractual right to choose them from a prescribed list of available funds and exchange funds at market value, possibly involving a relatively small handling fee. While this results in a pricing problem, as the available funds might have wildly varying volatility, the hedging problem can be far more severe if some of the funds in the list are not hedgable, ie, their basis risk is so high that it exceeds the benefits of hedging. Even if they are hedgable, the information flow of the policyholder's funds choice to the hedging unit must be very timely to ensure that the hedge works efficiently: "funds choice risk".

Policyholder behaviour risk

The "policyholder behaviour risk" which we have discussed in the pricing risk section also implies hedging risks. Let us assume that a certain asset-dependent policyholder behaviour has been assumed when determining the hedging portfolio, ie, assuming 10% lapses for in-the-money situations. Thus, a hedge portfolio for the remaining 90% of the policyholders has been set up. If, in reality, the asset-dependent policyholder behaviour is different and only 5% of the policyholders lapse, there will be a shortfall for 5% of the policyholders, and this in an in-the-money situation. This could result in substantial hedging losses.

Liquidity risk

The dynamic-hedging approach is not a static-hedging approach and as such requires frequent transactions: "rehedging". Owing to market constraints, hedging instruments which were initially liquid could become illiquid over time or even cease to exist. This risk is called "liquidity risk".

Counterparty credit risk

The hedging instruments, eg, swaps, involve counterparties which may fail to serve their obligations. The resulting risk is called "counterparty credit risk".

Key-person risk

Setting up a dynamic-hedging programme requires considerable skills and know-how. These skills are in high demand and it is not clear from the beginning that it is possible to retain this talent for the whole duration of the hedging operations, a time which can easily exceed 30 years. Actually, this is a "key-person risk", which the author has frequently observed to cause problems and which thus should not be underestimated.

Operational risk

The hedging programme typically consists of a complex series of processes, some of them IT-related. These processes must be performed regularly in a timely manner and without mistakes. The "operational risk" involved is considerable and far exceeds the typical level of operational risks in an insurance company.

Correlation risk

As we have already mentioned, most of the underlying funds are hedged by a benchmark index, which may consist of several asset indexes, even with different denomination currencies. Each of these asset indexes is then hedged independently. But the volatility of the benchmark index will depend on the correlation between these asset indexes (and, in fact, between the currencies involved) and thus changes in this correlation can result in hedging losses. We call this risk "correlation risk".

Bond credit-spread risk

Some of the above-mentioned asset indexes may be bond indexes. Typically, these are not hedged directly, but rather the underlying interest rate risk is hedged by using the characteristic features of the bond funds, eg, duration. While this obviously introduces a new basis risk, as this duration may change over time, it also introduces a "bond credit-spread risk", as the bond funds may include bonds which are exposed not only to interest rate risk but also to credit risk.

Pricing credit-spread risk

A further credit-related risk is more difficult to spot. The valuation of the guarantee to the policyholder is typically based on market rates of instruments which are thought to have similar credit quality, eg, swap rates. The underlying assumption is that insurance liabilities have the same credit quality as swap instruments and a lower credit quality than government bonds. But this may not always actually be the case. In times of market turbulence, the credit standing of banks might deteriorate substantially, resulting in very high swap rates. This implies low (theoretical) values of VA guarantees if swap rates are used for valuation. But this does not imply that the value of the obligations towards policyholders really decreases; we just observe the effect of using an inadequate pricing parameter, ie, swap rates. In fact, an interest rate which better reflects the quality of the obligations towards policyholders should be used. Depending on the circumstances, this could be interest rates more closely related to (but not necessarily equal to) government bond rates. This does imply that these interest rates (and not swap rates) should be hedged. If the hedging is based on swap rates, then a considerable "pricing credit-spread risk" arises.

Liquidity for collateral risk

Some hedging instruments may provide a perfect hedge for the guarantees under consideration, but this implies that in the case of a positive development they decrease in value while the potential regular payments from the insurance company to the counterparty stay fixed or even increase (eg, for an interest rate swap). This implies that the counterparty has a considerable counterparty default risk with the insurance company and will require a substantial collateral in liquid assets immediately. But the guarantee charges of the policyholders will be due in the future to a large extent and do not yet represent a liquid asset. Thus, the insurance company must finance the collateral to the counterparty. As the amount of the necessary collateral can be huge and arise very early, we have a considerable "liquidity for collateral risk".

Transaction cost risk

Dynamic-hedging operations require regular transactions. These, however, are typically associated with transaction costs, eg, in the form of bid–offer spreads. While these costs should be reflected in pricing, they can increase over time, resulting in a "transaction cost risk".

Cost of capital risk

VA products are under scrutiny from regulators, who typically require a substantial amount of risk capital. Regulations may change over time owing to developments out of the control of an individual insurance company, eg, political developments or insolvencies of competitors. Thus, risk capital requirements may increase, causing a need for liquidity and causing higher costs of capital for VA products, which then may appear underpriced: "cost of capital risk".

Cost of risk-management risk

The same developments may lead to more onerous risk management and reporting requirements, which in turn are more costly: "cost of risk management risk".

Opaqueness premium risk

The financial community may not understand the risk exposure of VAs or new VA features and regard the company's financial situation as more opaque when exposed to VAs. It might also be the case that these exposures are not communicated adequately to investors. This will result in an increase of the premium for opaqueness and thus lower share prices more than necessary: "opaqueness premium risk".

From the above descriptions we can see that the risks associated with a VA are typically not eliminated but only transformed, along what we could call a chain of risks.

The "shortfall risk" may be hedged using a dynamic-hedging approach, but this gives rise to a whole bunch of "hedging risks". Mitigating these hedging risks typically results in yet further risks, eg, hedging long-term volatility using an over-the-counter instrument results in increased counterparty risk. And we have seen lately that hedging counterparty risk using credit default swaps does not always work perfectly, and so on.

So there does not appear to be a "silver bullet" which eliminates all risks associated with VAs. Instead, one risk will typically be transformed into other risks, typically increasing operational risks. But we all hope that the remaining risks are those which are under better control than the original market risks.

6

Valuation of Variable-Annuity Contracts

Vinay Kalro, Jay Blumenstein and Joe Zhao

Swiss Re

As we have seen in the preceding chapters, VA products can be split into two parts:

- a common unit-linked contract, the base contract;
- an embedded option, reflecting the minimum guarantees.

The embedded option, as we will see, has a financial-market component and an insurance risk component.

In this chapter we will focus on valuing the unit-linked contract and the impact the insurance risks have on the value of the embedded option.

An insurance company that issues a variable annuity (VA) will be subject to the cashflows generated by each policy: all fees, costs, commissions and the payouts of the embedded guarantees. To value such cashflows, we must compute the replication cost; namely, the price of a portfolio of financial instruments that yields the same cashflows as the VA.

Depending on the actuarial assumptions, we may be able to invoke the "certainty-equivalent" approach in order to obtain the closed-form solution for any linear components of the VA. (In the same vein, pricing a forward contract does not require any simulation; it is merely the stock times discounted by the dividend: the risk-free rate differential present value factor.) Specifically, if the actuarial assumptions are such that the notional in force is not market dependent (eg, mortality and lapse are independent of the capital markets), we are in such a scenario. For a more in-depth discussion of the certainty equivalent approach, see Chapter 22.

The risk-neutral market-consistent framework states that the expected cashflows, assuming all assets grow at a risk-free rate, give

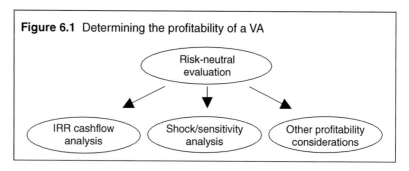

Figure 6.1 Determining the profitability of a VA

Risk-neutral evaluation

IRR cashflow analysis

Shock/sensitivity analysis

Other profitability considerations

the replication cost. A major difficulty is that VAs are dependent not only on financial variables but also on many unhedgable features, namely actuarial assumptions (eg, lapse, mortality, withdrawal and annuitisation utilisation).

Due to the fact that frictional costs (eg, for capital and hedging) play a role, pricing is not simply a risk-neutral run with the "best estimate" actuarial assumptions; Figure 6.1 shows other additional steps required to determine profitability.

- Internal rate-of-return (IRR) cashflow analysis, or timing of cashflows associated with issuing a VA (this includes capital and reserve).

- Shock/sensitivity analysis: given the uncertainty of the actuarial assumptions, how robust is a hedged VA in the face of actuarial assumption uncertainty? This helps to determine what type of target risk margin to consider.

- Macro considerations, such as risk of future accounting rule changes (eg, what happens if reserve or capital requirements change in the future?), diversification within the insurance company's risk portfolio (eg, longevity versus mortality-risk considerations), likelihood of reinsurance, ability to hedge, etc.

MARKET-CONSISTENT VALUATION
Base contract

By definition, these are cashflows generated from the base contract, not considering claims generated from guarantees or additional rider fees.

As the value of the base contract is typically linear in all exposures, we can use the certainty-equivalent approach and assume that all assets earn the risk-free rate. Therefore, we can apply a deterministic approach. (This requires the notional amortises deterministically, eg, no dynamic lapse, etc.)

To value the base contract, we need to compute the following two items.

- Development of the total account value, ie, expected remaining notional at each point in time t. This is achieved by taking age, gender, mortality, lapsation and utilisation of withdrawal or annuitisation features into account.

  The type of riders often has an impact on lapse behaviour; for example, withdrawal products and annuitisation products with fixed maturities have different surrender charge periods and thus different expected lapsations.

- The fees (paid by the policyholder to the insurer) and costs (paid by the insurer to external parties) incurred: part of these are determined by how policyholders choose their fund allocation (different funds result typically in different fees). The base product will often include lapse fees, mortality, expense and administration fees, rebates from investment management fees (sometimes also called retrocessions) and possibly a maintenance fee (the policyholder is required to pay this fee if the account value goes below a certain value). Costs include commissions to brokers, which are in both up-front and trailing form, as well as internal administration expenses to process the policies.

Finally, a given set of actuarial assumptions (mortality, lapse, withdrawal behaviour, annuitisation behaviour, etc) dictates the trajectory of account notional over time, from which we can compute the present value of the fees, costs, commissions and claims.

Embedded options in guarantee riders

The valuation of embedded options offered to policyholders is accomplished in a risk-neutral market-consistent framework based on the concepts of no-arbitrage theory, ie, by determining the price of creating a replicating portfolio. While the details of determining this price are described in the next section, we want to focus on the key issues and components to be considered for a pricing framework. These are as follows.

- Market data: this includes interest rates and volatility, foreign exchange rates and correlation, equity index volatility surfaces and correlations between the different underlying indexes and rates. We also need to factor in repurchase costs and swap spreads in order to derive the appropriate forwards for risk-neutral pricing.

- Actuarial assumptions: these pertain to the assumptions on mortality, lapse and withdrawal behaviour. Mortality and lapse at each time step can be modelled deterministically (the law of large numbers) or as stochastic variables (Ho *et al* 2006).

Within the deterministic methodology we compute for each policyholder the mortality rate m (using attained age, gender, policy age (for improvement factor, etc)) and lapse l (using policy age, moneyness, etc). Then we assume that a proportion of the policyholders die consistently with the average mortality rate, and we compute a death claim for that portion. A similar procedure is used for lapses. Withdrawal behaviour is modelled by splitting each policy, ie, allocating a portion of each policy to each withdrawal delay bucket; similar splitting is done in other dimensions (eg, thresholds before step-up is elected). For active blocks, the number of policies already in withdrawal could be higher than implied by the assumptions and then we need to consider shifting policyholders over from adjacent to satisfy the empirical observations (for example, the assumption would specify 30% withdraw immediately, 30% start withdrawal in two years, another 30% start in five years and 10% never withdraw; if realised data indicates that after one year we have 50% withdrawing, then we would move 20% over from the two-year bucket; if realised numbers are more drastic (say 70%), then we deplete the two-year bucket and take another 10% from the five-year bucket). An alternative to the splitting approach is to randomly assign policyholders to different withdrawal buckets while maintaining the overall withdrawal distribution. (For example, if we had 100,000 policies and wanted to apply a simple assumption: 50% withdraw immediately, 50% withdraw in year five, we could either have each policy "split" into two policies with half the notional, each part exhibiting either the immediate withdrawal behaviour or the five-year delay, or randomly assign 50,000 policies to withdraw immediately and 50,000 policies to withdraw in year five. Both approaches perform equally well in the authors' experience; the latter tends to break down when there are a small number of policies, such as in a cellular approach.)

- Policy data: when considering prospective business, pricing is done using synthetic cells representing policyholder demographics for new business. For valuation of ongoing business it is essential to consider the actual seriatim data, ie, the data given by the existing policies. Often such data consists of hundreds of thousands of policies, which are further split to incorporate policy-owner behaviour (eg, withdrawal delay, guarantee resets and step-ups), effectively creating blocks of millions of policies. Pricing using conventional techniques then becomes an arduous task, especially given that risk management of such blocks requires the calculation of a grid of several price points. Practical techniques to speed up the calculations include parallel processing and use of a specialised control variate.[1]

The estimated relative performances of different methodologies on a typical VA product are

- Excel spreadsheet model $\sim O(\text{weeks})$,
- single processor brute force C++ implementation $\sim O(\text{days})$,
- single processor C++ implementation with specialised variance reduction $\sim O(\text{hours})$,
- parallel implementation with variance reduction $\sim O(\text{minutes})$.

This speed-up is a tremendous advantage considering we have to compute hundreds of pricing points routinely.

IRR cashflow analysis

If we have hedged perfectly, and our actuarial assumptions were realised, then how do the net expected cashflows play out over time? How does the IRR from such a calculation relate to the cost of capital of the insurance company? Table 6.1 outlines the analysis and also incorporates capital and reserve requirements incurred from issuing the policy.

Table 6.1 Sample IRR calculation

	Day 1 (US$)	Year 1 (US$)	Year 2 (US$)	Year 3 (US$)	Year 4 (US$)
Fees					
M&E Fees	0	79,405,151	75,595,358	70,739,017	64,124,254
Investment management fees	0	21,050,270	20,063,205	18,793,762	17,043,955
Lapse fees	0	2,146,776	3,514,133	2,813,970	598,804
DB rider fees	0	0	0	0	0
WB rider fees	0	21,298,723	21,770,627	21,553,776	20,605,740
IB rider fees	0	0	0	0	0
AB rider fees	0	0	0	0	0
Total rider fees	0	21,298,723	21,770,627	21,553,776	20,605,740
Total fees to insurance company	0	123,900,919	120,943,323	113,900,525	102,372,753
Claims					
DB claims	0	(1,736,029)	(3,107,139)	(3,947,235)	(4,453,422)
WB claims	0	0	0	0	0
IB claims	0	0	0	0	0
AB claims	0	0	0	0	0
Total claims	0	(1,736,029)	(3,107,139)	(3,947,235)	(4,453,422)

Table 6.1 Sample IRR calculation (*Cont.*)

	Day 1 (US$)	Year 1 (US$)	Year 2 (US$)	Year 3 (US$)	Year 4 (US$)
Increase in hedge cost reserve	0	(14,293,572)	(14,293,572)	(14,293,572)	(14,293,572)
Hedging gains/losses	0	1,736,029	3,107,139	3,947,235	4,453,422
Total income	0	109,607,346	106,649,750	99,606,953	88,079,181
Maintenance	(59,709,593)	(9,207,326)	(8,705,804)	(8,143,806)	(7,391,949)
Commissions	(149,794,957)	0	(32,863,345)	(30,343,114)	(36,247,279)
Other costs and expenses	0	(18,585,138)	(3,628,300)	(3,417,016)	(3,071,183)
Increase in CARVM allowance	130,675,265	10,937,798	(41,269,220)	(86,329,063)	(786,354)
Net gain	(78,829,284)	92,752,680	20,183,081	(28,626,046)	40,582,416
Tax on net gain	(17,342,443)	20,405,590	4,440,278	(6,297,730)	8,928,132
Increase in economic reserves	0	89,203,725	(5,476,076)	(5,420,526)	(9,958,630)
NII on economic reserves	0	4,543,762	4,322,079	4,047,025	3,649,111
Tax on NII on economic reserves	0	999,628	950,857	890,346	802,804
Distributable cashflow	(61,486,842)	(13,312,499)	24,590,101	(13,751,110)	44,459,221
IRR		21.76%			

The result shows an IRR of 21.76%. Note the consideration of all balance sheet items incurred from issuing a VA. This includes, for example, a commissioners annuity reserve valuation method (CARVM) allowance, which is basically an asset that is due to the fact that the required capital to hold is the total account value minus lapse fees (ie, the cash-surrender value). Therefore, there is a "phantom asset" that amortises every year as the lapse fees decrease. Note that the lapse fees are typically put in place to create such an asset which offsets the upfront commission costs.

Table 6.2 Case study data

Mortality shift	Lapse shift	AV (%)								
		80	80	80	100	100	100	120	120	120
		Rates (bps)								
		Down 75	Flat	Up 75	Down 75	Flat	Up 75	Down 75	Flat	Up 75
Down 5%	Down 25%	1.13	1.53	1.85	1.33	1.72	2.03	1.25	1.69	2.03
Flat	Down 25%	1.27	1.63	1.92	1.46	1.81	2.10	1.39	1.78	2.10
Up 5%	Down 25%	1.40	1.73	1.99	1.57	1.90	2.16	1.52	1.88	2.17
Down 5%	Flat	2.46	2.48	2.51	2.47	2.50	2.51	2.47	2.49	2.51
Flat	*Flat*	*2.56*	*2.56*	*2.56*	*2.56*	*2.56*	*2.56*	*2.56*	*2.56*	*2.56*
Up 5%	Flat	2.65	2.63	2.61	2.64	2.62	2.60	2.65	2.62	2.60
Down 5%	Up 25%	3.40	3.15	2.94	3.22	2.97	2.78	3.23	2.97	2.76
Flat	Up 25%	3.47	3.20	2.98	3.27	3.02	2.81	3.29	3.01	2.79
Up 5%	Up 25%	3.54	3.25	3.02	3.33	3.06	2.84	3.35	3.05	2.82

In the case study, we consider the following scenarios: AV ±20%, flat rates ±75bp, flat mortality ±5%, flat lapse down/up 25%. (For a withdrawal benefit (WB), we typically also consider withdrawal utilisation in such an analysis). The results show that the hedged position is still net positive P&L in all situations. Note that the hedge position is identical for the mortality and lapse flat row (fifth row), as in this case where the realised actuarial assumptions equal the actual actuarial assumptions, the hedge is in fact perfect, so the hedged position will equal the risk-neutral price in all market scenarios.

Shock/sensitivity analysis: how robust are the cashflows?

The other angle in pricing is how robustly the hedge will perform if the realised actuarial experience is different from the actuarial assumptions (ie, we consider the net position: VA liability–hedge) under different market and actuarial situations (see Table 6.2). This analysis helps an insurance company to compute the appropriate cushion to the straight profit and loss, so that they can be confident that for, say, 99% of the scenarios this is a positive trade. A key element for this analysis is a sense of the extent to which the actuarial assumptions can change, in the sense of a probability distribution to arrive at such a statistic. Note that market moves and actuarial shocks are not necessarily independent; for example, the presence of a dynamic lapse implies that the lapse-down and market-down scenarios should have higher weights than lapse-down and market-up scenarios.

1   An efficient control-variate method can be understood as follows: set $P_i = P + (P_i - P)$, where P is the average payout and P_i is the policy-specific payout. Owing to the fact that policies have very similar attributes, the variance of $(P - P_i)$ is much smaller than the variance of P_i itself. By choosing random paths per policy, we effectively simulate the mean payout P on a large number of paths, while cancelling the errors in $(P - P_i)$ across the random chosen paths per policy. This is just one example of a typical control-variate approach.

REFERENCES

Boyle, P., and M. Hardy, 2003, "Guaranteed Annuity Options", *Astin Bulletin* 33(2), pp. 125–52.

Dellinger, J. K., 2006, *The Handbook of Variable Income Annuities* (New York: John Wiley & Sons).

Ho, T. S. Y., S.-B. Lee and Y.-S. Choi, 2006, "Practical Considerations in Managing Variable Annuities", Working Paper, Thomas Ho Company Ltd.

Milevsky, M. A., and S. E. Posner, 2001, "The Titanic Option: Valuation of the Guaranteed Minimum Death Benefit in Variable Annuities and Mutual Funds", *Journal of Risk and Insurance* 68(1).

7

Valuation of Variable-Annuity Guarantees

Kirk Evans
Samsung Life

As we have seen in the preceding chapters, variable annuity (VA) products contain elements that are similar to capital market options and other elements which are similar to more traditional insurance products. This dual nature needs to be considered when valuing VA guarantees. Only then will we gain an accurate assessment of the risk VA guarantees impose to the seller and thus possible to determine the appropriate charge for VA guarantees.

In this chapter, the focus is on the guarantee elements of VA products. The VA guarantee's similarity to the capital market options derives from the fact that its value is tied asymmetrically to the VA's underlying fund performance. Most VA guarantees (GMDB, GMIB, GMAB, GMWB and GLWB) are similar to capital market put options and provide a payout if the performance of the underlying funds (net of fees) does not meet some minimum level of return over a specified period of time. However, there are some less popular VA guarantees, such as the Enhanced Earnings Benefit (EEB), that is intended to cover tax liability by providing a payout to the VA guarantee-holder if the underlying fund performance (net of fees) exceeds a specified level, similar to a call option. Regardless of whether VA guarantees are similar to a put option or a call option, the valuation considerations are the same.

Even though the VA guarantees do have characteristics in common with capital market options, they possess significant insurance characteristics that need to be considered when determining an appropriate charge for the guarantee. Unlike capital market options, VA guarantees are typically life contingent. We have seen in the preceding chapters how these features are appropriately reflected in pricing. We also have seen that the guarantee element should be priced using the risk-neutral approach. We will elaborate on this approach in this chapter.

RISK-NEUTRAL VALUATION

To reflect the fact that the VA guarantees derive their value from the performance of underlying funds and have asymmetric exposure to the capital markets, we need to use risk-neutral valuation, a well-known concept of financial economics, as the basis for properly determining the value of this guarantee. Risk-neutral pricing is rooted in the concept that in complete markets (markets where contingent cashflows are determinable and can be replicated with liquid market-traded instruments) no-arbitrage or the law of one price governs. The basic premise is that two instruments with identical future cashflows under all future scenarios have the same price. The following is a simple binomial example used by many textbooks to demonstrate this basic principle of risk-neutral pricing.

We assume the following:

- a continuous risk-free rate (r) of 5%;

- a one-year time interval;

- a stock, whose current price (S_0) is US$100, which has two possible values after one year,

   - an increase to US$150 ($S_u$),

   - or a decrease to US$50 ($S_d$);

- an individual who has a portfolio (P) consisting of Δ shares of stock described above and Ω units of a risk-free bond (at time 0 the risk-free bond's value is US$1 per unit) and sells a put option with a one-year maturity and strike price of US$100 on the described stock.

After one year the put option will have a payout of US$0 if the stock price increases and a payout of US$50 if the stock price decreases. Say that the option-seller holds the correct number of units of Δ and Ω to ensure that the value of their portfolio at the end of one year exactly matches the payout of the put option they sold.

The value of the portfolio (P) now and in the future must then be

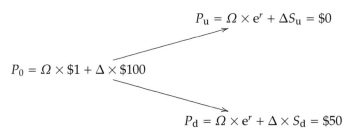

$$P_u = \Omega \times e^r + \Delta S_u = \$0$$

$$P_0 = \Omega \times \$1 + \Delta \times \$100$$

$$P_d = \Omega \times e^r + \Delta \times S_d = \$50$$

Solving the two equations at the end of one year for Δ and Ω, we get $\Delta = -0.5$ and $\Omega = 71.3422$. The negative Δ indicates that the stock is sold short. Under the no-arbitrage concept, the value of the put option must equal the value of the portfolio, since they have the same payout under both future states. Therefore, the value of the put option at time of sale is $P_0 = (71.3422 \times \$1) + (-0.5 \times \$100) = \$21.3422$.

Note that, in this put-option pricing example, we did not need to know the probability of the stock increasing in value versus decreasing in value or the expected return on the put option. We can value an option without knowing the real-world expected return of the underlying asset. This is because the option's price is relative to the stock's price and the probability of future increase or decrease in the stock's future price is already embedded in its current price.

The Black–Scholes–Merton option-pricing model for European puts and calls on non-dividend-paying stock is based on the above concept, but assumes an infinite number of continuous paths plus some additional assumptions, such as the following:

- stock prices follow a geometric Brownian motion;
- interest rates and volatilities are constant;
- trading is continuous with unlimited short selling;
- both the borrowing and the lending rate are the risk-free rate;
- markets are complete;
- there are no costs associated with trading, ie, no taxes, no bid–ask spreads, etc.

These assumptions led to the Black–Scholes–Merton differential equation, which is independent of risk preference. We need only to know the current stock price, the risk-free rate and the underlying stock's expected future volatility. This result is significant, because we do not need to know the investor's risk preference in order to value the option. In other words, investors could also be risk-neutral. It is assumed that they can completely hedge away risk and therefore do not require a risk premium. The drift and discount rate for all assets are the risk-free rates. The Black–Scholes–Merton differential equations for a European call (c) and a European put (p) on a non-dividend paying stock at time 0 are

$$c = S_0 N(d_1) - Ke^{-rT}N(d_2) \quad \text{and} \quad p = Ke^{-rT}N(-d_2) - S_0 N(-d_1)$$

where

$$d_1 = \frac{\ln(S_0/K) + (r + \sigma^2/2)T}{\sigma\sqrt{T}}$$

and

$$d_2 = \frac{\ln(S_0/K) + (r - \sigma^2/2)T}{\sigma\sqrt{T}} = d_1 - \sigma\sqrt{T}$$

Here S_0 denotes the stock's price at time 0, $N(x)$ is the cumulative probability distribution function for a standardised normal distribution, K denotes the option's strike price, r is the risk-free rate of return, T is the time until the option expires and σ is the volatility of the underlying stock.

The Black–Scholes–Merton framework is the basis for financial economics option-pricing methodology and should be applied, among other methods, when valuing VA guarantees to ensure that the insurer is receiving proper compensation for the capital market option risk they are assuming. Unfortunately, closed-form solutions, such as the Black–Scholes–Merton differential equation, only exist for relatively simple options that do not have any underlying actuarial components such as lapse rates, benefit utilisation, life contingency, etc. As a result, in order to value the VA guarantees under this framework, we typically use stochastic Monte Carlo simulation.

Monte Carlo simulation is a widely used method in many disciplines, including finance, to model uncertain or random events that cannot be described by closed-form solutions. The basic process for modelling VA guarantees using Monte Carlo simulation is as follows:

- define input parameters for underlying funds to be modelled;
- generate the resulting scenarios randomly using the defined input parameters and the specified probability distribution;

- calculate the VA guarantee's cashflows along each of the generated scenarios using the VA guarantee's contractual design and the underlying actuarial assumptions (lapse rates, mortality rate, benefit utilisation, etc);
- discount the cashflows back to time 0;
- aggregate the results in a fashion consistent with the analysis being performed, ie, for a risk-neutral valuation we would average across all scenarios the resulting discounted cashflows from each scenario to obtain the option value.

Using Monte Carlo simulation, it is relatively easy to capture the path dependency of typical VA guarantees. Another approach to valuing VA guarantees that has been gaining traction lately is the replicating-portfolio approach. Under this approach, it is necessary to determine a market-traded asset portfolio that replicates the VA guarantee's cashflows under a defined set of financial scenarios. This approach adds another level of complexity. This approach is described in Chapter 22.

STOCHASTIC SIMULATION

Financial economics tells us that the value of any asset is the expected present value of its future cashflows. For derivatives, such as options, the expected present value needs to be determined under the risk-neutral measure.

In some cases, as we have seen above regarding the Black–Scholes–Merton formula, it is possible to derive closed-form solutions for the value of financial instruments.

The complexity and path dependency of the VA guarantees typically does not allow derivation of an analytic expression to value the instrument.

In these cases, the value, ie, the expected value under the risk-neutral measure, is estimated by using Monte Carlo simulation, a method frequently used to price exotic or complex options. For this approach, a sufficiently large number of scenarios describing the capital markets are drawn according to the distribution prescribed by the risk-neutral measure. A sufficiently large number of scenarios are achieved when convergence is reached. Convergence is reached at N number of scenarios when any set of N scenarios generated from the prescribed risk-neutral measure produces the same value

Table 7.1 SPX implied volatility surfaces (%) as of October 31, 2008

Maturity	ITM									
	50	70	80	90	100	110	120	130	140	150
1M	84.0	75.6	69.0	60.7	51.7	43.7	37.7	33.6	30.8	28.7
3M	70.6	64.2	59.3	53.5	47.5	41.9	37.4	33.8	31.1	29.0
6M	62.0	55.9	51.9	47.4	43.0	39.0	35.5	32.7	30.3	28.4
9M	57.4	51.7	48.1	44.3	40.7	37.4	34.5	32.0	29.9	28.2
1Y	54.2	48.9	45.8	42.5	39.4	36.5	34.0	31.8	29.9	28.2
3Y	45.2	41.4	39.6	37.8	36.2	34.7	33.3	32.1	31.0	30.0
5Y	42.9	39.8	38.4	37.0	35.7	34.6	33.5	32.5	31.7	30.8
7Y	41.9	39.2	38.0	36.8	35.8	34.8	33.9	33.1	32.3	31.6
10Y	41.3	39.0	38.0	37.1	36.2	35.4	34.6	33.9	33.3	32.7

Source: JP Morgan.

Table 7.2 South Korean spot-swap curve as of March 31, 2009

Maturity	Rate (%)
3M	2.48
6M	2.50
1Y	2.86
2Y	3.30
3Y	3.55
4Y	3.70
5Y	3.79
7Y	3.87
10Y	3.98
12Y	4.01
15Y	3.96
20Y	3.90

Source: Bloomberg.

for the instruments being valued. Usually, N needs to be 1,000 or more to reach convergence.

The scenarios are calibrated such that the resulting values of observable financial instruments calculated using the calibrated scenarios coincide with the observed market prices of such instruments. The calibration process will vary depending on the economic scenario generator used.

Then the discounted cashflows of the contingent claim we want to value is determined for each of these scenarios. According to the law of large numbers, the average of these discounted cashflows across the scenarios is an estimate of the expected value or, in this case, option value.

The key to this type of valuation is the scenarios used to generate the cashflows and the discount rates used to present value those cashflows. For pricing options, including VA guarantees, it is necessary to use market-consistent scenarios. Only if the scenarios are market consistent will we know that the calculated option cost is reflective of the appropriate price for the option risk assumed, given the current market consensus. The market consistency is achieved by using market-observed parameters, such as implied volatilities and appropriate risk-free rate curves, to generate the scenarios.

These inputs are obtainable through sources such as investment banks, Bloomberg, options brokers, etc. For more developed markets, the implied volatility is a surface where the implied volatility varies by in-the-moneyness (ITM) and maturity. Typically, the swap curve is used for the risk-free rate term structure in valuing options. Table 7.1 shows a sample implied volatility surface and swap curve.

Various models utilise the implied volatility surface differently. A simplified approach, such as the Black–Scholes–Merton approach, assumes that the volatility is constant throughout the projection and would use the implied volatility that reflects the ITM and maturity of the instrument being valued on the valuation date. More sophisticated models use the entire implied volatility surface either implicitly (eg, the stochastic volatility model) or explicitly (eg, the local volatility model).

As with the implied volatility surface, various models use the spot-swap curve differently (see, for example, Table 7.2). Some models assume a constant risk-free rate throughout the projection and may use the spot swap rate that corresponds to the maturity of the instrument being valued on the valuation date. Typically, with Monte Carlo simulation, forward rates are calculated off the spot-swap curve and used as the drift and discount rate for the future time periods in the projection. A more sophisticated approach is to stochastically model future forward rates.

Before generating the final scenarios, we can ensure market consistency by calibrating the scenarios to observed prices of financial instruments, like bonds and options at various maturities and at various levels of in-the-moneyness. There are various market-consistent risk-neutral scenario generators and calibration techniques we can use to accomplish this. This is explored further in Chapter 8.

Once the market-consistent risk-neutral scenarios have been generated, the process for valuing the guarantee is relatively straightforward. All we need to do is project the option's cashflows along each scenario and discount back by the appropriate discount rate (risk-free rate) for each time period along each scenario. The average present value of cashflows across the scenarios is the option value. It is worth mentioning that risk-neutral valuation is a pricing mechanism, which does not recognise real-world risk premiums and makes no attempt to reflect the expected future state of the world. Therefore, the distribution of results has no meaning. Only the average of the present value of the results across scenarios has a meaning. This is the option's financial economic value or risk-neutral price.

Monte Carlo simulation utilising market-consistent risk-neutral scenarios is a commonly used basis for valuation of VA guarantees, but unfortunately VA guarantees have a very long maturity compared with capital market options and therefore there may not be observable capital market parameters for implied volatilities or risk-free rates at maturities equal to that of VA guarantees. Under these circumstances, we are forced to use our best judgment, based on the information available, to extend the implied volatility surface and risk-free rate curve to the maturity needed. Given that VA guarantees are not market tradeable, it is not crucial that there is market consensus as to their option value, but it is crucial that the calculated option value is reasonable and appropriate to ensure proper compensation for the company assuming the capital market option risk and to allow for the costs of hedging.

REFLECTING INSURANCE CHARACTERISTICS OF VA GUARANTEES IN THEIR PRICE

As stated previously, VA guarantees have significant insurance risks in addition to their capital market option risks. The risk-neutral valuation assesses the financial economic value of VA guarantees at a point in time assuming a specific set of actuarial assumptions, which provides a solid basis for valuing VA guarantees but does not provide the final price. Given that VA guarantees have more uncertainty, or more risk, than pure capital market options, the charge for a VA guarantee should be different from its purely risk-neutral valuation. Below is a list of some of the key differences between VA guarantees and pure capital market options that need to be considered when determining the final price for VA guarantees.

- The price is set; capital market option prices change almost continuously as the market conditions change. Insurance prices are set, or at least very sticky, for new sales for a period of time, usually years. Given this, it is important that the price of VA guarantees is valued using risk-neutral parameters that reflect more than just a single point in time. We need to use parameters that will cover the cost of the option over the sales period (which admittedly is a guess).

- The underlying is typically mutual funds, while most pure capital market options have a single stock or a specific index as their underlying or at most a defined fixed basket of indexes. The underlying of VA guarantees is usually a set of actively managed mutual funds with various investment strategies. In addition, the contract-holder usually has some leeway to select the fund mix they desire as well as to change the mix over time. This adds uncertainty regarding what the future underlying will be. This additional risk factor should also be incorporated in the pricing.

- Lapse rates: if the VA contract-holder wants to cancel the contract before maturity, they lapse the contract for the cash-surrender value. Pure capital market options are sold back into the market at the current market price. To reflect this lapse risk in pricing VA guarantees, it is standard practice to assume dynamic lapse rates that reduce lapses as the guarantee becomes more in-the-money. In addition, to assess the risk associated with the uncertainty of the future lapse rates, we should look at different levels of basic lapse rates and various dynamic lapse formulas when valuing.

- Benefit utilisation: some VA guarantees permit the contract-holder's discretion regarding benefit utilisation. The practices to capture this vary. The safest approach is to assume that the contract-holder is always optimally efficient in exercising the benefit. But the reality is that most contracts are sold to cover an insurance need and the contract-holder may have other goals besides maximising the value of the VA guarantee. To reflect this, we may use a dynamic utilisation function that increases the contract-holder's efficiency of exercising the VA guarantee as the benefit becomes more in-the-money. We should also include the risk associated with the uncertainty of future benefit utilisation in the valuation.

- Life contingency: most VA guarantees are life contingent. The uncertainly regarding future mortality or longevity needs to be incorporated in the valuation. This is discussed in more detail elsewhere.

- Long maturity: the life of VA guarantees is usually much longer than a traditional capital market option. This poses problems for the calibration of the risk-neutral scenarios. There may not be observable inputs, such as implied volatility and risk-free rates, that extend to the life of the VA guarantee. Under these circumstances, we are forced to set these longer maturity parameters using our best judgment, given the context of the valuation.

- VA guarantees do not exactly fit the risk-neutral framework; most of the key assumptions of the risk-neutral framework do not apply directly to VA guarantees. VA guarantees are not market tradeable and cannot be replicated at issue (ie, hedging requires rebalancing over the life of the guarantee at an uncertain cost and effectiveness). These differences are significant and should be considered when valuing VA guarantees.

- Cost of capital: insurance companies are required to hold reserves and capital to back the VA guarantees. The cost of holding this capital needs to be reflected in the VA guarantee's pricing.

These items are additional risks or uncertainties that the capital market option does not have and cannot be fully captured by performing a single risk-neutral valuation. Sensitivity testing on these uncertain components is necessary to assess the level of risk and the risk profile for these items. After completing the sensitivity tests, the company may need to add a margin on to the risk-neutral cost to cover these additional risks. From the author's experience, it is not uncommon for the additional margin to be as high as 30–50% of the risk-neutral cost.

Ignoring reinsurance, the insurance company will be holding the liability for the VA guarantee until lapse, death or maturity. The resulting economic impact to the insurer selling the guarantee is based on how the future real world plays out. This is true even if the VA guarantee risk is hedged, since the hedge will have to be rebalanced over time under uncertain future market conditions. Given this consideration, it may be useful for the insurer to assess the real-world profile of the VA guarantee including its risk management strategy once the pricing and the risk management approach have been determined. There are several approaches that can be taken to perform this analysis. It is important to note that this analysis needs to be performed in a fashion that is consistent with the risk management approach for the VA guarantee liability and the insurer's particular risk tolerance.

A common approach is to test the adequacy of the VA guarantee's price by assessing its sufficiency across a real-world scenario set. In this analysis, unlike under the risk-neutral measure, we are trying to capture the distribution of the potential future markets. It is recommended to derive the underlying parameters by calculating the historical returns and volatility of the markets of interest (markets/indexes that represent the VA's underlying funds). The parameters should be calculated over a long historical period that captures several market cycles and covers a time period longer than the maturity of the VA guarantee being valued. It is common practice to use a 30- to 50-year period.

The modelling approach is similar to the risk-neutral valuation, except that now we are valuing the cashflows across real-world scenarios, have a VA guarantee fee cashflow to compare with the VA guarantee claim cashflows, incorporating a specific risk management strategy such as hedging and we want preserve individual discounted cashflows by scenario. In this analysis, we are not just trying to capture the average results across scenarios, but we also want to rank the results to determine the point at which the VA guarantee's fee does not cover the contingent claims. This can be accomplished by ranking the

(present value (PV) VA guarantee's claims)

$-$ (PV VA guarantee's fees)

We may also want to assess the point at which a deficiency occurs with the company specific risk management strategy. For a hedging risk management strategy, we may compare

$$[(\text{PV VA guarantee's claims}) + (\text{PV hedging costs})]$$
$$- [(\text{PV VA guarantee's fees})$$
$$+ (\text{PV hedging instrument's payouts})]$$

Each company will have to set the percentile or contingent claim expectation (CTE) level at which it is comfortable for shortfalls to start occurring, ie, the point where (PV VA guarantee's claims) > (PV VA guarantee's fees).

The CTE measure is the average of $100\% - X\%$ scenarios results where $X\%$ is the point of interest (ie, 90% CTE is the average of the 10% worse scenarios).

CONCLUSION

The valuation of VA guarantees is an iterative multi-step process; the VA guarantee's charge is typically taken out of the underlying funds, thus reducing the fund's net return over time, which in turn affects the potential claims.

Step 1. Risk-neutral valuation of the VA guarantee. This step usually requires several passes until the fee level converges. The first pass may be run without a VA guarantee fee. The successive passes are run with the latest VA guarantee to assess the fees impact on the claims produced.

Step 2. Determine the appropriate margin to be added for the risks associated with the VA guarantee's insurance elements. The practice here will vary by company. Some companies may build in an implicit margin during the risk-neutral valuation (see step 1) by deliberating using conservative assumptions. Others may use best estimate assumptions during the risk-neutral valuation and build in an explicit margin after calculating the best estimate risk-neutral cost.

Step 3. Determine the risk-profile of the VA guarantee under real-world distribution to assess the adequacy of the resulting VA guarantee's charge.

- If the charge from step 2 is not sufficient at the targeted per-centile, the charge may have to be raised and the real-world distribution reassessed.

- If the company has a specific risk management strategy for the VA guarantee, it is recommended to also assess the real-world profile of the VA guarantee with the risk management strategy.

Step 4. The final step, not covered in this chapter, is to integrate the VA guarantee into the overall VA contract's pricing and risk profile. VA contract pricing is covered in Chapter 6.

No matter which process is used to value VA guarantees, it is crucial that its dual nature is recognised and that an appropriate charge is levied to compensate the company for all of the risks and costs associated with VA guarantees.

8

Models Used to Quantify Risks in Guarantees

Daniel Heyer

Nationwide Financial

We have seen in the preceding chapter how variable annuity (VA) guarantees are priced in principle. We have also seen that stochastic simulation is typically used to value these guarantees. What we have not seen are the details underlying stochastic simulation models. This chapter will focus on these models and their implementation.

At their heart, VA guarantees are complex derivative instruments that protect policyholders against very specific types of financial risk. To properly manage these risks, the insurer must carefully understand the types of financial uncertainty that are being assumed with each benefit and ensure that their market models incorporate these types of randomness.

For example, the Guaranteed Minimum Accumulation Benefit (GMAB) ensures that the policyholder's account will not lose money over a specified investment horizon. To value this benefit, the insurer must have a model that captures the distribution of asset returns over specific time horizons, reflecting features like variance, skewness, kurtosis, etc. At the same time, however, the path of account returns up until the benefit's maturity is irrelevant; only the cumulative returns matter. Understanding this distinction allows a wide spectrum of models for valuing GMAB policies. For example, the two scenario-generation models visualised in Figure 8.1 yield identical return distributions at each maturity and identical GMAB values, even though the evolution of the return paths over time is quite different.

As another example, consider a ratchet Guaranteed Minimum Death Benefit (GMDB). In its richest form, when you die, this benefit guarantees that your beneficiaries will receive the highest account value you have ever held. Like the GMAB, this benefit is linked to the

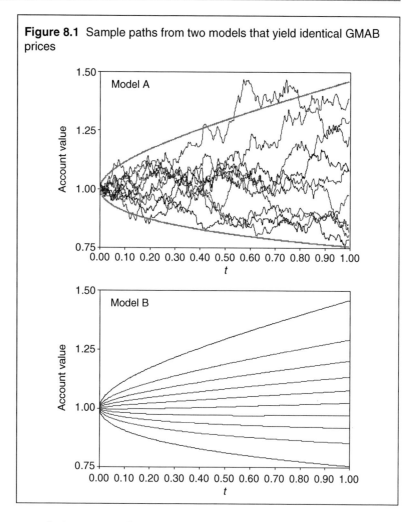

Figure 8.1 Sample paths from two models that yield identical GMAB prices

cumulative return distribution, but at every point in time (because death can occur at any time), and in comparison to the highest value attained along each path. In this case Model B clearly does not capture the risk associated with this ratchet feature and cannot hope to yield a reasonable value.

Finally, the insurers' risks have become increasingly subtle and complex as the VA-guarantee market has matured. This complexity makes it ever more difficult to identify the financial phenomena that must be incorporated into scenario-generation models. For example, Guaranteed Lifetime Withdrawal Benefits (GLWBs) guarantee that periodic withdrawals from an account will never exhaust that

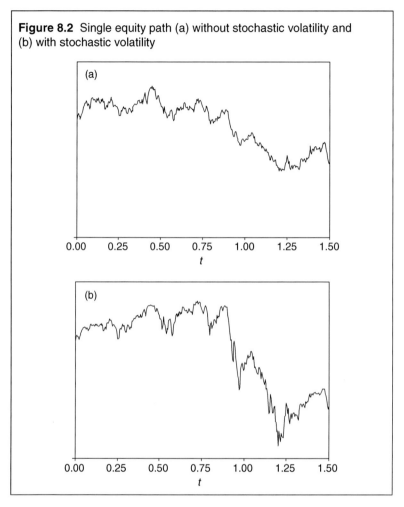

Figure 8.2 Single equity path (a) without stochastic volatility and (b) with stochastic volatility

account. This type of guarantee is adversely impacted if the account value is depressed when a withdrawal is made, even if the market quickly recovers. Accordingly, the GLWB can only be properly valued with a scenario-generation model that captures the potential for sharply depressed market levels.

Figure 8.2 illustrates a model that uses stochastic volatility to capture this short-term market-drop risk. The Black–Scholes model is a simple geometric Brownian motion and evolves relatively smoothly over time. With the introduction of stochastic volatility, however, the equity process shows pronounced cycles, with occasional steep drops followed by sharp recoveries. This sort of behaviour is typical of real-world market scenarios and important to proper valuation of GLWBs.

Hopefully these limited examples have made it clear that a deep understanding of the guarantee being valued is necessary before any scenario-generation model is selected. Some basic questions whose answers will aid development of this understanding are listed below.

- What are the benefit's critical dates (ratchets, withdrawals, payouts, etc)?

- Does accumulated value matter? Do short-term variations in level matter?

- What matters right before a critical date? What matters right after it?

- What can change the amount of the benefit payout? What can change the timing of the benefit payout?

- Is interest rate risk primarily from discounting (present-valuing claims) or do interest rates affect the amount of the payout?

The answers to these questions help to develop an understanding of the VA guarantee and guide the modelling process.

STOCHASTIC SIMULATION

The core of any simulation problem is the ability to specify the under-lying stochastic processes as stochastic differential equations (SDEs), which capture the relevant features discussed above. For example, the classic Black–Scholes model is specified as

$$dS = \mu S \, dt + \sigma S \, dW$$

From this equation we can see that the change in S is proportional to S and consists of a time-deterministic drift μ and a random component with volatility σ. A set of these stochastic processes describing each risk of interest forms the heart of the scenario-generation model.

Once the relevant equations have been specified for equities, inter-est rates, currency exchange rates, credit default rates, etc, it is pos-sible to derive the pricing partial differential equation (PPDE), the master pricing equation that describes the value of any derivative security valued in this model universe. In general, the PPDE can be quite difficult to solve, especially when the derivative security involves path-dependent features like ratchets, withdrawal dates, etc. Fortunately, there is a mathematical technique, the Feynman–Kac Theorem, which allows us to convert the PPDE solution into an expected value computed over a set of specific random scenarios: the so-called risk-neutral scenarios. While there is a natural tendency to think of these scenarios as some sort of parallel financial universe, this thinking can lead to unhelpful "misintuition". Risk-neutral scenarios are better viewed as a mathematical "trick" for solving partial differential equations, and the PPDE in particular.

The procedures for deriving the PPDE and risk-neutral scenarios matched to the chosen stochastic processes require a working understanding of stochastic processes, stochastic calculus, no-arbitrage principles and a few other mathematical tools. These topics are covered in most texts on derivative mathematics such as Neftci (2000).

Once the risk-neutral stochastic processes have been determined, they must be simulated. Continuing the case of the Black–Scholes model above, the risk-neutral scenarios are specified by the SDE

$$dS = (r - \tfrac{1}{2}\sigma^2)S\,dt + \sigma S\,dW$$

Most textbooks suggest simulating this process over discrete time steps using the first-order Euler discretisation, a discrete-time approximation (all that a computer can manage) of the continuous SDE. This discretisation involves replacing dt by δt and dW by $Z\sqrt{\delta t}$, where Z is a standard normal variate. This simple discretisation works for most applications where the time step δt is small and the time-deterministic drift function is not too complicated. For larger time steps and more complex drift functions (particularly mean-reverting functions) higher-order discretisations are required. This topic is covered in more advanced simulation texts such as Kloeden and Platen (1992).

Proper attention to discretisation can greatly simplify simulation and significantly reduce computational time. Poor discretisation can lead to unintended and unexpected consequences. For example, we may choose an interest rate model that has a simple closed-form solution for bond prices. This choice means that any cashflow in the simulation can be easily present-valued using this analytic bond-price formula. If the interest rate model is poorly discretised, however, simulated bond values will not match the analytical value and the analytic shortcut may yield distorted results. As a general rule, consistently applying a flawed model (using the "wrong" rate simulation and discounting with the "wrong" simulated bonds) yields far better results than inconsistently apply a perfect model (using the "wrong" rate simulation and discounting with the "perfect" analytical bonds).

THE MENU OF MODELS

When selecting a model we must consider the application as well as the nature of the VA guarantee. For pricing, risk management and embedded-value-type calculations, it is important to accurately reflect all relevant risk sources over relatively long timescales. These considerations generally mean developing highly customised models that are not available in any textbook. The statistical techniques for analysing market data and uncovering the underlying stochastic processes are advanced and require a deep understanding of stochastic calculus.

For hedging, it is also important to reasonably reflect the prices of tradeable hedging assets: puts, swaps, futures, hybrid securities, etc. This objective, however, creates some complications. The liquid-asset market generally consists of less complex risks than VA guarantees and this market is largely concerned with value changes over the next three to six months. These features lead to common market models for hedging assets that are relatively simplistic (ie, highly tractable) and are tuned to short-timescale features of the market.

Nevertheless, these asset models are intuitively understood, are covered in most textbooks and are a good place to start. Table 8.1 provides a brief summary of common market models, their statistical characteristics, and risks to which they might apply.

Each of these models has its trade-offs. Hull–White and Cox–Ingersoll–Ross (CIR) models have analytic formulas for bonds and common options, but tend to be too tame over long time horizons. The lognormal rate models tend to be too wild over long time horizons. Naive approaches to these limitations (eg, shocking rates paths, regime switching, capping lognormal rates, etc) can be problematic for long-dated VA guarantees. Similar issues arise for equity volatility models.

Table 8.1 A spectrum of common interest rate and equity volatility models

Model	Var.	VC	CTS	MR	Comments
Interest rates					
Hull–White	MMR	Normal	Y	Y	Good for short-term discounting; allows negative rates
Extended CIR	MMR	Non-central χ^2	Y	Y	Good for long-term discounting
BK	MMR	Lognormal	Y	Y	Good for long-term discounting and valuing mild rate optionality
LMM	Yield curve forwards	Lognormal	Y	N	Use when benefit payout is a function of future yield curve
Equity volatility					
BS	—	Const. vol.	N	N/A	Commonly used for quoting option prices
Dupire	Inst. vol.	Function of equity level	Y	N/A	Not good for path-dependent options
Heston	Inst. vol.	Non-central χ^2	Y	Y	Not good for long dated skew
SABR	Inst. vol.	Lognormal	Y	N	Need to consider consequences; no mean reversion

BK, Black–Karasinski; BS, Black–Scholes; CTS, capture current term structure; Inst. vol., instantaneous volatility; LMM, Libor market model; MMR, money-market rate; MR, mean reverting; Var., variable modelled; VC, short-term volatility character.

CALIBRATION

Before discussing calibration it is important to understand the difference between implied volatility and realised volatility. Implied volatility is best thought of as "price" and not as a volatility at all.

Why is this so? Option prices are a function of many moving parts, including strike, maturity, equity level, rate level, etc. Two different options are certain to have different prices, but how different should they be? Traders express price using a standardised model (generally Black–Scholes or the Black model) and the "implied" volatility is the volatility that must be used in that model to get the observed price. This approach automatically adjusts out obvious price factors like maturity and strike, leaving the volatility as a measure of relative cost. These relative costs help traders understand supply/demand impacts, unusual market conditions, etc. The key here is that implied volatility is linked to a specific option and to a specific pricing model. Applying implied volatility to different options or models is problematic.

For dynamic-hedging purposes, however, we are primarily concerned with the realised volatility of basic equity indexes. For this application, the model volatility is adjusted to reflect the best-estimate statistical behaviour of realised volatility.

For most applications, it is critical that the interest rate model reprices the current yield curve. For this reason, almost all practical interest rate models either model the yield curve directly (eg, the Libor market model) or include a time-dependent drift function that is mechanically adjusted to match the current yield curve (eg, for the money-market rate models). In either case, reproducing the current yield curve is so formulaic that the term "calibration" hardly applies. (The Black–Karasinski model is a notable exception, however.)

For the money-market rate models, calibration is used to determine the mean-reversion speed of interest rates and the instantaneous volatility of interest rates. This information can only come from a historical analysis of interest rates or from the prices of interest rate options. But these models are not typically used for pricing interest rate options and cannot generally capture a broad spectrum of option prices. Rather, these models are designed to model bond prices (present-value discount factors) and the impact of short-term volatility in discount rates. Accordingly, these model parameters are often historically calibrated.

If these money-market rate models must be adapted to re-pricing interest rate options, however, some care must be exercised in selecting the proper model. Interest rate options have a term structure of implied volatility, just like equity options. Each money-market rate model has an associated family of volatility term structures that it is capable of generating. For example, the Black–Karasinski model yields a very flat volatility term structure, while the CIR model can generate hump-shaped term structures. It is important to match the proper model with the observed implied-volatility term structure.

The Libor market model has been explicitly designed to re-price many common interest rate options and contains "an embarrassment of parameters" (Rebonato 2004). These parameters describe the volatility of forward rates at different maturities, their correlation and possible time dependencies as well. Calibrating all these parameters in a parsimonious and stable way requires a great deal of sophistication. Rebonato's book provides a practical introduction to specifying and calibrating this model.

Similarly, when modelling equity returns we need to consider whether implied volatility or realised volatility is being modelled. As discussed above, implied volatility is linked to a specific set of options that will form the calibration targets. And, as for interest rate calibration, we must also be careful to match the proper model with the observed implied-volatility term structure. When calibrating for dynamic hedging, however, we are primarily concerned with the realised volatility of basic equity indexes. For this application, the model volatility is adjusted to reflect the best-estimate behaviour of realised volatility.

As a general rule, we should ensure that the feature being calibrated is something that is controllable by the model. For example, calibrating a Black–Scholes equity process to options exhibiting skew is pointless; the Black–Scholes model incorporates constant volatility and simply cannot match skew. While this example is obvious, calibrations often include "calibration razors" or stylised facts that the modeller wishes to incorporate directly into the simulation. We should always make sure that these features are actually controllable by the model parameters being calibrated.

MODEL RISK AND OTHER PRACTICAL CONSIDERATIONS

A significant practical risk is flawed model implementation arising from coding blunders, improper discretisation, etc. A two-pronged approach helps limit these concerns.

- List all statistically testable features of the model. Then use the sample output to test them. For example, are scenarios intended to be driftless, grow at risk-free rates, generate specific distribution forms, etc?
- List all features of the model that have analytic results (bond prices, option prices, steady-state distributions, etc) and then use the sample output to test them.

Together, these two approaches help to verify that we have implemented what we intended.

But were our intentions appropriate for the task? In any modelling exercise the greatest risks are the unanticipated risks, particularly the risk regarding assumptions that are built directly into the scenario-generation model form itself. The best way to combat this risk is to have a suite of models available that span a range of forms and assumptions.

Coupled with deep intuition for VA guarantees, a suite of models can quickly reveal any shortcomings in modelling, assumptions or analysis. The models listed in Table 8.1 range from tame to wild, from mean reverting to unconstrained. A good practice is to value VA guarantees at a variety of market levels, maturities, etc, using each of these models. We should be able to anticipate the effects of switching between models and the magnitude of those effects. Exploring unanticipated results helps to avoid oversights and build sound intuition. Similarly, regularly studying the changes in hedge asset prices help us understand the risks that drive value.

CONCLUSION

Variable annuity guarantees are complex derivative instruments that protect against specific, often subtle, types of financial risk. To properly model these risks, we must have a careful understanding of which market features drive benefit payouts. Armed with this understanding, we can select appropriate financial models and formulate the risk-neutral Monte Carlo scenarios for valuing those guarantees. When implementing this risk-neutral model, discretisation requires care, and calibration must be matched to the intended use of the model. Finally, all aspects of the model must be continually tested and evaluated. Each new market situation or model application is an opportunity to challenge our intuition and broaden our understanding.

REFERENCES

Kloeden, P. E., and E. Platen, 1992, *Numerical Solution of Stochastic Differential Equations* (Springer).

Neftci, S. N., 2000, *An Introduction to the Mathematics of Financial Derivatives*, Second Edition (New York: Academic Press).

Rebonato, R., 2004, *Volatility and Correlation: The Perfect Hedger and the Fox*, Second Edition (Chichester: Wiley Finance).

Models Used to Quantify Actuarial/Policyholder Behavioural Risks in Guarantees

Tze Ping Chng, Matthew Wion

Ernst & Young

The value of a variable annuity (VA) guarantee depends on many factors, not least the options made available to the policyholder. The policyholder's options to surrender the policy, vary the timing and amount of withdrawals, vary the timing of annuitisation and inject or transfer policy funds can all have an impact on the frequency and severity of the guaranteed benefit payout. Unpredictable usage of those options as well as its asymmetric dependency on the capital markets make policyholder behaviour a critical yet challenging assumption to quantify and model. It impacts on most aspects of VA product management, including product design, pricing, valuation, capital management and risk management.

Common themes have emerged when evaluating policyholder behaviour. For example, the view that policyholder behaviour varies depending on the perceived value or in-the-moneyness (ITM) of the guarantees. ITM is a term used to indicate the relative value of the guarantee compared with the associated contract value. If the value of the guarantee is greater (less) than the contract value, the guarantee is in-the-money (out-of-the-money). If the value of the guarantee is equal to the contract value, the guarantee is at-the-money. Later in the chapter, common definitions of ITM are discussed for the different VA guarantees. Given that many guarantees are relatively new and contain waiting periods, there is an insufficient amount of credible data upon which to develop and base policyholder-behaviour formulas. Thus, there are varied practices when implementing behavioural formulas, including the types of formulas used, the factors that may impact on behaviour and the degree of sensitivity to those factors.

In this chapter we discuss the models, suitable approaches and considerations needed in order to quantify policyholder-behaviour risks in VA guarantees. We discuss policyholder behaviour in regard to the following possible policyholder options: lapse, annuitisation, withdrawal, regular premium payments and asset allocation. We also discuss the impact of product-design flaws. The chapter will conclude with a discussion of practical considerations when modelling policyholder behaviour.

LAPSE

Lapse represents one of the most important policyholder behaviours that drive the ultimate guarantee cost. As guarantee charges are collected regularly from policy issuance, policyholders that lapse prior to the maturity of the guarantee have paid for a guarantee that they have never utilised. It is common practice for companies to vary the lapse-rate assumption based on the ITM of the guarantees. The reasoning is straightforward: if the guarantee is perceived to be worthwhile to the policyholder, ie, is in-the-money, then we are more likely to anti-select against the issuer by continuing to receive the guarantee. Alternatively, if the guarantee is of little or no value to the policyholder, ie, is out-of-the-money, the policyholder may choose to lapse the policy so that no further charges are collected. When developing the lapse-rate assumption for modelling purposes, companies typically start with a base lapse rate and apply a dynamic lapse-adjustment factor, which varies based on the value of the guarantee. Given the lack of industry studies and the uniqueness of various company-specific factors such as product designs, commission schedules and distribution channels, most companies use their own experience studies as the starting point for setting the base lapse rate (PBITT Working Group 2008a).

Consideration can also be given to the policyholder perspective. The cause of lapsation can vary, stemming from the need either for funds or for more attractive alternative investments, but surrendering a policy does not come without a cost. Besides potentially paying a surrender charge penalty, the policyholder forgoes the tax deferral privileges (in certain countries like the US) and insurability. To the extent that these effects impact on behaviour, experience studies

Table 9.1 Common ITM definitions that are used when determining the dynamic lapse-adjustment

Guarantee	Common ITM definition
GMDB	Guarantee value/account value
GMAB	(PV) Guarantee value/account value
GMIB	Guarantee income/current annuity income
GMWB	Guarantee value/account value or PV benefit/account value
Lifetime GMWB	PV benefit/account value

typically provide the mechanism to build that impact into the base lapse-rate assumption.

The dynamic lapse-adjustment factor can be one-sided or two-sided. A one-sided factor is capped at 1.0, meaning that the dynamic adjustment only acts to lower the ultimate lapse rate. A two-sided factor increases the ultimate lapse rate beyond the base lapse rates if the guarantee is deeply out-of-the-money. A one-sided factor adjustment is more popular (PBITT Working Group 2008b, p. 5), as companies typically believe that increasing the ultimate lapse-rate assumption beyond the base rates has the impact of lowering the ultimate guarantee cost and is thus not regarded as conservative. It is also common practice for companies to apply a floor to the dynamic lapse-adjustment factor, as most believe that a small group of policyholders will always lapse, regardless of the ITM of their guarantees, purely due to (unexpected) cashflow or liquidity needs.

The ultimate lapse rate is given by the following equation

$$\text{ultimate lapse rate} = \text{base lapse rate} \times \lambda \qquad (9.1)$$

where λ denotes the dynamic lapse-adjustment factor, one-sided ($\lambda \leqslant 1.0$) or two-sided ($\lambda > 1.0$).

A sample dynamic lapse-adjustment factor is given by (American Academy of Actuaries' Life Capital Adequacy Subcommittee 2005)

$$\lambda = \min\left[U, \max\left[L, 1 - M \times \left(\frac{\text{GV}}{\text{AV}} - D\right)\right]\right] \qquad (9.2)$$

where U denotes the cap or maximum, L is the floor or minimum, M denotes sensitivity, D is the trigger point and GV/AV (guarantee value divided by account value) gives the ITM. Assigning values to these parameters requires either judgment calls of the VA writers or calibration through actual experience study data. As the guarantees embedded in the VA products are not alike, different definitions of ITM are applied, such as those shown in Table 9.1. As GMDB is a death benefit, which means it is only possible to receive the benefit upon death, many companies do not apply a dynamic lapse adjustment to GMDB-only VA products (PBITT Working Group 2008b, p. 4) in the US. However, in other parts of the world, applying dynamic lapse adjustments to GMDB is more common, as experience (including that from traditional life products) has shown that policyholders are sensitive to the value of a death benefit, and therefore may be more inclined to persist when the guarantee is in-the-money until the value is realised. Other commonly used dynamic lapse-adjustment factors include linear, stepwise, exponential, arctangent and parabolic formulas. This classification refers to the dependence of the lapse rate on the ITM.

As a GMAB guarantees a minimum account balance at expiration, the dynamic lapse-adjustment factor should also incorporate the time-to-maturity element when determining the degree of adjustment. The closer a policy is to the expiration of the GMAB, the more sensitive a policyholder is to the ITM. For products with multiple guarantees, eg, GMDB and GMAB or, more recently, hybrid GMAB/GMIB, some companies compute two lapse adjustments separately and apply the more conservative factor.

We typically need to go through a full bull-and-bear-market cycle in order to understand lapse behaviour. With the massive asset price declines in 2008, many guarantees at the time of writing in July 2009 are deep in-the-money. Therefore, now is a perfect time for VA writers to test out their dynamic lapse formula. Regardless of the functional forms of the dynamic lapse adjustment selected, we should always perform a reasonability check and ask if the adjustment rate makes sense. For example, does the ultimate lapse rate go down when the guarantees are in-the-money?

Figure 9.1 demonstrates the degree of dynamic lapse adjustment under various commonly used dynamic lapse formulas. A cap of 100% and a floor of 50% are applied to these formulas. Note that the parameters for these formulas are set hypothetically; in reality we can expect significantly different dynamic lapse-adjustment patterns if different parameters are used.

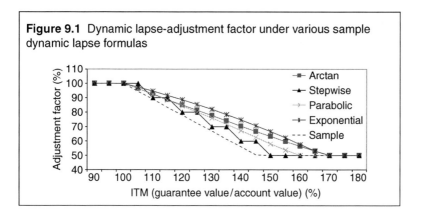

Figure 9.1 Dynamic lapse-adjustment factor under various sample dynamic lapse formulas

Other factors that should be taken into consideration when determining ultimate lapse-rate behaviour include product design, surrender charge schedules, distribution channels, commission schedules, perceived reputation and geographical differences. Experience has shown that distribution channels play a major role in driving the ultimate lapse experience. A company's existing product can experience a higher lapse rate as a result of the introduction of a competing product with a more attractive commission rate. The geographical and cultural differences across the different regions around the world also exhibit very different lapse patterns. For example, a product sold in Japan is expected to have a lower lapse rate than a similar product in the US. Even so, we must not make the generalisation that lapse rates are always lower in Asia. There are significant variations throughout Asia, and jurisdictions like Japan, Korea or Hong Kong do not necessarily share similar lapse patterns.

Product design is one of the best ways to manage policyholder behavioural risks. For lapse rates, companies typically offer incentives such as a loyalty bonus to improve persistency. Similarly, trail commission or commission chargeback can be deployed to encourage distribution channels to promote policy retention.

ANNUITISATION

Experience shows that in the absence of a guarantee, annuitisation of VA contracts is not a common action. This could be a function of policyholders not interested in surrendering the upside market potential and the relatively low payout rates typically provided within the base policy. As a result, VA models include either a very low or no base annuitisation assumption.

The GMIB is designed to provide a guaranteed amount of annuity income in the case where the contract value is depressed and/or the annuity purchase rates at the time of annuitisation are lower than the guarantee. The guaranteed annuity income provided by the GMIB is typically based on a benefit base which is independent of the contract value at annuitisation, and guaranteed annuity purchase rates defined at the time the policy is purchased. Common definitions of the benefit base are a return of the initial premium, the initial premium increased at a specified annual rate or the maximum account value at pre-specified periods such as each policy anniversary.

There is typically a waiting period of 5–10 years before the GMIB annuity income can be elected. Once past the waiting period, the policyholder has the option to annuitise the then current contract value at the then current annuity purchase rates or annuitise the GMIB benefit base at the guaranteed annuity purchase rates. The value or ITM of the guarantee is equal to the difference in these two sources of annuity income. The presence of the GMIB could alter how policyholders view the value of the annuitisation feature.

Several factors could impact on the timing and degree of GMIB utilisation. Among the most common are the ITM level of the guarantee, the age of the annuitant and the duration of the policy particularly as it relates to the waiting period. For a GMIB, the ITM is usually determined by comparing the value of the guaranteed annuity payments (GMIB/a_x^G) with the current annuity payments (AV/a_x^C); that is

$$\text{ITM} = \frac{\text{GMIB} \times a_x^C / a_x^G}{\text{AV}}$$

When presented in this way, a policy is in-the-money when the ITM > 1, that is, the guaranteed annuity payment is higher than the current annuity payment. Alternatively, the policy is out-of-the-money when ITM < 1 and it would be more valuable to annuitise the contract value at current annuity rates than the GMIB at guaranteed rates. The age of the policyholder can also play a role, due to differences in the need for income as well as tax implications such as potential tax penalties, eg, for distributions under age $59\frac{1}{2}$ in the US. Annuitisation formulas can account for age-based variations by adjusting the ITM formula or the annuitisation rate itself. Finally, it is common to expect a spike in annuitisation when the benefit first becomes available after the waiting period, subject to the level of ITM and age considerations as discussed.

Although these economic and demographic drivers are important, there are other factors that impact on whether or not a policyholder will annuitise. For instance, annuitising a VA liquidates the investment in the underlying funds, thus forgoing an upside market potential, as well as giving up the liquidity feature of a VA. These disincentives may limit the number of policyholders who annuitise. It is common, therefore, to include a maximum annuitisation rate in the dynamic annuitisation formula. Again, this maximum rate may vary for the spike annuitisation.

Here are a few final points to consider when modelling annuitisation rates. Similar to lapse rates, common dynamic annuitisation formulas include linear, stepwise, exponential, arctangent and parabolic formulas. Guaranteed annuity payments, which in many cases are for life, introduce longevity risk. Improving mortality could prolong benefit payments, increasing the risk to the insurer. Therefore, it is now common to reflect mortality improvements when calculating the guaranteed annuity payments. In practice, GMIB payments are rarely modelled explicitly as cashflows until run-off. Rather, the commuted value of the guaranteed payments is calculated and assumed to be paid.

WITHDRAWAL

Withdrawal behaviour has become an increasingly critical assumption as the number and types of guaranteed minimum withdrawal benefits (GMWBs) have magnified. GMWB designs guarantee a withdrawal amount, commonly 4–7% of the benefit base, to be paid for a fixed period or for life. The guarantee cost is very sensitive to the level of benefit utilisation. The level of benefit utilisation in turn can vary based on a number of different factors such as the ITM of the guarantee, age, qualified versus non-qualified status, distribution channel and product incentives. A single dynamic formula is usually not sufficient to capture the many dynamics that could impact on the withdrawal utilisation. An increasingly popular approach to modelling the level of withdrawal utilisation is to separate the business into different withdrawal cohorts.

Table 9.2 Some definitions of withdrawal cohorts

Cohort	Withdrawal (%)	Percentage of policy
1	0	10
2	f(ITM)	80
3	Max	10

There are different approaches to developing cohorts and to allocating a block of business to those cohorts. Although the forms may vary, the general concept is to recognise the potential variations to both the timing and amount of withdrawal utilisation. Many companies will assume that those who have already begun to make withdrawals will continue to do so at the current withdrawal level, or at the maximum withdrawal level if higher. If a policyholder is enrolled in a systematic withdrawal plan where the amount withdrawn is known, companies are likely to reflect that information in the utilisation modelling. If withdrawals have not yet started, there are two different ways of viewing the withdrawal utilisation. It may be assumed that the policyholder begins withdrawals immediately, or when first available if there is a waiting period, but the amount of the withdrawal varies by cohort. For example, Table 9.2 defines three cohorts. Cohort 1 assumes no withdrawals are taken, cohort 3 assumes that the maximum withdrawal percentage allowable by the product is taken, while cohort 2 uses a dynamic formula based on the ITM of the guarantee to determine the withdrawal percentage. Once these cohorts are defined, the allocation of the block can be set as shown in the last column of the table. The percentages allocated to each cohort must total 100% but can be fluid based on actual experience.

This is a relatively straightforward example and clearly other cohorts can be defined. For those cohorts with behaviour that is dynamic, the dynamic assumption will typically be based on the ITM of the guarantee.

Alternatively, it may be assumed that 100% of the withdrawal is utilised but the timing of the withdrawal varies by cohort. For example, Table 9.3 illustrates cohorts that vary by age and the timing of the first withdrawal.

Table 9.3 Cohorts that vary by age and the timing of the first withdrawal

Age	Allocation at time of first withdrawal (%)				
	Immediate	5 years	10 years	20 years	Never
Under 50	0	10	25	50	15
50–59	5	25	40	15	15
60–69	40	30	15	0	15
70–79	55	25	5	0	15
80+	65	20	0	0	15

Given the uncertainty around the timing of withdrawal utilisation, some product designs have an automatic withdrawal provision that requires withdrawal upon certain policy durations or attained age. Some companies believe that guaranteed cost declines when the initial withdrawal is delayed. Therefore, they provide an enhanced benefit base for each year of deferral in order to promote such behaviour. Other considerations include qualified/non-qualified tax considerations such as penalties in the US for withdrawals before age $59\frac{1}{2}$ and the required minimum distribution (RMD). Longevity risk, as with the GMIB, may require mortality improvements to be modelled.

REGULAR PREMIUM

While most policies in the US and Japan are single premium, regular premium payment policies are increasingly common in Korea, Hong Kong and continental Europe. The modelling of expected premium payment therefore becomes an additional consideration when it comes to policyholder-behaviour modelling. As regular premium products typically come with a target premium amount, it is common for companies to model only the target amount. This is also because any top-up premiums are usually not covered in the guarantees.

ASSET ALLOCATION

Many VA guarantees require the policyholder to elect an asset allocation model, restrict the underlying funds that can be selected or limit the overall percentage that can be allocated to specific funds. For those designs that include automatic rebalancing as part of the allocation method, the underlying models should reflect that rebalancing through time. Beyond that, it is not common to see transfers across accounts explicitly modelled. Consideration should be given to tail events and whether or not those would trigger an asset allocation event. For example, an extreme market downturn, such as we saw at the end of 2008, may result in the stop-loss mentality of shifting funds from equity funds to fixed-income funds. While rational thinking would lead us to believe that policyholders would keep their investments in equity funds in the presence of a guarantee like those found in VA, experience shows the opposite taking place. In the US, the VA assets invested in equity funds dropped from 60% to 45% (NAVA 2009, Table 4) within a year of the market crash in 2008.

DESIGN/PRICING FLAWS

In late 1990s, some of the VA products in the US were issued with a dollar-for-dollar withdrawal provision. This provision reduces both the guarantee amount and the account value dollar-for-dollar for each dollar withdrawn. This became an issue after the NASDAQ market bubble burst in 2000–1, leading to guarantees that were in-the-money. Some policyholders, after becoming aware of this design flaw, exploited the VA writers by drawing down the account value significantly. Assuming the guarantee amount is US$1,000, and the account value is US$500, the account value would need to double in value to break even. However, if the policyholder withdraws US$400, there will remain only US$100 in account value and US$600 in the guarantee amount after the withdrawal for a dollar-for-dollar policy. This means that the account value would have to increase sixfold to break even.

As most companies today still price based on an expected level of lapses to support the guarantee cost, we need to consider the potential impact on the day when all policies become totally rational. While this is not likely to happen in the near future, knowing its impact allows companies to better understand their risk profile in the worst-case scenario.

PRACTICAL CONSIDERATIONS AND CONCLUSION

As we have shown in this chapter, there are many considerations to be made and options to take when developing models to quantify policyholder-behaviour risk. The theories and reasoning that drive the formulas may break down in practice due to unforeseen policyholder reactions and irrational behaviour. The lack of credible data makes the task even harder, as the dynamic models in large part have not been validated. For example, the dynamic models do not reflect the tendency for policyholders to persist when market performance is good and lapse when market performance is poor. In fact, most dynamic formulas assume precisely the opposite behaviour, due to the presence of the guarantee. Even with guarantees in place, policyholders may put more value into the stability of their current holdings than in the future guarantee. Life events will play a role regardless of market performance. A lapse or withdrawal may be driven by need rather than the ITM of the guarantee.

There are other modelling decisions that could impact on the policyholder-behaviour assumptions. Monte Carlo stochastic modelling exercises may require seriatim data to be grouped into model cells. Cell grouping may distort behaviour patterns and thus it is important to be sure that the key drivers of dynamic behaviour formulas are covered in the cell compression criteria. The ITM of the guarantee, a key driver of most dynamic behaviour formulas, will vary within and across the economic scenarios used in the modelling and thus careful consideration should be given to the interest and equity model choice (see Chapter 8). It is important to note that the ultimate projected dynamic policyholder behaviour is only a reflection of the expected behaviour under the scenarios generated by these models.

Finally, setting assumptions for policyholder behaviour is not a static process. The formulas should be periodically evaluated as new experience emerges. This is especially true during volatile market movements, such as those experienced in 2008. It is those bull-and-bear-market cycles that can substantiate or refute the policyholder-behaviour formulas and how they predict behaviour in tail events. It is critical to understand the elements that are most sensitive and have the largest impact on the liability value and the risk. Experience studies are the primary source of data. Sufficient levels and frequency of data collection are necessary for the experience studies to be credible and useful. The process should include a mechanism to update the dynamic formulas based on the actual experience obtained. Such a mechanism also allows VA writers to respond to the emergence of an increasingly rational group of policyholders in the future.

REFERENCES

American Academy of Actuaries' Life Capital Adequacy Subcommittee, 2005, "C3 P2 Report", June, p. 78.

NAVA, 2009, "NAVA Reports Fourth Quarter Variable Annuity Industry Data", March 18, Press Release, URL: http://www.irionline.org/news/article/id/249.

PBITT Working Group, 2008a, "Policyholder Behavior in the Tail Variable Annuity Guaranteed Benefits Survey: C3 Phase II 2007 and 2008 Results", Society of Actuaries' Policyholder Behavior in the Tail Working Group Report, September, p. 11.

PBITT Working Group, 2008b, "VA Survey", Society of Actuaries' Policyholder Behavior in the Tail Working Group Report, September.

Section 3

Managing Risks in Variable Annuities

Introduction

Kannoo Ravindran

Annuity Systems Inc and Háskólinn í Reykjavík

Since the introduction of variable annuity (VA) contracts in the marketplace in 1952 by the Teachers Insurance and Annuities Association–College Retirement Equity Fund (Poterba 1997), the VA contract has gone through several metamorphoses before reaching its current state of existence. Although there are many reasons for this explosive growth and proliferation over the decades, some obvious examples are

- changes in tax regulations,
- regulations governing what the insurance companies can sell to a consumer versus a bank, mutual fund company, etc,
- evolution of population demography,
- growth of consumer knowledge-cum-risk-appetite.

Until the late 1990s, whenever a product was launched by an insurance company it was quite often the case that it had a reinsurer behind it taking on all the risks embedded in the product for some pre-specified premium. With this approach, the direct companies ran a profitable business by collecting a spread over-and-above the basic costs associated with retail distributions, infrastructure and reinsurance (to name but a few), while the reinsurers got compensated for taking on the market and actuarial risks.[1] It was also coincidentally at this time when the conventional wisdom among reinsurers was that

- market risks like mortality risks can be diversified (and hence the more policyholders the better) and
- the long-term put options embedded in these contracts were almost worthless.[2]

Since the late 1990s, when the reinsurers started recognising that they were underpricing the risks (ie, were not compensated sufficiently for the risks they had assumed), they started pulling out of the market quickly. Given that these reinsurance treaties did not have any agreements in place to prevent a reinsurer from turning off the tap on the flow of new business, the direct writers, after having been dependent on the reinsurers for a long time, now faced a conundrum. As a consequence, they were left with the following choices:

- to take on the risks unhedged,
- to stop offering the reinsured retail products on an ongoing basis or
- to take on the risks and try to get them managed internally using a slew of risk management methods.

Given that the second option is not really viable, since implementing it could result in a potential loss of revenue in other business lines, insurers writing this business tended to opt for the first choice over the third for the following reasons:

- ease of implementation;
- they shared the reinsurer's sentiment that historical long-term returns imply the guarantees are nearly worthless;
- they were unable to justify the cost associated with building the appropriate infrastructure required to run an internally managed hedging programme;
- riders were not allowed any marking-to-market provisions for the purposes of reporting in financial statements;
- they did not know where and how to start;
- they recognised the fact that the first option gives shareholders instant gratification and hence a better compensation for the senior management, especially when senior management has a view that the possibility of a downturn in the long-term market return is extremely remote.

After a string of highly publicised losses by writers of these risks, both the regulators and rating agencies started paying more attention to companies taking on such risks. As a consequence, companies have been discouraged from taking on such risks naked, so much so that, whenever the accounting standards allow the VA riders to be marked-to-market, it is highly likely that insurance companies run some kind of an internal hedging programme.

RISK MANAGEMENT

While Section 2 focused on the quantification of risks and tools used to quantify these risks, this part of the book will discuss how companies go about managing their risks. As is well known, the basic building blocks for managing these risks involve a combination of taking on the risks naked and use of reinsurance treaties, capital market instruments[3] and product development.

The balance of how much of each to manage is very much an art and is therefore subjective. As a consequence, this balance tends to change across companies, depending on

- the objective of the hedging programme,[4]
- the types of risk a company wants to manage,[5]
- the amount of money a company wants to spend on the hedging programme (including the cost of infrastructure).

Given the above framework, it is important for writers of VA products to understand and accept the fact that there are certain types of risks inherent in this product that simply cannot be hedged, regardless of the nature of the hedging strategy, while there will be others that are a function of the hedging strategy being implemented. As a consequence, in running any kind of hedging programme it is imperative for an insurance company to understand how well risks that are supposedly hedged are indeed hedged and how much of the risk just cannot be hedged given the nature of the business; this is further discussed in Section 4.

SUMMARY OF SECTION 3

This part comprises five chapters, starting with an overview by Rajeev Dutt of all the risk management strategies that are used in practice. We then continue with Adam Stolz's discussion (Chapter 11) on ways of using product development to manage risks embedded in VAs as a first line of defence. Michael Winkler contributes the third chapter (Chapter 12), in which he discusses the reinsurance market and use of reinsurance to manage risks. Yves Lehmann continues this discussion in Chapter 13, on the use of capital market instruments to manage risks. This part of the book concludes with an discussion from Kannoo Ravindran (Chapter 14) in which he suggests that all these varying strategies can be put together in practice to better manage the risks.

1 Counterparty risks were never discussed or questioned as long as the economics of the transaction made sense to both parties.

2 This was simply due to the fact that, upon analysing historical long-term returns, the probability of long-term negative return was very unlikely and hence the put options were almost worthless.

3 Examples of these are index futures and options, interest rate and equity swaps, interest rate swaptions, hybrid equity market options spanning both the interest rate and equity asset classes, volatility/variance swaps and other customised hedges.

4 This refers to fact that the hedger could manage the true economic risks versus risks associated with fluctuations in the financial statements (arising from the fact that liabilities cannot be marked-to-market, while the assets can) versus risks associated with fluctuations in required capital arising from what the conditional tail expectations look like.

5 Since the objectives identified are very much a function of equity market risks, volatility in equity market risks, interest rate risks and volatility in interest rate risks (to name but a few), an example of this could simply be managing the volatility in interest rates.

REFERENCES

Poterba, J., 1997, "The History of Annuities in the United States", National Bureau of Economic Research, Working Paper 6001.

10

Overview of Commonly Used Risk Management Strategies

Rajeev Dutt

Milliman

The current variation of insurer-offered retirement guarantees was made possible by the advancement of financial risk management practice in insurance companies and investment banks after the collapse of the variable annuity (VA) reinsurance market in early 2000. For current benefit designs, product development and pricing with a strong focus on the company's risk management framework are the essential elements when bringing new products to market. The advancement and acceptance of sound financial risk management practices have facilitated the development of living benefits that target the primary goals of retirement planning: protecting capital and providing income, while keeping pace with inflation.

RISK MANAGEMENT TECHNIQUES

VA guarantee writers have the choice of insuring the risks directly, transferring them to a rated counterparty (ie, reinsurer or investment bank) or some combination of the two. For most risk management approaches, a hedging programme of some sort will ultimately be used to transfer some of the risk to the capital markets.

There are a number of possible objectives to choose from when setting the hedging strategy. Ordinarily, a fine balance (due to the company's overall risk management objectives) is determined between managing economic risk, financial statement risk (due to the accounting treatment of the benefit designs) and capital requirements (due to issuers's jurisdiction and the regulatory environment for guarantee-type products). In practice, this is very much driven by what the company is most uncomfortable assuming, and can potentially vary across companies.

With the markets of late 2008, companies re-evaluated the cost-benefit relationship of managing accounting risk as it became more apparent that the primary risk was high realised volatility. Implied volatility is the market's expected view of future realised volatility; however, this expectation deviates for long-term options (a space where the market is fairly illiquid and not transparent). In addition, full market consistency may not be available for insurance liabilities as insurance guarantees are illiquid and long term in nature.

As there are generally no capital market instruments available to hedge actuarial (eg, behavioural, mortality, longevity) risks, conservative product pricing and ongoing experience monitoring is essential. Whatever financial risk management strategy is ultimately selected, it must be updated or rebalanced frequently such that the hedge in the future is insulated from the impact of the past experience deviations, while keeping in balance with the philosophy that the past cannot predict the future.

The following list presents an overview of the five commonly used risk management strategies. While all of the listed techniques have been in place for some time with the VA players in North America, there is no reason why these risk management solutions could not be used within any financial market outside North America.

Naked or no risk management

This approach, where capital provides for the ultimate claims, was dominant in the early days of Guaranteed Minimum Death Benefit (GMDB) guarantees, before the market crash of 2001. The rationale behind the strategy was based on high rates of assumed equity growth paired with high guarantee charges. At the time, the likelihood of a significant market decline was misestimated. In early 2009, there were still a few VA writers who used shareholder capital to satisfy regulator concerns of severe and sustained market declines. The problem with this approach is that management's view of the necessary buffer may be quite different from what the market actually experiences.

Static hedge

A static hedge attempts to replicate the future cashflows of the liability at a certain point in time based on expected policyholder behaviour and persistency. This usually involves purchasing a series of exotic equity options with a range of expiration dates and strikes which are typically established through an investment bank's structured-solutions service team. Accordingly, issues around transparency regarding the counterparty's creditworthiness need to be considered. In addition, the transaction cost must be considered in light of the pricing assumed within the product offered by the insurance company. Static strategies are not easily adaptable to the inevitable differences between the actuarial assumptions and the emerging experience.

Semi-static hedge

Due to the complexities associated with a static-hedge position, including the transaction costs paid for structured options, basic static hedges are rarely used in practice. A semi-static hedge is a variation of the static hedge in that the company uses a "semi-static" strategy to attempt to achieve a perfect static hedge by dynamically adjusting the hedge periodically, to allow for experience deviations of the existing block. This type of hedge needs to be refreshed with the addition of new business to the portfolio.

Dynamic hedging

Dynamic hedging is a common method of managing a portfolio of asset protection guarantees. A dynamic-hedging strategy replicates the liability by dynamically matching the sensitivities (or first- and second-order "Greeks"). Dynamic-hedging strategies insulate the net position of the portfolio from small movements in the capital markets. Rebalancing the hedge portfolio as markets move ensures that the underlying hedged position is managed against larger capital market movements that accumulate over longer periods of time. The amount of risk coverage depends on the sophistication of the dynamic-hedging strategy. In contrast to static or semi-static hedging, this approach allows for more flexibility and potentially lower cost, albeit complicated and infrastructurally heavy (due to the need to replicate this risk internally).

Being the current industry trend, dynamic hedging uses plain vanilla, liquid instruments (ie, predominantly exchange-traded instruments so as to reduce the transaction costs) to hedge the embedded option liability. The dynamic nature of this strategy requires that hedge positions are continuously updated to reflect emerging policyholder experience and market conditions. As the product sophistication of the industry increases, dynamic hedging is becoming the industry standard, with best practices continuing to evolve. Regulators and rating agencies also recognise the effectiveness of dynamic hedging as a risk mitigating technique, although currently no full capital relief is given for this type of strategy.

Reinsurance

This is one solution that could potentially allow the guarantee manufacturer to mitigate all capital market and actuarial risks. Basis risk, which represents the ability of the hedging instruments to track the underlying liability, can essentially be eliminated with a reinsurance solution. The reinsurance treaty terms ultimately dictate the coverage available, and mutually acceptable pricing may not accommodate all levels of desired insurance.

This form of coverage was available before the collapse of the markets in early 2000. It reappeared and was vibrant until the volatility shocks of late 2008. With reinsurers freely entering and leaving as market players in the equity guarantee space, the reinsurance risk management solution may never be a complete or permanent solution for the typical VA writer. Nevertheless, several large blocks of VA reinsurance exist today.

11

Using Product Development to Manage Risks

Adam Stolz

AXA

Product development is the process of designing, implementing and launching a new product. This occurs in many different industries; the focus here is on developing variable annuity products in the insurance industry and, most notably, how the design of these products can be used manage risks from an insurance company and customer point of view.

Product design is the most important aspect of risk management for variable annuities with guarantees. Once a guaranteed product is sold there is no going back. The choices of what to guarantee, how much to guarantee and what flexibility to offer are fundamental questions for risk management, and also fundamental questions for customer and marketing appeal. Therein lies a double-edged sword.

The starting point for any product design should be simplicity: the simpler the concept, the easier it is to understand, model and manage the risks and also the simpler it is to explain to customers, distributors and other stakeholders. As we saw during the 2008–9 financial crisis, complexity can lead to many unforeseen and undesirable consequences. Unfortunately, there are many things that get in the way of this aim of simplicity, namely

- local tax and insurance regulations,
- continual competitive demands for more sophisticated and complex products,
- distribution and customer feedback favouring a variety of features,
- financial and product professionals' desire to make the product more complex.

RISK APPETITE

The purpose of variable annuity (VA) product design should be to push through these constraints as much as possible so as to develop the best trade-off between the consumers and the insurer. Risk is the business of insurers and so without it they would not exist; but too much risk could potentially result in the insurer not being around to fulfil its obligations to the customer 10, 20 or 30 years hence. Furthermore, for these products, most of the risk is linked to financial markets, and so there is a systemic risk impacting on all policies; the traditional insurance philosophy of diversification across policies to manage the risk would not work well here.

Therefore, products should be designed to transfer risk from the customer to the insurer, and for the insurer to pass much of this risk to capital markets through hedging, with the insurer being comfortable that the residual risk remaining can be managed to within defined limits of value, capital and income. This concept of "risk appetite" should be central to any product-design decision. Meeting risk-appetite limits for VAs is as important, if not more important, as meeting performance targets in a central scenario.

The definition of value, capital and income (see Table 11.1) can vary significantly between different insurers and different countries, and will likely change over time due to new International Financial Reporting Standards (IFRS)/solvency capital rules.[1] While a risk appetite framework is important, it can quickly become complex. Thus, we should rely on other drivers of risk management in the product design.

Table 11.1 Components of product risk/return framework

Risk/return framework	Performance targets central scenario	Risk appetite limit in stress scenario (examples)
Value	To be defined in	In absolute terms
Capital	line with	As percentage of product central scenario
Income	company targets	As percentage of company-level results

RISK DRIVERS

Even without sophisticated models, we can still make some quite important statements about the risks of different product designs. The following features all lead to a higher cost of the guarantee and also potentially higher residual risks after hedging:

- higher guarantees;

- more frequent ratchets, resets (and similar features);

- a higher share of equity and other risky assets;

- more customer options, eg, additional premiums, deferral period option, dollar-for-dollar withdrawals, fund switching;

- regular premiums;

- combinations of the above which can potentially compound the risks.

The important aspect here is that just increasing the guarantee fee for these features will not be sufficient to manage the tail risk in a stress scenario. Other risk management measures will also need to be taken, including some of the following:

- adaptation of hedging strategy (including reinsurance);

- sharing of risks with the customers, eg, penalties for certain behaviours, the ability to reprice or change the guarantee for in-force policies in defined cases;

- imposing stricter limits in the product design in regards to consumer options;

- setting aside extra capital in order to cover shortfall in adverse scenarios.

Even with these and other measures, the additional risks assumed by offering such guarantee features may be too high and so should not be included. Insurers need to be careful not to include features where the risk exposure cannot be quantified. Any new feature, even if offered by competitors, should be fully understood, measured and be able to be managed before being offered to consumers. As past experience shows, what may have been a cheap feature based on historical experience can potentially become very expensive, as customers become more educated and market conditions change.

It is not uncommon to see insurance companies adding features over time to please customers and distributors and to enhance competitive positioning. While each incremental feature to an existing product design may not yield a severe exposure, the resulting overall product design may contain more risk than can be managed over time. For this reason, continued education and engagement with all product stakeholders is a must for any ongoing product development process.

PRODUCT EXAMPLES

To illustrate the concepts described so far, we will now discuss examples of the use of product design to enhance risk management.

Deferral period option

Consider a single premium VA with a Guaranteed Withdrawal Benefit for Life (GWBL). These products are normally structured to provide guaranteed income for retirement, and there is a deferral period before the first withdrawal, during which a customer earns a deferral bonus for each year of waiting. The customer often has a choice on the length of this deferral period.

Let us consider the risk of this option from a pricing and hedging perspective.

- Pricing. The aim would be to set a price that would cover the cost of the guarantee in a stress scenario. This usually occurs when the product has some built-in incentive for policyholders to behave in a certain way in an adverse market scenario (eg, immediate lifetime withdrawals or all withdrawals at the end of the 10-year deferral bonus period). However, sometimes there is no obvious single optimal point, and to price the risk correctly we should value optimal behaviour across a range of deferral periods, ie, like an American option. This may lead to a price much higher than the baseline assuming expected behaviour. From a customer perspective, this may lead to a price much higher than they are willing to pay.

- Hedging. Even if the option is fully priced, there is still a chance that unhedged risks can lead to adverse income after hedging. With pricing, we can be conservative in our approach, but hedging an assumed behaviour that maximises the value of the guarantee may lead to volatile results if customers behave in a different (ie, sub-optimal) manner.

To better manage the risk of this option we can consider the following design alternatives.

- Fixed deferral period. This could be set at the start date of the policy, taking into account the expected retirement date for the customer. If the customer needs income at a different date, then they would have access to the capital on a pro rata basis when needed. This design should lead to a lower price for the customer.

- Flexible deferral period, with an optimal point. Pricing and hedging could be done by assuming that the customer chooses the optimal starting date for withdrawals, but keeping the flexibility for the customer to choose another date if they wish.[2]

Fund and fee structure

Many distributors and customers like the ability to choose between different funds to be included in their VA offer. This in turn has led to a common open-architecture fund structure with a large range of actively managed funds being offered.

From a risk management point of view this design has a number of bad properties:

- there is no difference in guarantee price or treatment of funds that are difficult to hedge (eg, sector-specific, corporate bond, property funds) and those that are easy to hedge (eg, index trackers which are used as underlying for widely traded derivatives contracts);

- there is no difference in guarantee price for funds with higher fund management fees, giving a higher drag on the account balance and as a consequence contributing to a higher cost of guarantee;

- there is a sub-optimal diversification between different asset classes, leading to a higher cost of guarantee, and normally a higher guarantee fee for the customer.

On the other hand, there are probably a large number of customers who do not use or care for the features of open architecture, especially if this feature is more expensive than a more basic fund structure. Having said that, the fund revenue is an important source of margin for VA providers to help subsidise the cost of the guarantee, which as a result can serve as a resistance to any change.

Given the slew of problems above, we now propose a few potential design alternatives to better meet the interests of both customers and insurance companies:

- use of index trackers to minimise the cost to the customer and focus the product on having the best value guarantee;
- use of fund allocation to maximise diversification while being able to offer some non-index funds to give some alpha to clients;
- use of guided architecture to give the customer a choice of funds, but with constraints on the amount to be invested in any one fund, sector, etc.
- a choice allowing consumers to elect any combination of the above, but with lower prices for the more basic features (eg, index funds) and higher prices for enhanced features (eg, funds that cannot be easily replicated by tradeable indexes).

Commission and fee levels

For the most part, variable annuities are sold and not bought. Further, variable annuities are complex products that require significant time for an advisor to explain and support. To incentivise the sellers of variable annuities it is important to pay a sufficient level of commission. Based on market practice in 2008–9 we see

- US commission rates of about 7% upfront (or equivalent) for the vast majority of sales,
- commission rates in other markets (eg, Europe, Japan) of about 4–6% upfront (or equivalent).

Commission needs to be earned back by the insurance company through fee revenue, so the higher the commission, the higher the fees. Higher fees have two important impacts:

- a lower return for the customer and higher return for the insurance company in up-markets;
- a higher cost of guarantee for the insurance company in down-markets (as the guarantee is independent of fees from a customer perspective).

So, having lower commissions will lead to lower fees, which will be better for the customer (in up-markets) and better for the insurance company (in up- and down-markets). But of course, lower commissions will be worse for the seller/advisor and generally lead to lower sales and market-share.

During the 2008–9 financial crisis, we saw significant losses from insurance companies' variable annuity businesses, but excellent returns for customers (due to the guarantees) and excellent opportunities for distribution (due to the attractiveness of variable annuity guarantees in an uncertain financial environment).

The question going forward is whether we will see any reduction to commission and fee-levels for the benefit of insurance companies (and customers) at the expense of sellers and advisors. Given the success (especially in the US) of third-party sales of variable annuities, it will be difficult to change, but this nevertheless may be a necessary step to achieve a more sustainable approach to the manufacturing of these products in the medium to long term. For a commission reduction to be successful, it will probably require simpler product designs, and more effective product support, in order to reduce the time taken by sellers and advisors to explain and manage variable annuities. In 2009, we have already seen a number of insurance companies launch new simpler variable annuities, some with reduced commission and fees, others with the same commission and fees as existing products. Only time will tell which strategy has the most success in the long run.

CONCLUSION

Product design has been, and will continue to be, the most important aspect of risk management for variable annuities with guarantees. As insurance companies' risk appetite evolves, and their ability to understand, measure and manage risk advances, we will see an ever-changing variety of product designs being offered both in the US and around the world. But the most successful companies are likely to be those that have the greatest insight into what is driving the need for customers and distributors in the variable annuity market and exploit this insight to offer the best combination of product features, commission and price, as well as a peerless ability to explain and support these products over time.

1   It is important to note that two insurers with differing frameworks would end up with two different product designs.

2   Although in this case it would still be prudent to include in the pricing/hedging model the probability of the consumer choosing a different deferral period (as this consequently affects the value of the guarantee).

12

Using Reinsurance to Manage Risks

Michael Winkler

New Re

An experienced investment banker once said: "The only perfect hedge is when someone else owns [the risk]".[1] (After the recent experience of the financial-market crisis in 2007–8, which was in the first instance a credit crisis, we may add "and if this other party is creditworthy enough to finally meet the obligations".)

Variable annuity (VA) writers were very aware of this basic idea right from the early days of offering guaranteed minimum benefits on their products. It naturally follows that the history of VA reinsurance has always been closely linked to the history of VA covers.

HISTORY OF VA REINSURANCE

Early Guaranteed Minimum Death Benefit (GMDB) covers in the 1990s were cutting edge for the product developers, who were initially not used to doing the pricing for these covers. The traditional entry point for a reinsurer was to provide pricing support to their clients and then back this up by taking the risks for an agreed price. However, in the early days, the pricing methodologies used by many of the reinsurers were not very sophisticated. An example of this is evidenced by the fact that GMDB covers were priced using actual claims costs instead of realising that this will rarely be a good indicator for future claims costs.

In those days, reinsurers provided very onerous VA covers, offering price guarantees for new businesses over a two- to three-year period (Ruark 2005). The ceding companies, however, did not fully appreciate these generous covers and left many of their portfolios without any reinsurance. Meanwhile, the reinsurers did not hedge the financial-market risks that they had assumed and were similarly exposed to market crashes.[2] Over time, the GMDB covers proved to be a very competitive market in which the insurance companies tried to differentiate themselves by making incremental changes to basic guarantee design.

By adding more bells and whistles (or, more often, slightly bigger bells and louder whistles) without charging a higher price for the extended cover, insurance companies tried to make their product more attractive. Although these changes were usually pretty modest on their own, because the competitors did the same the products' features quickly became more aggressive, finally resulting in a lot of additional options for free. Despite this, the reinsurers felt that there was no reason to worry, due to the fact that they were only exposed to low claims costs in the past.

When the stock market crashed in 1998, many insurers and reinsurers learnt the lesson that proper pricing and hedging of the guarantees is crucial. As a consequence, many reinsurers withdrew from this business and the VA reinsurance market almost dried up. As can be seen from their annual reports, many reinsurers suffered from this first experience far beyond the start of the new millennium, so much so that attempts to hedge the legacy GMDB exposures at a later stage could not entirely undo the problems.

On the other hand, the pain felt by the VA providers during the crash in 1998 (and again later, in 2001–2) increased their risk awareness and "forced" them to improve the quality of their risk management significantly. Feeling confident that they could properly manage the risks of VA reinsurance, reinsurers (re-)entered the market over the past few years. Since reinsurers tend to hedge their financial-market risks, we find that

- prices are a lot closer to those of investment banks,
- prices for new business are no longer guaranteed for long periods, and
- reinsurance of in-force blocks of business has become more common.

This increased risk-consciousness of the reinsurers has impacted on the primary insurance market, promoting the move towards products for which risk management can be more effective. Despite all the lessons learnt, there are still some products that do not appear to embrace "adequate" risk management.[3] Unfortunately, such products have a certain impact on the insurance markets due to their effect on customer expectations. Fortunately, this typically lasts only for a limited period, since such approaches are not sustainable in the long run.

As a result of the financial-market crisis in 2007–8, the hedging costs for VA business have increased significantly (which has been reflected in the reinsurance premiums). On the one hand, this has meant that fewer in-force transactions have taken place than in previous years. On the other hand, market conditions have re-emphasised the importance of a comprehensive risk management approach. For many insurance companies (even for those running their own in-house hedging programmes for which reinsurance can be considered as a tool for risk diversification) this has meant renewed consideration of reinsurance. The willingness to accept exotic, unhedgable risks dried up after significant losses were reported in this area at a time when the awareness of counterparty credit risk increased significantly.

DRIVERS FOR REINSURANCE

Many VA writers typically use reinsurance when launching a new product. The reason for this stems from the fact that these writers do not have access to all the necessary technical skills and as a consequence need pricing, product design and risk management support once the product has been launched. This is very similar to other lines of business where new entrants first rely on reinsurers to cope with the uncertainties of a new product, in both the design and assumed risks.

Although a VA writer may plan to do their own risk management in due course, implementing such programmes may not be efficient until a critical mass of in-force business has been built up. For a new product line this can present a challenge even for a big company, since it will take some time to reach the necessary scale. During this time, the company will be exposed to financial risks which may be quite material. In this situation, reinsurance can be used as a stop-gap strategy during this initial period. Furthermore, the reality of the matter may be that the critical mass is never reached over the planned time horizon. In such an instance, reinsurance can continue to be the most optimal risk management strategy.

When writing new business, a VA writer may not be certain that they would be able to achieve adequate volume to justify the investment in their own risk management infrastructure. In this instance, reinsurance can be used to test and judge the market as to whether critical mass can be achieved. In fact, reinsurance can be used even when the VA writer decides to set up their own risk management programme. Since it takes time to recruit and train the necessary skilled staff and build the appropriate systems, having reinsurance in place during this period of build-up will be a useful risk management strategy.

For back-end loaded products, there might be a significant surplus strain in the first year which can be compensated by a reinsurance commission; so financing of new business is a another driver for VA reinsurance (just like many other traditional products).

Companies with their own hedging programmes might decide on reinsurance for completely different reasons, such as risk diversification, managing or mitigating the significant operational risk of the hedging activities or coping with particular deficiencies of their own hedging programme. A new product line may also bring some of the same challenges that were described earlier for a new VA writer.

These days, insurance companies are increasingly trying to optimise their capital position. As a consequence, in addition to reinsuring business exceeding their own capacity, companies also use reinsurance for the following statutory reasons:

- to move the business to a more favourable regulatory environment through reinsurance;
- to ensure favourable regulatory treatment for the use of reinsurance over other risk management options.

International insurance groups use internal reinsurance arrangements as a tool to centralise risk management and benefit from the economies of scale or to take advantage of a certain regulatory treatment. For the centralised internal reinsurer, the considerations for external reinsurance are the same as for a stand-alone VA writer. Furthermore, the ability to centralise is also affected by the peculiarities of the products in local markets, and this can in turn limit the economies of scale. External reinsurance may also be used to address any limitations that may arise.

A new driver for reinsurance is the story a company wants to tell to its investors. Companies that have had their fingers burnt by financial-market risks in the past can now use reinsurance and communicate to their shareholders that they have fully reinsured their VA business. Doing this helps to increase their credibility in the marketplace among shareholders and puts to rest concerns regarding exposure to such products, contrary to some of the recent press releases in regards to VA writers incurring heavy losses due to the lack of a prudent and effective risk management programme.

TREATY CONCEPTS

The most common reinsurance agreement focuses only on the guarantees of the product. The reinsurance benefit is the positive difference between the guarantee level and the actual fund value at the time of the claim. In certain specific circumstances it may be beneficial to the parties for the fund management to be transferred to the reinsurer as well. However, this is usually not required.

The reinsurance premiums are normally expressed in basis points of the fund value. This means that the dollar value of the premiums is lower when the guarantees are in-the-money (and therefore valuable) and higher when the guarantees are out-of-the-money. Alternative charging structures for reinsurers are based on the single premium or on the guarantee levels and are therefore less sensitive to policyholder behaviour (eg, high lapses in the case of out-of-the-money guarantees have less impact on the overall profitability, since the corresponding reinsurance charges are not higher than those for the other scenarios.) Such an approach needs to be considered at the product-design stage if alignment between the reinsurance premiums and customer charges is desired.

As long as the guarantees are fully transferred to the reinsurer, the statutory treatment of the reinsurance agreement is clear in most regulations. Due to the fact that the reinsurer is now liable for meeting those guarantees, the original risks are replaced by the counterparty risk of the reinsurer. As long as the reinsurer can meet its liabilities, the ceding company will be able to pay the guarantees. This is commonly referred to as "reserve credit for reinsurance", which means that the ceding company no longer has to establish its own reserves for the guarantees. Instead, the insurer may have to hold a reserve or capital provision against the counterparty risk of the particular reinsurer taking over the guarantee risks.

In most cases, ceding companies are looking to pass the guarantee risks to the reinsurer in a comprehensive way. However, there are still cases where the reinsurance agreements provide a limited risk transfer. This is clearly the case wherever the ceding company chooses to retain some risk in order to align the interests of both parties. For example, as in traditional reinsurance arrangements, a certain proportion of any significant mortality risk would be retained by the ceding company (otherwise the ceding company would be not interested in doing underwriting and claims management properly). Similar considerations can be applied to certain policyholder behaviour risks like lapses or fund switches as well as to the basis risks associated with internally managed funds. If there is a chance for the primary insurer to steer these risks, there should be an incentive for them to do so (namely a corresponding retention of that risk). Furthermore, the views of the reinsurer and primary insurer on those risks might differ significantly, and applying conservative pricing and sharing of the upside arising from that might not allow for competitive pricing; in this case, it makes more sense if the ceding company simply retains those risks (outside of a certain corridor).

Companies sometimes look for cheaper cover and would like to introduce certain limitations for that purpose. As a consequence, they may want to either retain the risk associated with a small drop in account value (deductible) or ask the reinsurer for cover up to a certain account value drop (cap). In the US, some aggregate claim caps are additionally put in place, stemming from a time when hedging of the financial-market risks was not yet established and reinsurance companies wanted to limit their exposure with other measures.

For all limited covers, getting reserve credit for the reinsured risks may not be straightforward even if the particular regulatory environment recognises full covers. Regulators tend to assess the unhedged risks in a more conservative way, resulting in these partial covers not being capital efficient.

OUTLOOK

As VA markets develop, there will always be a significant number of companies looking for VA reinsurance, either just for the starting phase or as a long-term risk management solution. VA reinsurance is often the only way to enable small and medium-sized companies to enter the VA market if white labelling is not available. For large

companies (even those with their own hedging platform), VA reinsurance can be a bridging solution until the in-house risk management is fully established or used as a long-term risk diversification
tool. Given all the uncertainties of an emerging VA market, reinsurance can also help to keep the business risks associated with the new
product under control.

Regulators in many countries seem to favour reinsurance as a
risk management tool due to the fact that it is easier to assess than a
company's own hedging programme with all its operational risks.
Furthermore, reinsurance can lead to a certain standard setting in
the market and can shape the market in such a way that proper
risk management procedures can be applied. However, many VA
regulations are yet to be developed and finalised, thereby making
it difficult to predict whether reinsurance will be an attractive risk
management option.

The shareholders of VA writers pay close attention to the risk management of these products. As a consequence, there is a strong need
for a sound reinsurance programme in favour of an in-house hedging
due to higher transparency. Companies whose hedging programmes
have shown particular deficiencies in the past will have difficulty
explaining why the planned changes in their hedging strategy will
now lead to a much more robust and favourable outcome.

It is not yet clear whether customers will accept the more restrictive policy provisions required by reinsurers or the higher costs for
less restrictive provisions. If there are still VA writers adopting a
more aggressive approach (and hence more attractive guarantees) in
a particular market and neither regulators nor shareholders are stop-
ping them from doing so, risk management, including reinsurance,
will take longer to establish.

Where VA reinsurance is a well established risk management tool
and the related counterparty risks are properly managed, the regulators, the shareholders and the insurance clients can be more confident that the long-term guarantees of their VA products will finally
be met.

1   David Komansky, former CEO of Merrill Lynch, discussing the turmoil in the bond market
    in 1998 (*Wall Street Journal*, September 22, 1998).

2   The justification for not hedging was due to the "diversification over time" philosophy that,
    in the long run, sufficient premiums will be collected to cover the losses, since market risks,
    like mortality risks, can be diversified.

3 One reason for such products hitting the market is the fact that these features were supported by reinsurers who have taken relatively benign views of the risks involved and have subsequently withdrawn from the reinsurance marketplace.

REFERENCES

Ruark, T. J., 2005, "Where Does the Time Go?", *Reinsurance News*, August, No. 56.

13

Using Capital Markets to Manage Risks

Yves Lehmann

Société Générale/Catalyst Re

Despite the fact that Guaranteed Minimum Benefits (GMxBs) – the new frontier between capital markets and insurance – have been around for a while, the problems revealed in 2007 and 2008 were not much of a surprise. The recent crisis has also taught us some of the following lessons about this new business.

- Economically, GMxBs are essentially exotic (complex, path-dependent, multi-asset based) options. Their management requires actuarial skills, market access and extensive experience in derivatives risk management. Stand-alone development by GMxB writers has led some of them to ignore and misprice certain risks. Due to competitive pressure, business has become unsustainable, especially in the US. Fortunately, the market is maturing quickly.

- GMxB pricing is also driven by regulatory capital and accounting arbitrage. For instance, while financial options are marked-to-market, some of the GMxB options are marked-to-model.[1] Naturally, GMxB issuance has concentrated on the cheapest options at the expense of the VA writers.

- Commercially, GMxBs are distributed like financial products. In the US, distribution by third-party banks and independent financial advisors increased from 55% of sales in 1998 to 68% of sales in 2007. In Japan and Europe, distribution is mostly done by commercial banks and independent brokers. The consequence is a much more fickle client base than traditional insurance clients.

Table 13.1 Different capital strategies

Strategy (insurance language)	Translation (capital-market language)	Pros and cons
Do nothing (self-insurance)	Selling naked put options	Very capital intensive (especially in a downturn)
		Viable only if issuer capital cost is abundant and cheap
Dynamic hedging	Implicit parameter and model arbitrage	Potentially minimise accounting volatility and regulatory capital
		Insurer may ignore some risks (eg, basis risk)
		Operationally heavy, not economical for mid-sized insurance companies
Core hedge	Explicit parameter arbitrage	Minimise economic capital
		Insurer decides which market parameters it wishes to hedge
		May create accounting volatility
Core reinsurance	Core hedge plus reinsurance wrapper	Selective risk transfer of market and insurance risks
		Optimised allocation of economic capital
		Accessible for mid-sized insurance companies
Full reinsurance	Back-to-back	Lack of capacity (withdrawal of traditional reinsurance companies)
		Considered as expensive (compared with accounting and statutory capital standards)

DIFFERENT CAPITAL STRATEGIES

After selling GMxB embedded options, there are several different ways a GMxB writer can use capital markets or reinsurance to manage its risks. Table 13.1 provides a brief overview of these strategies.

LISTED DERIVATIVES AND INTERNAL HEDGING

Until the late 1990s, most insurance companies did not hedge their GMxB related risks. Despite this strategy not being sustainable, a few companies (on a smaller scale) are still deploying this actively.

Listed futures and options have significantly reduced the variance of expected profit and loss (P&L), especially under actuarial stochastic models. However, the results vary greatly depending on the model and parameters chosen.

Given the complexity of GMxB embedded options, losses could have been expected to arise from the most exotic features, for instance, correlation or smile risks. Although it may seem surprising that at first glance the major losses have come from the most basic risks, such as tracking error (which everyone thought was under control), on a closer look this should not come as too much of a surprise if we recognise the fact that tracking error impacts on the balance sheet almost immediately, compared with vega mis-hedges (which can only bleed over time) given the fact that many of the hedgers in this business run a delta-hedging programme and assume volatility risk.[2]

Delta hedging and tracking error

In 2008, most VA writers were adversely affected by basis risk (or the tracking error between the fund returns and replicating index returns).

Traditionally, there has been no explicit provision for basis risk. Funds are expected to mean-revert around their benchmark indexes.

The notional on which an insurer assumes tracking error risks depends on both the delta of the put option and the expected lapse rate. Unfortunately, these factors change over time.

Basis risk: a numerical illustration

The following simple numerical example shows how internal hedging can give a "myopic" perspective of optional risks, and the

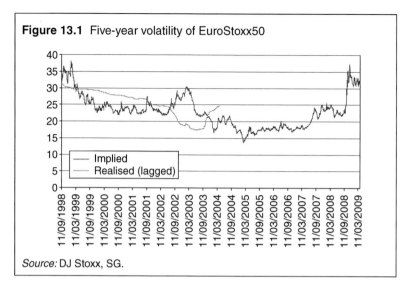

Figure 13.1 Five-year volatility of EuroStoxx50

Source: DJ Stoxx, SG.

unstable nature of VA risks, which was not anticipated in actuarial models.

Let us assume that, at inception, your GMxB option has a "delta" of 20% and you anticipate that 50% of your clients will surrender without exercising the option: your basis risk is on 10% (20% × 50%) of your GMxB notional.

However, this result is not very stable. One year later, if your funds have lost 60%, the picture is quite different. Your option would have a delta of 80%, and your clients are much less likely to lapse; it is anticipated that 90% will hold the product to maturity. Your basis risk is now on 72% (80% × 90%), a sevenfold increase in one year.

Vega hedging

Unlike the case for basis risk, many insurance companies made a conscious decision not to hedge their volatility risk despite the fact that, contrary to popular belief, implied volatility was not expensive. In fact, when we look at the five-year rolling volatility since 1998 (see Figure 13.1), implied volatility was slightly lower than realised volatility.[3]

Until 2007, implied volatility was generally recognised as particularly "cheap", thanks to abundant liquidity in the capital markets. However, it started rising in 2007 and spiked upwards in autumn 2008, just as the equity market went down.

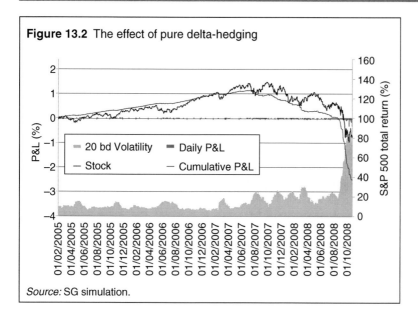

Figure 13.2 The effect of pure delta-hedging

Source: SG simulation.

Insurers who had relied on pure delta-hedging (without vega hedging) were hit twice, once on their realised P&L (impact of higher realised volatility) and then again on their embedded value (impact of higher implied volatility).

Figure 13.2 illustrates the first effect over 2007 and 2008, for a GMxB pure delta-hedging replication, ignoring basis risk and implied volatility effects. It can clearly be seen that the P&L (denoted by the grey line) is actually positively correlated to the stock market, since higher volatility generally tends to happen in a bear-market environment.

There is nothing wrong with insurance companies making a conscious financial decision not to hedge vega risk. However, such financial decisions should be kept separate from the GMxB pricing, and the corresponding capital should be provisioned for investments.

If not done properly, internal hedging can become myopic, and hence can lead to very large surprises after a few years. As a consequence, it should not be used as a convenient way to ignore certain financial risks (which is sometimes encouraged by lenient regulatory capital standards).

As we have seen, internal hedging is not without its hidden risks. At the other extreme, transferring all the risks to a reinsurer appears to be the safest approach to managing these risks (with which the hedger is now exposed to counterparty risks and a possibly expensive cost associated with this risk transfer).

Core hedge

Unlike dynamic hedging, core hedging (sometimes also known as cashflow hedging or quasi-static hedging) is about robustly hedging long-term cashflows. For instance, in 2004 a leading French insurer set out to hedge its Guaranteed Minimum Death Benefit (GMDB) book with a series of hybrid options. Instead of hedging delta, rho and vega separately, the insurer built a stable hedge portfolio, which was rebalanced only a few times a year.

Implementing a core hedge does not necessarily mean that the insurance company transfers all financial risks to its counterparty. It is possible for insurance companies to retain long-term volatility risks and hedge the cashflows arising using this underlying volatility assumption. As a consequence, the option premium can be adjusted *ex post* based on a realised volatility. Another alternative is to have a variable notional hedge. Thus, if volatility turns out to be higher than initially projected, the insurance company would know the additional costs in advance.

Internal hedging versus core hedging

There are three main differences between internalised dynamic hedging and core hedging.

- Operations (linked to daily trading) are outsourced to the bank, which benefits from economies of scale and lower transaction costs.

- The insurance company can therefore focus on long-term risk management, which is its core skill.

- Rather than taking "implicit bets" hidden in actuarial models, the insurance company takes explicit views on the risks it wants to retain (eg, volatility risks, basis risks, actuarial risks). The insurance company can also choose to cap those risks, depending on its global asset-liability management strategy.

Core hedge ranges from "micro-hedge" (a portfolio of hybrid options on basket of indexes) to parametric hedge (a proxy hedge in order to minimise the variance of the residual risk, on the actual book).

Core reinsurance

Core reinsurance goes one step beyond core hedge, and incorporates reinsurance and structuring features. The main considerations for choosing core reinsurance include the following.

- Accounting treatment: for instance, in the US, GMDB and Guaranteed Minimum Income Benefit (GMIB) guarantees are not marked-to-market, unlike any capital markets asset used to hedge the risks. In such an instance, core reinsurance is accounted like the underlying risk, making it accounting friendly.

- Statutory capital: in many of the regulatory jurisdictions around the world, hedging programmes utilising capital markets instruments do not get full capital relief. In such an instance, reinsurance provides greater capital relief.

- Transfer of actuarial risks: behaviour (lapse) and biometric risks (mortality, longevity).

Initiated by MetLife in 2005 to hedge its GMDB risks, core reinsurance can be a meaningful strategy for in-force blocks exceeding US$100 million. The core reinsurance model has become pre-eminent in Japan (the largest market for VAs after the US).

CAPITAL MARKETS FOR ACTUARIAL RISK: ALTERNATIVE RISK TRANSFER

Alternative risk transfer (ART) is typically focused on property and casualty risks (eg, hurricanes, earthquakes, etc). The ART market for life insurance, which is still in its infancy, is expected to develop in the next decade to face the growing capital needs of life-insurance companies.

Mortality and longevity

Mortality-risk hedge instruments were initiated by Swiss Re through mortality catastrophe bonds, where the objective of these bonds was to release tail risks, linked to some national statistics.

Longevity risks involve huge systemic risks, with very long durations. In 2005, BNP Paribas tried to structure a longevity bond, with

EIB (European Investment Bank) as the issuer and PartnerRe as reinsurer. The bond was based on parametric data, and limited in duration to 25 years. This simply failed to take off, since the counterparties (ie, investors) were not willing to hedge their longevity risks.

In 2008, JP Morgan opened the market for longevity swaps. However, most transactions involving longevity risks still take the form of reinsurance or pension buy-outs, combining financial and longevity risks. A growing exception, however, is the secondary market for life settlements, as discussed below.

Looking ahead, we anticipate that capital markets will continue to play a growing role for management of longevity risk. The precedent is inflation, for which capital market activities have grown in the first decade of the 21st Century, at least in the major currencies. For longevity bonds, the catalyst might be the public sector and their pension systems, which often combine underfunding and a concentration of longevity risk.

Behaviour risk: lapse and switch

Lapse risk is already being securitised for traditional life insurance, through value-in-force securitisation. Depending on the scheme, the actual risk transfer can be more or less significant.

There is already a significant behaviour ART market in the US, based on residential mortgage-backed securities (RMBSs). Prepayment risk on US residential mortgages is philosophically similar to lapse risk on life policies. The financial technology is available; a market exists (although liquidity has dried up since 2008). RMBSs took off after the savings and loan crisis; for many insurance companies, starved of capital, behaviour risk transfer would be a welcome opportunity.

Secondary insurance markets: a threat or an opportunity?

Capital markets already play a role in insurance capital. The secondary market for life-insurance contracts has picked up significantly since 2004, mainly in the US and UK. It clearly shows that there are investors, both individual and institutional, for insurance risks.

Today, the market is clearly geared towards individual policyholders, at the expense of the insurance companies. Since the VA market is still young, the secondary market will not pick up for another five or ten years, when more sophisticated investors will enter the marketplace and policyholders/advisors become more knowledgeable about value of these guarantees, making it attractive for policyholders and financial intermediaries to trade in and out of them. However, the market would be developed at the expense of the original VA writers.

As secondary markets for insurance policies develop, VAs will become more and more like pure financial products. To prepare for this potential threat, VA providers need to anticipate the trend in their VA pricing and design of products.

CONCLUSION AND OUTLOOK

Despite the VA insurance industry facing its first major crisis, VAs are here to stay, due to a genuine demand for hybrid solutions spanning both the capital markets and insurance space. As a consequence, three industry developments that would be worth following in the near future are

- core reinsurance, as a middle ground between internal hedging and full reinsurance, with selective risk transfer,

- dynamic variable annuities, with financial options already embedded into the funds, as already pioneered in Europe,

- development of secondary market for VAs, which will adversely affect VA providers who did not properly price and manage lapse and switch risks.

1 Mark-to-model is an intermediate valuation between accrual and mark-to-market, used for valuation of illiquid embedded options. Essentially, the insurer will develop a stochastic model (as for mark-to-market) and use historical estimates as parameters. For instance, for 2008 one company valued some GMxB with a mark-to-market volatility of 35%, and other GMxBs with a "prudent estimate" volatility of 20%.

2 This is further fuelled by the following facts.

- In the hedging programmes run by many VA writers, bond funds do not tend to get modelled or hedged. Given how credit spreads have blown out since autumn 2008, the lack of replication (or appropriate replication) of these bond funds has resulted in a significant increase in the tracking error.

- The correlation between the fund and replicating index returns (which tended to be quite stable in trending markets in the past) has decreased recently, resulting in an increase in tracking error. This phenomenon is a side effect of the liquidity breakdown that occurred in 2008.

3 25.06% for implied volatility (at-the-money) versus 25.33% for realised volatility (five-year rolling period, start dates from March 1998 to April 2004).

14

Putting It All Together: From Dynamic to Static

Kannoo Ravindran

Annuity Systems Inc and Háskólinn í Reykjavík

It should not come as a surprise that any VA writer is exposed to risks arising from the guarantees offered to the policyholder. Therefore, before trying to get into this business, some of the important questions that a potential VA writer needs to ask itself are the following.

- What kinds of risks are taken on by entering such a market?

- Is this a profitable business in which to partake (taking into consideration the cost of capital/controls/infrastructure, etc)?

  - If yes, how much profit is expected to be made from this line of business?

  - If no, what kind of impact would it have on the market share associated with the other product offerings and how much would this eat into the overall profitability of the company if this is not been offered?

On the other hand, for a VA writer who is already in the business, the questions to ask will be more along the lines of aspects of risk management strategies and how best to implement them in a well-controlled, effective and efficient manner. Since it is only possible to manage risks that can be both quantified and monitored, given the focus of this chapter, we will only discuss the management aspect of this problem.

THE OBJECTIVE

Before thinking about any risk management strategy, it is important for the hedger to be able to answer the question: "What kinds of risks am we interested in managing?"[1] Given that a VA writer is simultaneously exposed to financial-market risks (ie, "economic" risks), financial statement volatility risks (ie, "accounting" risks) and regulatory capital volatility risks (ie, "regulatory" risks), it is intuitively reasonable to expect all these risks to be mitigated by a complete reinsurance cover.[2] In reality, it is difficult to find a complete reinsurance cover, let alone find one for a price that would keep the VA writer's operation profitable. As a consequence, it becomes imperative for the VA writer to decide on the available risk management strategies that can be deployed efficiently. This, however, gets tricky, since it is often the case that, for all these riders, the "economic", "accounting" and "regulatory" risks do not march in step[3]. Given this backdrop, the hedger would need to be able to prioritise and decide which of these three risks is most severe or if all three types are equally important. Furthermore, given that in the US markets some of these liabilities do not qualify as derivatives, or CEOs of these companies are sometimes more driven to show growth with little volatility in their income statements, alternative risk management methods are often unable to address all these concerns simultaneously in one clean sweep, like a complete reinsurance would or can do. As a consequence, the choice of risk management strategies used to manage the risks embedded in these products is a function of the products and the objectives. Once the objective of the risk management programme has been identified, the next logical question pertains to that of how many of the risks we can afford to hedge given the current market conditions. The amount to be hedged is usually obtained iteratively upon identifying the following:

- the hedging strategies that will be deployed;

- the annual budget set aside for the hedging programme;

- the potential consequences of the unhedged risks.

Since this chapter is focused on the hedging strategies used by a VA writer (and hence the cost and risks associated with each of these strategies), henceforth we will assume for the sake of convenience and readability that we are only interested in managing the "economic" risks.

STRATEGIES FOR MANAGING RISKS

The risks embedded in these products are quite complex. While complete reinsurance has been the traditional method of choice to manage these risks, the lack of reinsurers or complete reinsurance makes it imperative for direct writers of this business to look for other alternative risk management techniques. As detailed in the earlier sections of this chapter, the risk management strategies available to the hedger take a combination of the following forms.

Taking on risks naked

The strategy of not doing anything (sometimes also called "self-insurance") allows the writer to set aside the appropriate capital for not doing anything. The user of this strategy is completely exposed to the underlying risks. Having said that, this could very well be a valid risk-mitigating strategy if the size of the business is quite small, since the execution of any hedge would require a minimum transaction size that may not be feasible for a small business. In such an event, it would be prudent for the company employing this strategy to be able to have a trigger level for the size of the business, so that the hedging strategies mentioned below can be implemented. In practice, although hedgers using this strategy tend to not do anything about monitoring or quantifying their risks, it is prudent to be able to run the risk positions at least monthly to ensure that the risks embedded in the business are still well contained and to see whether any unforeseen risks have just crept out from nowhere.

Reinsuring risks

This strategy revolves around reinsuring risks partially or completely using whatever is available at the marketplace for a reasonable cost. A complete reinsurance, if available for a reasonable price, is the best solution for the direct writer, since, in addition to mitigating the economic risks, there are no risks associated with requirement of capital, fluctuations in deferred acquisition costs, etc. In practice, the reinsurance that is currently available in the marketplace typically has various restrictions, for example,

- finite capacity,
- limits on single claims,
- limits on total annual claim,

- the ability to change premiums.

In using this strategy, the direct writer is exposed to counterparty risks (since the reinsurer must still be in business in order to be able to pay out the claims as and when they become due). As a consequence, to implement this strategy prudently, direct writers should ensure that the reinsurers know how to manage these risks and are doing so proactively.[4]

Static hedging

This strategy, which involves the purchase of long-dated over-the-counter (OTC) options from investment banks, can potentially be very expensive for the following reasons.

- Lapse and mortality risks are still borne by the direct writer, since investment banks typically do not take on non-market-related risks.

- The availability of OTC options decreases as the maturity of these derivatives exceeds 10 years.[5]

- The derivatives purchased are usually linked to indexes (eg, S&P 500, FTSE 100, etc), while the guarantees on these products are on actively managed funds. As a consequence, this strategy introduces the hedger to basis risks.[6]

- The accounting and regulations associated with these products are usually not derivatives friendly for certain types of riders. Hence, although the hedging programme may be perfectly economically hedged with OTC options, it is realistic to expect less than 50% of capital relief and to be exposed to reported accounting fluctuations – a problem that is very nicely circumvented by the purchase of a complete reinsurance.

- The purchaser of these options can end up paying dearly for these long-dated options. Furthermore, the bid–offer spread associated with these options is quite large. Given that lapse/mortality risks are still borne by the direct writers, any fluctuations of the realisations from the prediction would result in slippages in the hedging programme. As a consequence, the hedger would need to rebalance these hedges, resulting in them potentially unwinding existing long-dated trades and incurring huge transactions costs.[7]

Like the reinsurance strategy, this strategy also exposes the direct writer to counterparty risks. Unlike many reinsurers, however, investment banks selling long-dated options do often manage their risks proactively.

Dynamic hedging[8]

This strategy essentially amounts to doing what is done under the static option, but in a manner that is less static. The key motivation of this strategy is to reduce the transaction costs embedded in the static approach by doing what the investment banks themselves do internally when they sell these long-dated OTC derivatives. Thus, all the associated regulatory and accounting problems relating to the recognition of the use of derivatives in a hedging problem still remain. Although this is philosophically similar to what investment banks do to dynamically hedge their risks, it used to be a foreign concept to many insurance companies. As a consequence, insurance companies embarking on this approach do not fully appreciate the complexities and the intricacies associated with this programme. If improperly done, this programme can be more disastrous than taking on the risks naked.[9] Properly implemented, this strategy would revolve around the use of liquid instruments like futures, equity options (both exchange and OTC), swaps and swaptions.[10] The details associated with the implementation of a dynamic-hedging programme are further discussed later.

Product development

This strategy basically relates to the ability to ensure the risks embedded in a product are well contained. Given the nature of the strategy, product development is something that is done even before a product is launched to the retail market. In practice, in the process of pricing of a product, the insurer has the ability to decide what kinds of guarantee it should offer to policyholders in relation to the restrictions imposed on policyholders (regarding fund switches, surrendering, withdrawals, etc). The primary objective of this strategy is to help contain risks that cannot be hedged by capital markets instruments. In practice, this is the first line of defence for risk management and hence it is imperative that every VA writer implement this before launching the product into the retail market. As a consequence, for the purposes of our discussion we will henceforth assume that this strategy is already put in place before the launch of the product.

PUTTING IT ALL TOGETHER

All the strategies mentioned have been deployed by VA writers in one form or another, depending on the ready availability and afford-ability of full reinsurance cover. In the absence of such availability and affordability, each strategy (including partial reinsurance) has its own merit, depending on the kinds of risk the writer wants to hedge and assume. However, in practice, it is not uncommon to see the writer implementing a hedging strategy without fully compre-hending the view taken or risks (or consequences) to which they will be exposed. Furthermore, it is disturbing to sometimes see a writer of such risks continue with their dynamic-hedging strategy even if a reinsurance cover suddenly becomes available at an affordable price (assuming the counterparty risks are acceptable).

Having pioneered and implemented a myriad of hedge strate-gies for clients, the author has found that what works best in prac-tice is something called a quasi-static-hedging strategy. This strat-egy is actually a hybrid of the dynamic hedging, OTC static option and reinsurance strategies. As a consequence, the instruments used for implementing this strategy include reinsurance and long-dated options in addition to all the liquid instruments used for a dynamic-hedging programme. The motivation for this strategy is driven primarily by the following facts.

- When market conditions are not sufficiently favourable to transact in long-dated options/reinsurance (ie, these are not available at reasonable prices), the hedger will use dynamic hedging/self-insurance to manage the risks.
- The long-dated options/reinsurance transacted into serve as cashflow hedges (assuming there are no fluctuations in both policyholder behaviour and mortality assumptions from the moment that the hedges have been put on) so as to pay out the policyholder claims as and when they arise.
- Any time a transaction takes place in long-dated option/re-insurance, it is customised in a manner so as to avoid the need to unwind the hedge.[11]
- Any residual risks are dynamically managed.

- The hedger constantly checks the reinsurance market for the ability to completely lay-off the unhedged risks inherent in the existing in-force. The purpose of this is to transact in deals whenever laying off the residual risks (on both an existing and roll-forward basis) becomes cheaper than continuing with the internal hedging programme.

The above comments on the use of a quasi-static strategy can be easily modified to entertain any views a hedger may have on interest rates, volatilities, lapses, etc.

THE ABC OF DYNAMIC HEDGING

Since the seminal papers by Black and Scholes (1973) and Merton (1973), dynamic hedging has been used by investment banks to dynamically and synthetically recreate option-type risk profiles arising from transacting with other counterparties. In the traditional sense of the word, dynamic hedging typically involves replicating the transacting (sold/purchased) options with liquid and short-term instruments (ie, cash, futures and short-dated option contacts).

The simplest form of dynamic hedging is delta hedging of the equity risks (which is analogous to duration matching in the traditional asset liability management framework) which also happens to be the most unstable hedging approach in non-trending and volatile markets. The most sophisticated form of dynamic hedging revolves around hedging all the "Greeks", which is analogous to almost doing a back-to-back trade.[12]

Delta hedging

The concept underlying a delta-hedging programme can be more easily understood via a numerical example.[13]

Example
A bank sells a six-month call option[14] for US$2.26, which gives the purchaser the right to purchase the underlying stock at US$40 on option expiry.

To delta hedge, the bank would first calculate the option delta and then transact into that many underlying stocks.

Table 14.1 illustrates a stock price path (taken over monthly intervals) in which the option finishes in-the-money after six months. As can be seen, the delta of the option starts from 0.70 (which means that

Table 14.1 An in-the-money path

Time (months)	Stock price path	Liability delta	CP (US$)	Loan* (US$)	Weekly loan interest (US$)
0	40.00	−0.70	2.26	−25.74	−0.17
1	41.00	−0.78	−25.91	−29.19	−0.20
2	41.50	−0.45	−29.39	−15.69	−0.10
3	39.75	−0.88	−15.80	−32.89	−0.22
4	39.00	−0.61	−33.11	−22.58	−0.15
5	38.75	−0.10	−22.73	−2.97	−0.02
6	40.50	−1.00	−2.99	−39.44	—

Amount received from option exercise	US$40.00
Amount owing on loan	−US$39.44
Net profit after hedging	US$0.56

CP, cash position before implementing transaction; *loan required to neutralise the delta.

the hedger would go out and acquire 0.7 shares of the underlying stock[15]). This delta level fluctuates over the six months, finally resulting in one share (implying that the hedger would have acquired this one share under this delta hedging programme). This share of course would be used to fulfill the obligation of the bank in which the hedger would either deliver this share to the option purchaser for US$40 (if it was physical delivery underlying this option) taking a loss of US$0.50 or cash in the share to pay the option purchaser a cash amount of US$0.50 (Hull 2008, pp. 364–5).[16] In the process, the hedger makes a profit of US$0.56 (taking into consideration the US$2.26 option premium received at the inception of the contract).

Table 14.2 illustrates a stock price path in which the option finishes out-of-the-money. As expected, the delta which starts at 0.7 slowly drifts out to 0, indicating that the hedger should not be holding any shares since the option is worthless and there is no risk from this obligation. In the process, the hedger incurs a loss of US$0.45 (taking into consideration the US$2.26 option premium received at the inception of the contract).

In theory, if the replication interval was small enough, doing this would allow us to replicate the option premium of US$2.26 with

Table 14.2 An out-of-the-money path

Time (months)	Stock price path	Liability delta	CP (US$)	Loan* (US$)	Weekly loan interest (US$)
0	40.00	−0.70	2.26	−25.74	−0.17
1	39.00	−0.56	−25.91	−20.45	−0.14
2	38.50	−0.45	−20.59	−16.35	−0.11
3	39.75	−0.60	−16.46	−22.43	−0.15
4	41.00	−0.79	−22.58	−30.37	−0.20
5	38.00	−0.10	−30.57	−4.35	−0.03
6	39.25	0.00	−4.38	−0.45	—

Amount received from option exercise		—			
Amount owing on loan		−US$0.45			
Net profit after hedging		−US$0.45			

CP, cash position before implementing transaction; *loan required to neutralise the delta.

no variance around this option premium, provided that this is done under a slew of assumptions (Hull 2008, pp. 286–7). Furthermore, at the moment the volatility and/or interest rate changes during the option life, running the delta-hedging strategy (no matter how small the replication interval) does not usually lead to a replication cost of US$2.26. The reason for this simply stems from the fact that, in order to mitigate against movements in volatility and interest rates, we would have to go beyond delta-hedging. As a consequence we would have to transact into options (to help manage the volatility risks) and interest rate swaps (to help manage the interest rate risks).

Hedging beyond delta

Delta hedging focuses on immunising the first-order changes in option values for changes in stock prices. This can be more aptly seen from the following equation

$$\Delta c = \left(\frac{\partial c}{\partial S}\right) dS + \text{higher-order terms}$$

where Δc represents total change in the call-option value, $\partial c / \partial S$ represents the delta (the change in call value for a small change in stock price) and dS represents the total change in underlying fund value.

Table 14.3 Another in-the-money path

Time (months)	Stock price path	Option delta	Option gamma	Option vega
0	40.00	0.70	0.10	0.10
1	39.47	0.62	0.12	0.10
2	39.94	0.65	0.13	0.08
3	40.35	0.69	0.14	0.07
4	42.37	0.93	0.07	0.02
5	42.43	0.97	0.04	0.01
6	42.57	1.00	—	—

Thus, in performing delta hedging, it is assumed that none of the higher-order terms in the above equation is relevant and, as a consequence, the optionality is assumed to be directly proportional to the option delta. It is this delta that we try to mirror by transacting into the appropriate futures or stock contracts so as to offset the delta of the call option, as demonstrated in the example earlier.

As mentioned previously, delta hedging tends to be quite unstable when volatilities and interest rates also move around. As a consequence, the above equation can be rewritten as

$$\Delta c = \left(\frac{\partial c}{\partial S}\right) dS + \frac{1}{2}\left(\frac{\partial^2 c}{\partial S^2}\right)(dS)^2$$
$$+ \left(\frac{\partial c}{\partial \sigma}\right) d\sigma + \left(\frac{\partial c}{\partial r}\right) dr + \text{other terms}$$

where $\partial^2 c/\partial S^2$ represents the gamma (change in delta value for a small change in fund value), $\partial c/\partial \sigma$ represents the vega (change in liability value for a parallel shift in volatility value[17]), $\partial c/\partial r$ represents the rho (change in liability value for a parallel shift in zero rate[18]), $d\sigma$ represents total change in underlying volatility value and dr represents total change in underlying zero rate.

Although the stock was used to hedge the delta risks, it unfortunately cannot be used to hedge higher-order Greeks like vegas and gammas, since a stock does not contain any optionality. Hedging gamma and vega risks requires the use of options. As a consequence, transactions would be made in different types of options so as to offset the gamma, vega risks.

Table 14.3 illustrates how gamma and vega vary for another in-the-money path.

Table 14.4 Available instruments at time 0

Type	Premiums	Delta	Gamma	Vega
Stock	40	1.00	0.00	0.00
One-month ATM option	0.69	0.58	0.28	0.05
Two-month ATM option	1.07	0.62	0.19	0.06

At time 0, recall that we bought 0.7 shares to neutralise the delta risks when we were hedging only the deltas. To hedge off all delta, gamma and vega risks we have to transact in three different instruments, of which at least two have to be options. Suppose, for the purpose of illustration, that we have the three instruments in Table 14.4.

Given these hedge instruments, the hedger would buy 2.64 two-month options, sell 1.46 one-month options and sell 0.08 shares.[19] In doing this, the hedger would be able to neutralise the option delta, gamma, vega of 0.70, 0.10, 0.10, respectively. Like delta hedging, the hedger would rebalance this position on the second month to neutralise all the Greeks again. This process is repeated until the maturity is reached.

Moving from theory to practice

From the sections presented thus far, the reader may be tempted to infer that in order to manufacture any option in practice, we need only to apply the delta hedging strategy or delta/gamma/vega hedging strategy. This is far from the truth, since the problem in practice is a lot more complex for the following reasons.

Transactions costs and trading limits

As can be seen from the above examples, to run a perfect hedging programme with zero slippage, we would need to monitor changes in the market (and hence the changes in portfolio[20] Greeks) and then neutralise these every time the portfolio Greeks deviate from zero. However, this may not be practical for the following reasons:

- markets may be not trading continuously during a 24-hour period,

- liquidity constraints may prohibit the number of transactions at a single time,

- notionals associated with the trades are typically in discretised units,

- transaction costs are incurred when putting on and unwinding the trades.[21]

To accommodate the practical considerations cited above, it is common to introduce the concept of trading limits to a hedge programme. This can be more easily understood by using the delta-hedging programme as an example. In this instance, the hedger would also have a dollar-value delta hedge exposure to work with. Thus, as long as the dollar-value delta of the portfolio does not exceed this threshold, the hedger does not need to rebalance the hedges to bring the portfolio delta back to 0 (although this could be done if the hedger so wished). However, should this portfolio delta breach the dollar-value delta trading limit, the hedger must rebalance the portfolio Greeks to bring it back within the prescribed trading limits.

Vega and rho limits

In practice, hedges are typically made against movements in delta, vega, gamma, rho (although this is very much a function of the trading limits and the option replicated). As can be observed, for short-term options (like the one discussed), the vega and rho risks can be easily managed using relatively shorter term options leaving the hedger exposed to small residual risks.[22] However, for longer option maturities, it is not advisable to hedge long-term volatility and rho risks using short-term instruments simply because the bigger the difference between the hedged option maturity and hedged assets maturity, the greater the lack of correlation between long-term volatilities/zero rates and short-term volatilities/zero rates. Hence, for a volatility/rho hedge to work effectively, the maturities of the hedged option and the hedge assets need to be as close as possible. From a hedging perspective this may be difficult to pull off in practice. Thus, to hedge a collection of transacted options, a risk manager would typically split the entire volatility–yield curve into potentially three buckets[23] so that all exposures in a particular bucket are hedged using assets maturing in that bucket.

Counterparty risks

When executing any hedge, a risk manager would in practice use a combination of the exchange and the OTC market instruments. While counterparty risk is a non-issue for exchange-traded instruments, it is indeed a problem for instruments trading in the OTC markets (especially if they have long maturities). Given the backdrop of collapses in investment banks like Lehman Bros, Bear Sterns, AIG FP, etc, it is imperative for the hedger to ensure that the counterparty of the OTC trade is going to be around to pay out on the acquired options. As a consequence, it becomes important for the hedger to think about ways to manage their counterparty risks.

Asset universe

Although the delta in the above example was hedged using the underlying stock, in practice it is the futures contract on the underlying that is used for hedging the delta risks.[24] The assets used in practice to hedge these risks can be summarised as follows:

- delta: futures
- gamma/vega: options
- rho: interest rate swaps.

There is one added complication that a risk manager faces in practice. The asset universe from which hedge assets are selected is quite large (unlike the examples discussed earlier), since there are usually quite a few derivatives instruments trading on a particular index/stock. Furthermore, when options are involved, the hedger has to make a choice on calls/puts, option life and option strikes, since each combination has a different price. As a consequence, a risk manager has to decide how best to select between assets (since cheaper does not necessarily mean better, given the residual/roll-over risks they may create).

VA related complications

In addition to the issues raised above, there are other problems encountered by the hedger of a VA portfolio. Examples of these are given below.

- Basis risks. Since the underlyings of VA products are typically actively managed funds and these funds do not actively trade as underlyings on the exchange, the hedger is only able to replicate fund returns with a portfolio of index returns. Given this backdrop, in addition to doing what has been mentioned above, the hedger is also exposed to basis risks.

- Realisation of behavioural/mortality assumptions. Unlike options that trade in capital markets, the optionalities embedded in a VA are very much driven by policyholder behaviour[25] and mortality assumptions. Thus, even if one is able to replicate the optionalities "perfectly" to the extent that there are no basis/delta/vega/rho, etc, risks, any deviation from the expected policyholder behavioural or mortality assumptions could potentially create huge unhedged risks. Given that this type of slippage cannot be hedged by any instrument in the capital markets instrument, the hedger has to "constantly" monitor and adjust the hedges as soon as the deviations from the expected behavioural and mortality assumptions become realised.

- Correlation risks. Since the guarantee provided to a policyholder is based on an account value (which is the sum of all deposits in the invested funds), the hedger is naturally exposed to the correlation between the invested fund returns. While the vega/rho risks can be somewhat hedged using index options and interest rate swaps, hedging correlation risks associated with the fund returns is almost impossible. What makes this an extremely difficult problem to manage is that this is very much a function of policyholders' fund holdings because the moment policyholders all switch to a single fund, the correlation risks immediately disappear.

Another aspect of the correlation risks that are inherent in many of the living benefit products is that relating to interest rate movements and fund returns. This stems from the fact that, when such guarantees are modelled, the models typically involve both stochastic interest rates and fund returns. Changes in this correlation assumption again cannot be hedged, making it important for the way such guarantees are typically modelled. As a consequence, the ability to estimate this correlation prudently becomes very important.

- Accounting of derivatives. Certain types of riders (eg, guaranteed minimum income benefits (GMIB) and guaranteed minimum death benefits (GMDB)) in the US and other countries are not considered as derivatives. Thus, running a dynamic-hedging programme, no matter how effective and efficient, can introduce volatility to the financial statements since the assets used to hedge are marked-to-market, while the guarantees hedged cannot be marked-to-market. As a consequence, the hedger may choose to focus on trying to manage the "economic risks" subject to some pre-specified acceptable volatility in financial statements ("accounting risks").

The above list represents a few of the issues faced by a hedger when running a dynamic-hedging programme. Before implementing such a programme, all the above issues must be addressed and quantified as much as possible. The practical way to do this is to simulate the actual risk management programme using the Monte Carlo method (or other numerically efficient simulator) by running it over sample policies both futuristically and historically to show what the distribution of the hedging cost looks like over various trading limits, transactions costs and market conditions. (This is discussed further in the next chapter.)

> This chapter is based on the author's 2008 unpublished working paper "What You Need To Know About Managing VA Risks?" Please contact the author for a copy.

---

1 Throughout this chapter, we will use the terms hedging and managing interchangeably.

2 This would be a reinsurance treaty in which all market and actuarial risks are transferred to the reinsurer.

3 By this, we mean that sensitivities of "economic" risks, "accounting" risks and "regulatory" risks can be markedly different for a dollar-value change in the underlying account value.

4 This is driven by the fact that the lack of the reinsurers' ability to do so has been the big reason for their exit from this marketplace. As such, it is imperative for direct writers to put in place "controls" and "business terms" to ensure that the reinsurers have in place a well-established risk management programme.

5 This term is very much a function of the markets, since in some markets the sweet spot tends to be more like three or five years.

6 This refers to the risks arising from replicating the returns of the actively managed funds by indexes.

7 This is further complicated by the fact that policyholders do switch between funds. Hence, what may initially be well replicated by a S&P 500 Index could very easily change to another index if policyholders start moving their investments to other types of funds that do not correlate well with the S&P 500 Index. In such an instance, the hedger has to unwind the

8 Insurance companies quite often use dynamic hedging to also mean delta hedging of the equity risks and/or delta hedging of the interest rate risks.

9 As evidenced by the blow-ups associated with the usage of derivatives by corporations and investment banks, these disasters happen from not fully understanding and properly controlling market risks, operational risks, etc. Examples of this include Orange County, Barings, Proctor & Gamble, etc.

10 Usually only used for living benefits that have a high convexity exposure to interest rate movements. More sophisticated dynamic-hedging strategies involve the use of variance swaps, equity return swaps, etc, depending on the risks assumed and mitigated by the writer.

11 The author's experience finds this to be the best way to risk manage these risks in the absence of complete reinsurance cover. However, doing this does require sufficient derivatives-trading and financial-market experience to know how many risks to lock-up and when to lock them up.

12 The term "Greeks" is used to describe all the partial derivatives (ie, sensitivities) of the option premiums with respect to the underlying. For example, if c denotes the option premium when the option life is t, the current stock price is S, the strike price is K, the annualised option volatility is σ and the continuously compound risk-free rate is r, then

$$\text{delta} = \frac{\partial c}{\partial S}, \qquad \text{gamma} = \frac{\partial^2 c}{\partial S^2}, \qquad \text{rho} = \frac{\partial c}{\partial r}, \qquad \text{vega} = \frac{\partial c}{\partial \sigma}$$

$$\text{theta} = \frac{\partial c}{\partial t}, \qquad \text{vanna} = \frac{\partial \text{vega}}{\partial S}, \qquad \text{speed} = \frac{\partial \gamma}{\partial S}, \qquad \text{zomma} = \frac{\partial \gamma}{\partial \sigma}$$

$$\text{vomma} = \frac{\partial \text{vega}}{\partial \sigma}, \qquad \text{ultima} = \frac{\partial \text{vomma}}{\partial \sigma}, \qquad \text{charm} = \frac{\partial \delta}{\partial t}, \qquad \text{colour} = \frac{\partial \gamma}{\partial t}$$

etc, where only the first four Greeks are used quite often in practice.

13 Although there are many financial textbooks that contain examples of delta hedging, we will give an example for the sake of completeness.

14 This assumes that the underlying stock is trading at US$40, the six-month risk-free rate is 8% and the six-month implied volatility is 12%.

15 This is contrary to the sale of a put option. When a put option is sold, the hedger has to go out and short sell the shares of the stock to delta hedge the risks.

16 This is due to the fact that the hedger would receive US$40 from the option purchaser for something that is worth US$40.50, in the process incurring a loss of a net amount of US$$(40.50 - 40)$.

17 In addition to this, we must look at non-parallel shifts in the volatility curve. This can be done in practice by partitioning the volatility curve into three time buckets (eg, 0–3 years, 3–7 years, beyond 7 years) which can also be thought of as short-term/mid-term/long-term buckets. Each segment is then shifted independently of the other two segments to understand the impact of the change in that segment. This would only complicate the analysis and discussion.

18 In addition to this, we must look at non-parallel shifts in the yield curve. This can be done in practice by partitioning the yield curve into three time buckets (0–3 years, 3–7 years, beyond 7 years) which can also be thought of as short-term/mid-term/long-term buckets. Each segment is then shifted independently of the other two segments to understand the impact of the change in that segment. . As in the volatility curve analysis, this would only complicate the analysis and discussion.

19 This is obtained by solving the simultaneous equations

$$(x_1 \times \text{stock delta}) + (x_2 \times \text{1-mth option delta}) + (x_3 \times \text{2-mth option delta}) = 0.7$$
$$(x_1 \times \text{stock gamma}) + (x_2 \times \text{1-mth option gamma}) + (x_3 \times \text{2-mth option gamma}) = 0.1$$
$$(x_1 \times \text{stock vega}) + (x_2 \times \text{1-mth option vega}) + (x_3 \times \text{2-mth option vega}) = 0.1$$

which simplify to the following equations:

$$(x_1 \times 1) + (x_2 \times 0.58) + (x_3 \times 0.62) = 0.7$$
$$(x_1 \times 0) + (x_2 \times 0.28) + (x_3 \times 0.19) = 0.1$$
$$(x_1 \times 0) + (x_2 \times 0.19) + (x_3 \times 0.06) = 0.1$$

Solving the above simultaneous equations gives $x_1 = -0.08$, $x_2 = -1.46$, $x_3 = 2.64$.

20 By "portfolio", we mean the collection of the transacted option and all the trades put in place to replicate the Greeks of the transacted option.

21 In the exchanges, the transaction costs typically take the form of a bid–offer spread, a fixed cost and a variable cost that would be a function of the volume traded. In the OTC market, the transaction costs typically take the form of a bid–offer spread. Thus, trying to rebalance continuously would be impractical.

22 Hedging the sale of a six-month option with one-, two-, three- or four-month options still means that the hedger is exposed to volatility–yield curves not moving in parallel (or spiking) between the maturities of the hedges and the six-month point. The closer the hedges are in terms of maturity to the six-month point, the smaller the residual risks (and hence the exposure to volatility–yield curve jumps and turns between these maturities).

23 These would typically be also called the short-term (0–3 years), mid-term (3–7 years) and long-term (more than 7 years) buckets. The divisions across these times tend to be very much a function of underlying markets. See also notes 17 and 18.

24 This simply stems from the fact that the transaction costs and capital associated with the use of a futures contract are much lower than those required for stocks.

25 By policyholder behavioural assumptions we mean assumptions relating to surrendering, partially withdrawing, annuitising, switching between funds, etc.

REFERENCES

Black, F., and M. Scholes, 1973, "The Pricing of Options and Corporate Liabilities", *Journal of Political Economy* 81, pp. 637–59.

Hull, J., 2008, *Options, Futures and Other Derivatives*, seventh edition (Englewood Cliffs, NJ: Prentice-Hall).

Merton, R. C., 1973, "Theory of Rational Optional Pricing", *Bell Journal of Economics and Management Science* 4, pp. 141–83.

Section 4

Monitoring and
Reporting Risks

Introduction

Kannoo Ravindran

Annuity Systems Inc and Háskólinn í Reykjavík

In order to successfully launch a VA product in the marketplace, insurers need to be able to

- quantify risks embedded in these products,

- manage the embedded risks prudently/effectively/efficiently and

- report accurately and monitor on a real-time basis both hedged and unhedged risks inherent in the risk management programme.

The first two points have been discussed in Sections 3 and 4, respectively, and so now we turn to focus on issues relating to reporting and monitoring of risks.

Senior management and board members are never in the trenches dealing with the day-to-day drudgeries of modelling, analysis and trade execution. As a consequence, it is important for an organisation to have (and continually encourage) clear communication channels between front-line practitioners and business line managers. Furthermore, it is imperative for any front-line practitioner to understand and fully appreciate the fact that whenever senior management feels uneasy about the risk exposure and the effectiveness of a hedging programme there is a strong likelihood that the hedging/business unit may be potentially shut down.

Hence, it is in the interest of a front-line practitioner to do whatever is required to ensure that business line managers are given clear, concise and accurate descriptions of exposure arising from the assumption and management of VA related risks. In this way, business line managers can be comfortable with the entire process, the risks taken and consequences of the risks taken. Given that business line managers do not have the luxury of time to delve into intricate details, a front-line practitioner needs to be able to filter all the technical details and condense them in a manner in which a business manager can easily understand the risk exposure that the corporation faces.

For reasons just discussed, it is important for a front-line practitioner to

- identify and quantify risks that need to be reported (including the frequency over which it is reported),
- articulate clearly, concisely and accurately what the hedged and unhedged risks are,
- show how well the hedging programme has worked thus far,
- attribute changes in mark-to-market values to factors so as to explain the lack of performance (ie, slippages) in a hedging strategy,

so that, in going through the reports, senior management can easily pinpoint what is (or can go) wrong and understand the consequences.[1]

RISK REPORTING

For a risk manager to be able to do a reasonable job in managing risks in a hedging programme, it is imperative that risks are well reported and monitored. As a consequence, time needs to be invested in designing a risk report so as to ensure that it captures all relevant aspects of the risks to which the company is exposed. While the look, feel and contents of a risk report can vary across companies,[2] there are certain common underlying philosophies that a report should capture. Examples of such philosophies are given below.

Quantifying risk exposure

Before attempting to quantify any risk, a risk manager has to accept that, whenever prevailing market conditions (eg, current yield curve/volatilities, etc) are not used to value an asset or a liability, an implicit view is taken. In other words, since valuation requires the use of inputs (assumptions) into a model, using anything besides the prevailing market conditions as inputs implies that a view has been taken on the market. While it is perfectly legitimate to take a view on how market conditions will evolve over time, it is imperative to report that a view has indeed been taken and hence quantify and report the exposure arising from this view, regardless of whether risks underlying the view are being hedged.[3]

So how do we go about reporting risk exposure? Although VA risk managers typically report the net delta, vega, rho, etc, risks associated with their assets and liabilities (something that many derivatives textbooks discuss when treating topics on hedging/replication), very few of them actually quantify and report risks associated with what can possibly go wrong (ie, from a what-if scenario-analysis perspective). Given the illiquidity of these liability guarantees, it is important for a risk manager to fully understand how well (in-sync) or badly (out-of-sync) the liabilities are correlated with the assets when inputs into models and assumptions change either incrementally or by jumps.[4]

Demonstrating effectiveness of the hedging programme

Although a successful past hedge performance is no guarantee of a successful future performance, senior management, board members, rating agencies and regulators rely heavily on historical hedge performance to maintain confidence about the effectiveness of the hedge programme. Given the relevance of historical hedge performance in decision making, it is important for risk managers to demonstrate in their risk reports how well their hedging programme has performed since inception. In this way, readers of the report can easily get an overview as to how well the programme has been working and how well the hedge objectives of the programme have been met.[5] (This is further discussed by Sauren in Chapter 16.)

Explaining slippages in the hedging programme

As any experienced VA risk manager knows, it is impossible to hedge against all risks underlying the VA guarantees.[6] Since slippages are inherent in any hedging programme, it is important to explain (or attribute) these slippages to fluctuations in assumptions or movements in markets, etc, so that senior management can better understand and appreciate if the slippages are due to bad trading decisions or poor actuarial judgements or simply unpredicted market movements. Called attribution analysis, this type of analysis is typically done on a monthly basis for both technical and strategic reasons.[7]

SUMMARY OF SECTION 4

This part of the book comprises four chapters, starting with a discussion by Mark Evans (Chapter 15) about measuring and reporting hedge efficiency. Evans talks about how attribution analysis can be used to understand efficiencies associated with a hedging programme. We then continue with Jorg Sauren's discussion (Chapter 16) on ways of measuring hedge effectiveness. He also discusses some of the practical issues to contend with in trying to implement some of these approaches. Mun Kurup and Warren Manners (Chapter 17) talk about their experience in running a hedging programme (and discussing if hedging in fact works in practice for such products), while outlining some of the issues to be dealt with in practice. This part of the book concludes with Chapter 18, in which Kanoo Ravindran raises questions and discusses issues that practitioners should seriously think about before attempting to implement a hedging programme.

1 While it is tempting to suggest that such risks should be reported in the same manner as risks are reported when running an exotic derivatives position, given the complexity and the interdependence of the risks underlying the VA guarantees, this is far from true.

2 This tends to be very much a function of the types of risks managed, objective functions of the hedge programmes and types of hedge strategies used.

3 As an example consider the situation where the hedger has a view that the volatility associated with the underlying index is 15% when the implied ATM forward volatility term structure of the same index ranges from 18% to 30% (assuming no volatility skew). Despite the fact that the hedger may be only running a delta-hedging programme (where the delta is computed using the 15% volatility), the risk manager should still communicate the risks arising from not using the market conditions instead of simply not reporting this aspect of the risk.

4 Senior management and business line managers in particular will be interested in this type of analysis so that they can make an informed decision as to whether they are comfortable with the type of exposure that they are taking on.

5 To make this information useful, the risk manager should also highlight, among other things, moments during history when the company's hedging strategies/objectives were changed/modified, or financial-market disasters took place (eg, collapse of markets after 9/11, bank bailouts).

6 While at first glance it is tempting to think that acquiring a complete reinsurance would completely remove all the risks, in acquiring such a reinsurance treaty the insurance company is in fact trading all the actuarial/market risks for counterparty risks (see the discussion by Ravindran in Chapter 18).

7 See the discussion by Mark Evans in Chapter 15.

15

Measuring and Reporting Hedge Efficiency

Mark Evans
AEGON

Attribution analysis is typically conducted every time an in-force file is updated. The purpose of this analysis is to explain away (or attribute) the changes in the values of the objective function that is measured and reported due to changes in the underlying factors (eg, in-force decomposition, equity market changes, etc).

An important part of hedging variable annuities is performing an attribution analysis. Attribution analysis serves both tactical and strategic purposes. On a tactical level, it identifies fast emerging trends, explains liability and hedge movements from period to period and serves as a control mechanism to audit the hedging activity and capture errors before trading errors result. Tactical attribution analysis should be run at the same frequency as the liability model is updated. Strategic attributions can be run less often, but focus more on how the hedge is performing economically, hedge effectiveness and whether any assumptions need to be reviewed. For the purposes of this chapter, we will assume that the liability model is updated each night following close of business and therefore the tactical attribution is performed daily. We will assume the strategic attribution is updated monthly. Furthermore, we will assume that the liability is evaluated with Monte Carlo simulation using risk-neutral techniques and that the hedges are intended to immunise the liability. Similar attribution techniques could be used for other hedging objectives such as hedging changes in financial statements.

Special consideration should be given to the use of random numbers when doing attributions. This can best be addressed by using the same random numbers for any given policy in the attribution. Otherwise, we could have a situation where two attribution runs produced a different result for a given factor when the factor did not change from one day to the next for that given policy. For various reasons, it may not be practical to use the same random numbers for a given policy indefinitely. Then perhaps random numbers could be updated for all policies periodically, but this should be an extra step in the attribution and the impact should be captured separately to avoid distorting other attribution items.

For ease of discussion, we will define the liability function as $L[S(t), I(t), F(t)]$, where $S(t)$ is the impact at time t due to equity levels, $I(t)$ is the impact at time t due to interest rate levels and $F(t)$ is the impact at time t due to non-capital market factors.[1]

CAPITAL MARKET VARIABLES

Examples of capital market variables impacting on variable annuity guarantees are equity levels, interest rate levels and volatilities of both equity/interest rate levels. Since the equity market risks embedded in a VA are hedged with derivatives on various equity indexes, in order to understand the impact of each index we would start with $L[S_i(0), I(0), F(0)]$, where $t = 0$ represents the time today and $S_i(0)$ refers to the current value of the index i. By looking at $L[S_i(1), I(0), F(0)]$, where this is the liability value calculated using the value of index i at the end of next business day, we can compute the impact of index i on the change in liability value from time 0 to time 1. We can calculate the delta and gamma contribution for index i from the index change using delta and gamma from the liability model. The total impact of index i minus the delta and gamma contributions will yield the higher-order Greeks for the index. The value of this higher-order Greek should be small compared with the delta and gamma associated with the same index, otherwise a calculation error is suggested and further research is warranted.

Once this is done, the cross Greeks can be calculated for each possible pair of equity indexes by increasing two indexes simultaneously and comparing that change to the sum of the changes for each index individually

$$\{L[S_i(1), S_j(1), I(0), F(0)] - L[S_i(0), S_j(0), I(0), F(0)]\}$$
$$- \{L[S_i(1), S_j(0), I(0), F(0)] - L[S_i(0), S_j(0), I(0), F(0)]\}$$
$$- \{L[S_i(0), S_j(1), I(0), F(0)] - L[S_i(0), S_j(0), I(0), F(0)]\}$$
$$= L[S_i(1), S_j(1), I(0), F(0)] + L[S_i(0), S_j(0), I(0), F(0)]$$
$$- L[S_i(1), S_j(0), I(0), F(0)] - L[S_i(0), S_j(1), I(0), F(0)]$$

Next, we calculate

$$L[S'(1), I(0), F(0)] - L[S(0), I(0), F(0)]$$

where $S'(1)$ represents the total change due to equity indexes. This will be approximately equal to the sum of the change from each index and the cross Greeks, with any difference being identified as higher-order equity cross Greeks. Only a small part of the total equity change should be due to higher-order cross Greeks. Lastly, we calculate $L[S(1), I(0), F(0)]$, where $S(1)$ is based on the actual equity returns of the variable annuity subaccounts and

$$L[S(1), I(0), F(0)] - L[S'(1), I(0), F(0)]$$

represents equity basis error.

When hedging with futures, the difference between cash prices and future prices often contributes noise to the daily attribution of delta (especially since futures trading tends to close later than cash trading), but this difference will mean revert to zero over longer time periods.

Interest rate changes impact on the value of variable annuity guarantees. Falling interest rates lower the drift rate in the Black–Scholes equity return function and increase the discount factors used to calculate the present value of cashflows generated by the guarantees. Both these items have the effect of increasing option costs, so variable annuity guarantees are very sensitive to interest rates. The total impact due to changing interest rates can easily be measured by $L[S(0), I(1), F(0)] - L[S(0), I(0), F(0)]$, but while the equity change can be decomposed into delta, gamma and higher orders easily, the decomposition of interest rate change impacts into rho, convexity and higher orders is complicated by the fact that interest changes occur along the yield curve and vary by tenor, whereas equity changes are only one dimensional. Approximation techniques must be used to allocate among rho, convexity and higher orders. Since some of the change due to interest rates is simply due to rolling up the curve, this effect should be captured.

There is also a cross term between equity changes and interest rate changes that can be sizeable, especially for options that are at-the-money or close to at-the-money. This can be calculated as

$$L[S(1), I(1), F(0)] + L[S(0), I(0), F(0)]$$
$$- L[S(1), I(0), F(0)] - L[S(0), I(1), F(0)]$$

When equity levels and interest rates move in the same direction, the cross term tends to have a negative impact. When equity levels and interest rates move in opposite directions, the cross term tends to have a positive impact. The liability change may also reflect the impact of changing equity and/or interest volatility assumptions if these are updated in the hedge programme itself. This is especially likely if volatility is hedged.[2]

Market activity will generate derivative cashflows and mark-to-market values that need to be reflected in the attribution. The impact of capital market factors on the derivative instruments in the hedge will be allocated by a decomposition paralleling the liability decomposition. This allows for actual to expected comparisons for each Greek.

Stock dividends need to be accounted for in the subaccounts and in the value of the derivatives. Transaction costs associated with trading derivatives should be reflected. Movements in interest rates and credit spreads as well as coupon payments and interest accrual will impact on fixed income portions of subaccounts.

Basis error is a large potential source of hedge inefficiency. Using multiple equity indexes can reduce basis error, but not necessarily substantially. The appropriate equity indexes can be determined by fund mapping using regression. The correlation from the fund mapping should bear a reasonable relationship to the equity basis error in the attribution. Although fund mapping should be reviewed frequently, it is reasonable to do this monthly for a multiple-index hedge. If the correlations change dramatically from month to month, then the stability of the amount of basis error appearing in the attribution is more likely to be poor. The weightings associated with the various indexes may vary noticeably from one month's regression to the next, which is not necessarily a reason for concern if the indexes are highly correlated with one another.

IMPACT OF POLICYHOLDER BEHAVIOUR

Policyholder behaviour is included in the difference between $F(0)$ and $F(1)$. An exit from the in-force through death or surrender will remove both the future-claims and future-guarantee fee revenue associated with the departing contract. Of course, a guarantee-related payment may also be generated by the termination. Dynamic policyholder behaviour can also come in via partial withdrawals, annuitisation, additional deposits from new contracts and existing contracts, voluntary resets of guarantee levels and transfer between funds.

Calculating the liabilities before and after reflecting each category of policyholder behaviour captures the impact of each such policyholder behaviour category. For strategic attributions, these actual impacts should be compared with the expected impact for the following two reasons:

- it indicates a need to review assumptions if actual and expected results are materially different,

- it is needed to allocate the total change in the liability to various components and, as will be discussed later, this requires identifying the expected impact of various customer behaviour categories.

The hedging model has to calculate the expected results implicitly in order to project the liability, although extracting said intermediate calculations may be challenging, especially if using externally developed software.

A determination can be made as to whether a customer behaviour assumption needs to be changed by reviewing actual versus expected results on a monthly basis. Standard statistical techniques including hypothesis testing can be used to determine whether a deviation between actual and expected results is statistically significant. If so, further analysis may be performed to determine how the assumptions should be changed. For example, if the impact from mortality is consistently running lower than the expected result, then subdividing the results by age, gender, etc, can lead to the determination of new model assumptions.

Dynamic policyholder behaviour can have a significant impact upon hedge effectiveness to the extent that actual results significantly deviate from expected results. This is likely to happen for several reasons. Firstly, it can be hard to predict dynamic behaviour under conditions that have not previously occurred. Secondly, predicting dynamic behaviour requires analysis across at least one additional dimension compared with traditional actuarial decrement analysis, leading to more complicated analysis. Thirdly, dynamic behaviour can change over time, especially as customers gain a better appreciation of the value of the guarantees. Furthermore, just like mortgage prepayments which are sensitive to interest rate levels, it is reasonable to expect customers to factor in the level of interest rates when valuing the worth of their guarantees. This introduces an important interaction between customer behaviour and interest rate convexity, which some variable annuity hedging models explicitly recognise. For these reasons, it is wise to test the sensitivity of the liability price and Greeks to variations in the dynamic behaviour functions, especially where there is large uncertainty about the accuracy of the functions. Since attribution focuses on price changes due to various factors, significant processing time can be saved by calculating only price for most or all of the attribution runs. The Greeks only need to be calculated once, and these may come from the hedge model.

LIABILITY

The attribution analysis needs to reflect liability cashflows associated with the guarantees. These consist of benefits paid beyond what would be due from the contract without the guarantee as well as fees collected or allocated for funding the guarantees. Tracking the benefits and fees separately along all dimensions of the attribution makes analysis easier, as the dynamics are quite different. Patterns may be obscured by looking at only the net of benefits and fees. The attribution should reflect interest imputed to the liability at the overnight rate.

The option Greek theta represents the change in option value with respect to time. For a capital markets option or other instrument, this can be calculated by standard formulas. A VA also has passage of time dynamics which we will refer to here as product theta. It turns out that expected product theta equals the sum of expected customer behaviour multiplied by -1. The actual product theta contains the various product-related (as opposed to capital-market-related) dynamics that fund the expected customer behaviour. In theory, product theta actual and product theta expected are equal, but in practice they are only approximately equal for most attributions due to various approximations and statistical noise. Product theta is necessary to reconcile total programme gain and loss to total programme actual versus expected in a complete attribution.

DETERMINING HEDGE EFFECTIVENESS

Estimating future hedge effectiveness is not an exact science and there are many reasonable approaches. One approach is to analyse periodic strategic attribution results via an R^2 (coefficient-of-determination) approach. Here the monthly liability movements with and without the hedge would be compared via an R^2 ratio to get at the standard deviation of hedge effectiveness. The monthly time period is somewhat arbitrary, but reasonable. It is also situational. For example, if hedging is performed using futures, the difference from different closing values mentioned above introduces timing noise that will mean revert over longer periods. On the other hand, if the R^2 calculation contains too few periods, there will be too few observations to be credible, and when ending and beginning market levels are about the same for a given period the attribution is likely to be mostly noise. The R^2 calculations should be based on each month's cash amount, not each month's hedged-to-unhedged ratio. This appropriately gives heavier weights to the months with larger market moves. Another approach is to consider each item in the attribution (or at least the material ones) and analyse the deviation of the actual from the expected for that item to get the efficiency for that item. Then the efficiency of all material items can be combined to get an overall efficiency, or applied separately by item in financial projection models.

Judgment should be used in the estimation of hedge effectiveness, and adjustments applied where appropriate. For example, emerging mortality experience may suggest a change in mortality assumptions. When this change is implemented in the hedging/attribution model, there will be a one-time change in the liability due to this change. If material, it is probably not appropriate to let this impact flow through into an R^2 calculation unadjusted.

The attribution can be used to assess the importance of secondary risks. For example, the attribution can measure the impact of cross terms between equity indexes as well as the cross terms between equity and interest. This is important, because the behaviour of these, particularly the cross terms between equity and interest, is likely to be different for a variable annuity minimum guarantee compared with common capital market structures because of the impact of dynamic customer behaviour.

A properly constructed tactical attribution analysis should be able to allocate the daily changes in liability and hedge instrument values. Sometimes there may be situations where some of the change is unexplained, creating an "other" category. If this is large, then an immediate investigation is warranted to make sure that there is not a problem with the attribution or the hedge itself.

Sometimes there are reasons for the attribution analysis and the hedge model to be run independently. This is likely since the many simulations required to create an attribution may not allow for as many scenarios as we may want to use for actual hedging runs. If they are run independently, the beginning and ending liabilities for the attribution and the hedge model should be within statistical boundaries due to differing numbers of scenarios and/or differing random numbers. Another possible reason for a large "other" is an operational error, such as a bad in-force file, capital market variable input error or software problems.

Even if the "other" is small, it is worthwhile discerning the source, as it may indicate a minor problem that could accumulate over time to something material, or indicate a problem that, while small now, could become larger under different market conditions.

It is possible to reduce "other" to amounts representing nothing more than rounding in a good attribution system.

1   This breakdown is not exhaustive, since we have not considered changes in equity volatilities/correlations, interest rate volatilities, etc.

2   The analysis of capital market variables can be viewed in terms of a multivariate Taylor series expansion.

16

Measuring the Effectiveness of a Hedging Strategy

Jorg Sauren

ING

Hedge effectiveness plays an important role in any hedge programme. In addition to aiding appropriate pricing of the variable annuity (VA) product, it has a big impact on the capital requirements and the volatility in the financial statements. Therefore, before setting up a metric to measure hedge effectiveness, it is important to answer the following questions about the scope of the hedge programme and intended coverage of the hedge effectiveness metric(s).

- What is the goal of the hedge programme? This can be anything from minimising the volatility in economic value of the in-force block of business to minimising earnings volatility to minimising capital requirements. Hedge effectiveness should tie in with the goal that the hedge programme intends to achieve.

- What risks are in the scope of the hedge programme? Is the hedge programme only focused on first-order (delta) exposures or does it also include second-order (gamma) exposures and volatility risk, etc? Are fees included in the scope? What risks are included in the effectiveness metric? Does this metric include all the risks that can be hedged or it is only focused on the risks in scope of the hedge programme?[1]

Some risks, such as dynamic lapse behaviour, cannot be hedged in the market, so hedge effectiveness is measured by assuming a model for dynamic lapse behaviour. However, it is always important to bear in mind that such assumptions can also have a crucial impact on the ultimate hedge performance.

Table 16.1 Effectiveness of the hedge programme

Risk factors in scope	1st-order (delta) effectiveness (%)	Higher-order (gamma) effectiveness (%)	Total effectiveness (%)
Equity level	95	50	90
Interest rate level	95	0	80
Equity volatility level	20	0	20
Foreign exchange level	80	0	75
Subtotal of hedged risk factors	85	30	75
Credit spread	0	N/A	0
Interest rate volatility	0	N/A	0
Total			70

AN EXAMPLE

In practice, we need a range of metrics to look at the effectiveness of hedging a single risk factor or a group of risk factors. Table 16.1 gives a fictive illustration of the effectiveness of the hedge programme.

In this example six different risk factors are distinguished. Equity level relates to exposure of equity funds (or funds with equity components) that the policyholder invests in, interest rate level relates to exposure to both bond funds the policyholder invests in and the interest rate sensitivity of the guarantees provided. As bond funds can also invest in "credit risky" bonds, there is also an exposure to the credit spread level. The guarantees of a VA contract result in implied volatility exposure. Increases in the equity volatility level typically make guarantees more expensive (the policyholder typically holds a long put option) and, similarly, increases in interest rate volatility make guarantees more expensive, especially for income benefits that guarantee a minimum annuity rate.

In the example, the hedge programme is using linear equity and interest rate hedges and short-term equity options to partly hedge equity gamma and equity volatility exposure. The overall hedge effectiveness of this programme is 70%. When zooming in on specific risks, we can observe that the exposure to credit spreads and to interest rate volatility is not hedged. As a consequence, looking only at the risk factors in the scope of the hedge programme produces an effectiveness of 75%. This observation can be broken down further by looking at a single risk factor and splitting between linear (delta) exposure and higher-order (gamma) exposures. The example is further explained in the section on value-at-risk, below.

How is first-order (delta) and higher-order (gamma) exposure split? The idea here is that first-order effectiveness tracks how well your hedge instruments track the sensitivity of a VA guarantee for small movements in risk drivers. It is, for example, difficult to get 100% hedge effectiveness for equity as there is a basis risk between the hedge instruments (typically index futures) and the equity fund exposures that are being hedged. The higher-order effectiveness is measured for larger changes in risk drivers, assuming there is a perfect first-order (delta) hedge. The total hedge effectiveness, eg, for equity, is how effective the hedge is for any change in equity markets; all three columns are calculated separately.

MEASURING HEDGE EFFECTIVENESS

What does a 75% hedge effectiveness in the above example actually mean and how do we measure this in practice? Roughly speaking, it means that our hedge programme has reduced the (economic) volatility of our VA liability by 75%. However, there is no unique metric to measure hedge effectiveness and the metric chosen depends on the approach chosen to measure it. Examples of these methods are given below.

Back-testing

This approach ties in very well with the attribution analysis that was discussed by Mark Evans in Chapter 15. It compares on a daily basis (assuming hedges are rebalanced on a daily basis) the change in the liability due to actual movements in market risk factors and the change in the hedge instruments due to the same market risk factors. It is feasible to break down the effectiveness to the level of the individual risk factor. The disadvantage is that this approach only tests the effectiveness given the actual market movements and does not give any information about the hedge effectiveness in much more volatile markets. So, before 2007–8 such analysis would not have given complete insight into the hedge performance in turbulent markets such as those experienced in that financial year. One element that complicates this approach is that all risk factors also have cross-impacts. Therefore, those risk factors that typically move highly correlated (such as equity indexes) should be back-tested in groups rather than individually.

Stochastic-on-stochastic simulation

This approach revolves around projecting the hedge strategy in a real-world scenario. At each time step along a simulated path, more risk-neutral simulations are required to determine the value of the liability and to rebalance the hedge strategy (eg, for delta hedging) using the then-prevailing simulated environment. This explains the name "stochastic-on-stochastic", which is also known as a nested stochastic calculation. The advantage of this approach is that you can project the impact of the chosen hedge strategy for a large number of real-world scenarios. It is also feasible to test the impact of changes in the hedge strategy, which makes this a powerful approach. However, the results are only as good as the model. If a certain risk factor is not modelled, then it is not feasible to see the impact on the hedge results. Furthermore, it is very computationally intensive to run such a nested stochastic calculation.

Since the stochastic-on-stochastic approach tries to simulate the real-world effectiveness of a hedge strategy, it is in theory the most precise way to look at hedge effectiveness. However, a large number of modelling assumptions need to be made to ensure that the simulation is manageable in terms of run-time, which in turn impacts on the simulated results significantly.[2] One way to solve the numerical issues associated with this approach is to use a replication-portfolio approach, as described in Chapter 22.

Value-at-Risk (VaR)

This approach is comparable to stochastic-on-stochastic simulation approach, as it projects the impact of the chosen hedge strategy over a large number of simulation paths. However, the main difference is that, in this approach, this projection is only for a single time step, making this approach much less computationally intensive. This time step should be short (typically one day) and tie in with the rebalancing frequency of your hedge. The hedge effectiveness is determined by the reduction in VaR at a given confidence interval that is achieved by the hedge strategy. This approach is also sometimes called earnings-at-risk (EaR) when the model measures the accounting value rather than the economic value. The advantage of this method is that it ties into internal models for capital requirements and looks at extreme scenarios for calculating the hedge effectiveness. Another advantage is that the VaR can also be used for setting trading limits. The disadvantage is that the outcomes of this method are also model dependent, although to a much lesser extent than the stochastic-on-stochastic approach. The wide use of the one-day VaR approach for banking trading books suggests that this method is considered one of the better ones for managing the risk of financial instruments.[3]

In practice, it is advisable to combine the back-testing approach with one of the simulation-based approaches. While the former should give a lot of insight into the impact of individual risk factors in day-to-day volatility in hedge performance, the latter gives a lot of insight into the hedge performance in more extreme real-world scenarios.

OTHER ISSUES TO CONSIDER
Model dependence of hedge effectiveness

The measurement of hedge effectiveness ties in very closely with the stochastic model that is used to project the value of the VA product. Most stochastic models project equity values and interest rates. More advanced models include stochastic equity volatility. The consequence of a simpler model is that the quality of the valuation of the VA and the measurement of hedge effectiveness are affected. Furthermore, when investigating the effectiveness of a chosen hedge strategy in more extreme market circumstances it is important to model all risk factors that have a significant impact on the value of the product in such extreme scenarios. One example is the impact of credit spreads. This factor was typically not modelled until 2007 and, as a consequence, had limited impact on the value of VAs. However, when credit spreads started to widen significantly in 2007–8, this resulted in a significantly lower value of some bond funds and increased the value of the VAs written on top of these bond funds.

Hedge effectiveness and market data

When using complex models for both pricing and risk management it important for the user to bear in mind that such models always need to be calibrated to market data. The typical tenors of VA products are often beyond the point that many markets are considered liquid. Even when long-dated hedge instruments are available to calibrate these models, there might be a bias in the pricing of such instruments due to supply–demand issues. Furthermore, even when market data is available, we would need methodologies to calibrate the model to this data, making this entire process more an art than a science.

Communicating hedge effectiveness

Hedge effectiveness is a good tool with which to communicate about the performance of a hedge programme: it is a metric that can be easily communicated to management. However, when communicating about a hedge programme and its effectiveness, it should always be made clear what is being covered, so that management is not surprised by losses on risks that are not covered by the hedge programme and its effectiveness metric. Combining hedge effectiveness with event risk scenarios can also be very useful in giving management insight into potential worst-case scenarios.

1   The former gives more information about the volatility in the results, while the latter focuses on how well the hedge programme covers its intended scope.

2   Due to its computation intensiveness, not all market risk factors can be individually modelled; this affects the simulated results. Furthermore, at each time step, model assumptions need to be made about the real-world scenario, etc, making this method more relevant to evaluating strategic decisions on changes in risk management strategy as opposed to a day-to-day effectiveness of a hedge programme.

3   Although we could argue that a longer horizon (eg, one week or one month) might be more applicable, given the fact that risks are typically longer dated, it is important to bear in mind that longer horizons might require rebalancing of positions, which would make the calculation more complex and computationally intensive.

17

Experience and Lessons Learned: Does Hedging Work?

Mun Kurup, Warren Manners

ING

The global financial crisis which started with a credit crunch at the beginning of 2008 has had a tremendous impact on capital and earnings of variable annuity (VA) writers. The fourth quarter of 2008 (2008 Q4) witnessed a sharp hike in implied volatilities and the economic slowdown and subsequent easing of monetary policy by governments meant lower interest rates (Figure 17.1). As a result, almost all VA writers, including those running sophisticated hedging programmes, experienced stress in some form or another, with many having to raise additional capital. Higher implied volatilities at levels beyond those at which typical stress testing was conducted in the years leading up to 2008 significantly increased the cost of hedging (delta), and at the same time lower interest rates meant a higher cost of future guarantees.

The Hartford Financial Services Group[1], which had VA assets under management (AUM) of US$75 billion at 2008 Q4, attributed their losses (close to US$400 million) to under-hedging of vega, basis risk and intra-day market volatility. Hartford claims that without their hedging programme losses would have been in the region of US$2.25 billion. Manulife Financial[2] and its subsidiary, John Hancock[3], with US$61 billion in variable annuity AUM, had to strengthen reserves to C$5,783 million as of December 31, 2008, compared with just C$526 million at year end 2007, creating a significant negative impact on Q4 earnings. Manulife, which raised C$4.275 billion in fresh capital in 2008 Q4, was not known to have run a comprehensive hedging programme prior to the global financial crisis. Problems with variable annuities at Old Mutual[4] started even before the financial crisis worsened. In the nine months prior to September 30, 2008, they had to increase their reserves to US$474 million

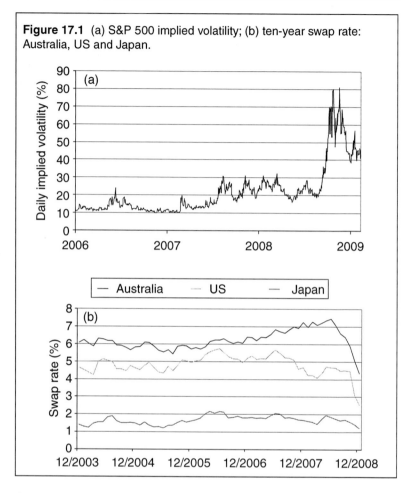

Figure 17.1 (a) S&P 500 implied volatility; (b) ten-year swap rate: Australia, US and Japan.

due to an increase in market volatility. This was attributed to aggressive product features in certain markets where products were subsequently withdrawn. These are just a few examples of how VA writers were affected by the crisis which started in 2008. The high-level take away from these experiences was that hedging programmes in general worked to limit losses in 2008 but did not completely live up to what was expected of such programmes.

WHAT WENT WRONG?

While there is no single reason behind the lacklustre performance of these hedge programmes, the list below covers the majority of losses incurred by the VA industry as a whole.

Lack of a holistic understanding by senior management

A comprehensive risk management policy that was well understood by senior business leaders was missing in many companies. Business leaders may have expected hedging programmes to
cover all market-related loses, while the hedging specialists may
have expected management to appreciate the limitations of the
programme.

Accounting asymmetries

Quite often VA writers chose hedging targets without fully considering the impact on other key financial metrics. In short, many companies have historically focused on hedging the economic fair value
of guarantees or the economic fair value of guarantees minus fees
(ie, the economic reserve) without fully evaluating the impact on the
accounting profit and loss (P&L). Accounting asymmetries tended
to arise when hedge portfolios were marked to market, while liabilities were valued under a prescribed accounting standard designed
to smooth changes in reserves. The result was that accounting P&L
volatility was exacerbated even when the hedge was performing
close to expectations.

Managed funds: a source of basis risk

A major source of earnings volatility for many VA writers came from
basis risk. Much of this basis risk was due to negative alpha generated by managers of actively managed funds. The alpha generated by active management is not hedgable through capital market instruments; thus, when alpha turns out to be negative, hedge
performance deteriorates. Performance of actively managed funds
over time can be expected to balance out, but can create significant
earnings volatility over the short term.

Ever richer benefits

The bear market experienced over 2001–2, coupled with intense competition and slimming profit margins, led to a benefits arms race
between the leading VA writers in the US in an attempt to gain
market share. Ratchet frequencies increased, roll-up rates increased
with compounding interest, guaranteed withdrawal rates (for WB
guarantees) increased for all ages, all without the necessary increase

in fees. These added bells and whistles had profound and unforeseen impacts on the performance of VA hedge programmes, which translated into increased P&L volatility.

Of particular concern was the impact of increasing ratchet frequencies. Embedded VA guarantees are effectively put options on the underlying fund offerings, but with the introduction of the ratchet feature companies were now exposed to upside as well as downside risk. This risk was fairly innocuous when ratchet frequencies were annual, but, as they increased to quarterly and monthly (even in some cases daily, and in other cases it was coupled with a roll-up base where the roll-up was applied on top of the ratcheted base), the delta of these guarantees began to swing wildly from negative to positive and back to negative with great regularity. Hedge positions established one day would need to be unwound the next. This meant that delta hedging programmes were unstable, costly and not particularly effective.

Hedging operations

Traditionally, hedging operations were not well integrated with the core insurance operations framework. This lack of integration meant that valuation models across functional areas and geographies were not always consistent. As a result, many organisations experienced operational surprises that contributed to P&L volatility. For example, valuation models used for hedging were often different from those used for financial reporting. These differences could be found, for example, in the actuarial assumptions, calculation and timing of liability cashflows, valuation techniques and modelling software. Additionally, lack of coordination between operational units that crossed geographic boundaries often led to misaligned hedging programmes. For example, valuations performed domestically were not always translated appropriately in order to ensure accurate hedging of international exposures.

WHAT CAN INSURANCE COMPANIES LEARN FROM THESE PAST MISTAKES?
Develop a comprehensive risk management policy and implementation plan

Understanding the implications of policy decisions by senior business leaders on the various capital and value measures as well as the impact on earnings viewed through various accounting and economic filters (US Generally Accepted Accounting Principles (GAAP), STAT (Statutory), International Financial Reporting Standards (IFRS), etc) is essential. This understanding extends beyond just the risks being hedged and includes unhedged as well as unhedgable risks.

A clearly defined risk policy that lays out what all the risks are, how they will be measured and managed and what the remaining residual risks are in terms of P&L and capital will help to bridge the gap between management expectations and reality. At a minimum, supporting analysis should include sensitivity testing, back-testing and stress testing of all key parameters, risk factors and risk mitigation strategies.

Effective implementation of the risk management policy with proper checks and controls in place is also important to ensure that market risk is not simply replaced by operational risk. The end-to-end process should be thoroughly examined for leakages and sub-optimal contributions to the intended goal.

Invest in tools, infrastructure and resources necessary to understand and manage the risks

The following are considered to be table stakes.

- Grid computing: the complexity of these embedded guarantees requires valuing them using Monte Carlo option-pricing techniques. This can be very computationally expensive and requires a robust grid-computing environment to do the job well. There are different types of computing grids – some that merely tie together a bank of personal computers, and more sophisticated distributed processing grids that optimise the use of available central processing units. The size of the VA book and available budgets will dictate the appropriate solution.

- Robust and redundant systems: these should be able to run and store valuations and Greeks on a seriatim (ie, policy-by-policy) basis as frequently as required.

- Strict adherence to clearly defined operational and governance guidelines: key personnel should regularly conduct drills to test the effectiveness of operations in the event of serious market corrections.

- Human resources with extensive experience in capital markets and insurance.

Develop a robust reporting framework to help senior management understand the risks and make prudent decisions on an ongoing basis

The development of a robust reporting framework to increase understanding and facilitate sound decision making is as much an art as is it is a science. There is a fine line between barely sufficient information and information overload, between over-simplifying and over-complicating. Striking the right balance will make all the difference in successfully navigating these waters.

Below are some examples of reports which should be included in a robust reporting framework.

Liability attribution reports

This report provides a detailed roll-forward of the liability from period to period, attributing all material sources of change. The attribution should be granular enough to identify both hedged and unhedged components. The hedged components should be carved out in such a way so as to facilitate ease of comparison with a similar attribution roll-forward on the asset side of the balance sheet (see the next section on "Hedge performance attribution reports").

The unhedged components are often neglected or consolidated under a single "unhedged" measure. This can be very dangerous, leading to poor decision making and undesirable P&L surprises. For good reason, companies have chosen not to hedge certain funds (for example, real estate or emerging markets) or certain sensitivities of their hedge target (for example, rho or vega risk). Other risks are simply not hedgable in the capital markets (eg, policyholder behaviour or fund manager alpha). Understanding how these decisions affect the P&L, along with the various other measures and metrics insurance companies tend to track, will help to establish priorities and effective use of finite resources.

Hedge performance attribution reports

This report provides a detailed roll-forward of the hedge performance from period to period. Here, the components of change in the hedged liability from the liability attribution report are compared with similar components of change in the hedge assets. To the extent to which the hedge assets do not perfectly offset the change in the hedge target, this report should attribute the causes of this hedge ineffectiveness. These attribution items reflect actual experience differing from expected experience. Some examples include basis risk, realised volatility risk and actual versus expected decrements (ie, mortality and lapses).

After all known sources of ineffectiveness have been identified, the remaining unexplained amount (there will always be a portion that cannot be explained) should be relatively small and unbiased. A way to track this visually is to keep a historical record of hedge performance and plot the unexplained amount against time. Over a sufficiently long time horizon (a year, for example), the graph should resemble a "white noise" process.

Risk profile report

This report provides a snapshot of the VA risk profile through various different lenses. It is often helpful to differentiate between asset risks, liability risks and the net of the two where relevant. We now give some examples (this list is not exhaustive).

- Greeks (ie, sensitivities):

  - first order (delta, theta, key rate rho, key rate vega);
  - second order (gamma, convexity);
  - cross terms (cross-gamma, cross Greeks, eg, change in delta relative to a change in interest rates).

- Tail risk:

  - VaR;
  - capital (economic, regulatory);
  - P&L stress tests (global financial crisis 2008–9; October 1987; Japan scenario).

- Concentration risk:

  - net amount at risk (NAR) by age band;
  - NAR by maturity (when claims are expected to come due);
  - NAR by in-the-moneyness;
  - exposure to large policies (more than US$1 million).

Hedge trade and position report

This report provides a summary of trade activity from period to period and a net position of hedge assets including notional amounts and market values. The report should include trigger price (market price at which a trade was triggered) along with trade price in order to see the impact of any delays in trading activity.

Funds assessment report

This report provides a summary of the performance of the funds underlying the VA guarantees. Performance should be measured over varying time horizons and compared with predefined benchmarks. This information is useful for portfolio managers as a feedback mechanism to help them to identify fund managers who are consistently performing poorly relative to benchmarks. Tracking items like style drift is useful when trying to attribute sources of basis risk.

Market activity report

This report summarises the changes in key capital market risk factors that affect the liability and the hedge assets.

Risk managers should look to supplement these reports with narratives and summaries that tie the hedge performance to the accounting P&L and explain why results may appear non-intuitive.

Use a blend of tools to manage risks

A capital markets hedge programme is only one of many tools available to help manage the risks of VA guarantees.

Other examples, meant to be used in conjunction with a capital markets hedge programme include the following.

Product characteristics

There are certain product features that can be managed in order to help to control the richness of the VA guarantees.

- **Underlying funds offering:** developing a well-defined fund selection process is an analytical and unbiased way of determining whether funds are appropriate offerings under a VA product. The selection process should focus on the amount of volatility introduced by the new fund and the hedgability of the fund. Hedgability is defined here as the ability to be tracked closely by a liquid capital market instrument.

The following is a list of general rules of thumb to be applied when selecting funds for a VA product.

- The offer of balanced funds or target allocation funds that limit exposure to equity markets will help to keep fund volatility relatively low and reduce the cost of hedging the guarantee.
- There is a strong argument that downside protection should be offered only for market beta (and not fund alpha). Limiting the number of managed funds and offering more index funds will greatly reduce basis risk in the hedge portfolio.
- Limiting the credit exposure in the funds offered will also help to reduce basis risk. Establishing fixed income fund mandates in order to invest only in government bonds will eliminate credit exposure.

Additionally, restricting the amount of switching between funds will increase hedge effectiveness and reduce the overall cost of hedging.

- **Ratchets and roll-ups:** ratchets and roll-ups contributed the most in terms of product richness in the run up to the financial crisis of 2008–9. They were ubiquitous in the industry, and not offering them would have damaged top-line growth (now, at the end of 2009, we are starting to see a scaling back by many players). If eliminating these features is not an option (particularly for mature markets), there are ways to limit their impact. For ratchets, the obvious answer is to extend the frequency of ratchets beyond one year. There are examples in Europe and Asia Pacific of two-year and three-year ratchets being offered. Where roll-ups are concerned, there are a number of options available, including reducing the roll-up percentage, offering only simple interest, extending the vesting schedule and keeping the roll-up base independent from the ratchet base.

- **Open-ended exposures:**
  - setting limits on the duration of coverage will help control longevity risks and limiting the duration of ratchets and roll-ups to a defined period will help to manage the tail exposure associated with capital market risk factors;

– another way to manage tail exposure is to subject the guarantees to global maximums (for example, roll-up base can go no higher than one-and-a-half times the initial premium, and the ratchet base can go no higher than twice the initial premium).

Natural internal hedges

Wherever possible, it is always prudent to take advantage of products that have offsetting exposures to particular risk factors and only hedge the net exposure. While this portfolio approach is optimal, it is not always practical (eg, prohibited by legislation, systems limitations, valuation limitations).

Reinsurance

While VA reinsurers have experienced issues similar to those of direct writers during the recent financial crisis, capacity is still available and investment banks are entering the markets in greater numbers, expanding the available reinsurance options.

Capital

Ensuring the availability of sufficient capital is the first line of defence in managing the risks of VA guarantees. Developing a robust way to accurately capture the tail exposure in a way that suits regulators, shareholders and executives has been, and continues to be, a challenge for the VA industry.

Insurance product portfolio diversification

To the greatest extent possible, insurers should look to manage their VA business as part of a balanced portfolio of products. Offering a diversified suite of products with uncorrelated exposures will help to dampen the P&L volatility that might otherwise arise when exposure is concentrated in one product. Establishing a cap on sales is one way to ensure VA exposure remains below a certain percentage of an overall product portfolio.

Prudent product development

Good risk management starts with good product design and, by following a few key principles, insurance companies can avoid many of the pitfalls seen in the past.

We give the following examples.

Take a balanced approach to risk and reward

The risk and reward of a product should be considered from the perspective of all key constituents: policyholders, shareholders and regulators. Increased competition for market share can lead to an untenable escalation of benefits (clearly evident in the US over the past decade) that unfairly favours the policyholder at the expense of shareholders. Regulators also feel the pinch, as their capital models tend to lag the industry and thus tend to underestimate the capital required to back these rich guarantees.

Guarantees should have a clear value proposition for policyholders, should be relatively easy to hedge to ensure shareholder value is maintained and should be able to fit into the existing capital standards in a way that does not arbitrage the system.

Keep it simple

This cannot be emphasised enough. Adding layer upon layer of complexity makes these products more and more difficult to value, to hedge, to understand and to communicate and ultimately leads to disillusioned customers, aggravated distributors and distressed management. Simple products that are easy to understand by all parties also reduce the risk of litigation by consumers who feel they were sold an unsuitable product under false pretences. Some examples of simplification include reducing the number of underlying funds, minimising the number of qualifications surrounding particular product features and keeping the fee structure simple.

Test results

Knowing how the value of new business, the internal rate of return, the P&L and the balance sheet will be affected by changes in underlying assumptions and risk factors is critical. Back-testing over severe market scenarios should be performed in order to determine how these metrics will vary and to see how bad things can get.

Certain risks, such as actuarial assumptions (eg, lapse, fund switching behaviour), cannot be hedged via the capital markets. Because there is not a lot of actual experience to draw from in the VA market it is important to understand the consequences of getting these assumptions wrong and how to mitigate this risk.

Manage the risk of in-force business

There are many ways of de-risking existing VA business. Examples of these include the following:

- optimising hedging and risk management operations;
- convincing customers to move to more balanced funds with less tracking error or even newer, lower-risk products in exchange for incentives;
- analysing reinsurance solutions including the purchase of deep in-the-money options (the challenge would be deciding on when to reinsure; eg, locking in market parameters as of 2008 Q4 may not be the optimal long-term solution).

THE FUTURE DIRECTION OF THE INDUSTRY

Since mid 2009 we have seen significant de-risking efforts by numerous VA players, including increased fees, reduced roll-up rates, reduced ratchet frequencies and reduced maximum allowable annual withdrawal amounts for all age bands.

There is reason to suspect that the pendulum may have swung too far towards risk reduction, in the process losing sight of the return on equity. This can be avoided if the risk–return proposition can be clearly articulated, clearly understood and managed in a prudent and controlled manner. One clear step in the right direction is the effort by some companies to develop projection models in order to understand their risk–return profiles beyond merely the present. These models can shed light on the issue in some of the following ways:

- how liabilities evolve over time;
- how different hedging strategies perform in different economic environments;
- which strategies are costly and which are cheap;
- where the leverage and pressure points are.

Thus far, life insurers have been the predominant writers of VA guarantees. The reinsurance market has seen capacity come and go with market conditions. While the current direct writers and reinsurers are likely continue to be the market leaders, it is only a matter of time before investment banks start emerging as service providers to the direct writers. Their services will include everything from full reinsurance to provision of basic hedging services. Additionally, the outsourcing of hedging services is also likely to grow, with more providers compared with the very few available today.

VA guarantees provide real value to policyholders and can be offered in a way that adds value for shareholders commensurate with the assumed risk. By following the simple but important steps outlined in the previous section, the risks can be well understood and managed to satisfy all constituents.

1   See http://www.thehartford.com.

2   See http://www.manulife.com.

3   See http://www.johnhancock.com.

4   See http://www.oldmutual.com.

18

Issues Related to Running a Hedging Programme

Kannoo Ravindran
Annuity Systems Inc and Háskólinn í Reykjavík

Writers of variable annuity (VA) products are typically exposed to an assortment of risks ranging across various asset classes like equities, interest rates, mortality (to name a few). Given how "underpriced" these guarantees are in the retail market, it is important for any writer of this business to be able to proactively manage the risks using a combination of one or more of the following methods:

- taking on the risks naked;
- reinsurance treaties;
- capital market instruments;
- product development.

While there is a large body of literature focused on how best to quantify such risks and how to go about managing them, very little has been written on issues inherent in running a hedging programme. In addition to outlining the risks associated with running a hedging programme, this chapter will outline questions that organisations should answer so as to ensure that running a hedging programme does not yield unwanted surprises.

RISKS UNDERLYING VA GUARANTEES PRE-HEDGING
In underwriting a VA product, the writer (before implementing any kind of risk management programme) is typically exposed to the following.

- Market risks: these are the risks associated with changes in the market variables that result in fund values (and/or interest rates, currency rates) falling short of what has been promised in the contract to policyholders.

- Actuarial and behavioural risks: since the pricing of this product is lapse, behavioural (eg, annuitisation, fund switching, etc) and mortality supported, these are the risks associated with adverse deviations in the actuarial assumptions from what was expected on average for the entire cohort of policyholders, leading to an exposure that is higher than that initially expected.

- Operational risks: these are the risks associated with the inaccurate or untimely capture of policyholder information (including investment allocations, annuitisations, withdrawals, etc) and subsequent inappropriate use of this information.

- Regulatory risks: these are the risks associated with the reserves/capital that need to be set aside for underwriting VAs. Included in this type of risk is the volatility on the balance sheet created by the selling of variable annuities .

RISKS INTRODUCED BY HEDGING

While it is a common belief among hedgers that any implemented hedging programme can only serve to reduce the risk exposure, given the nature and complexity of the risks inherent in VAs, and the continuing crisis in the financial markets, this belief is more a fallacy. In fact, when implementing any kind of hedging programme, it is imperative to understand that a hedger typically "swaps" the risks hedged for other types of risks (eg, counterparty, basis, liquidity, etc). This can be more easily observed by considering an example in which a hedger transacts in a complete reinsurance with no capacity limits in which 100% of the risks are transferred to the reinsurer. In such an instance, the risks a direct company is exposed to morphs from market, actuarial/behavioural, operational, regulatory related risks to that of counterparty related risks. Therefore, a hedger is typically exposed to the following types of risk.

- Capital markets (financial markets, basis, roll-over, liquidity, counterparty risks): these risks arise when implementing any capital-markets-based hedge,[1] since the maturities never extend as far as the mortality tables and any acquired hedge is typically indexed based. As a consequence, the hedger would be typically exposed to the following.

- Basis risks: exposure (slippages) due to "replicating" fund returns with a collection (basket) of index returns. In volatile markets, similar to what we have experienced since mid 2008, this has been a big source of exposure for writers of this business. This is further discussed in Section 6 of this book.

- Market risks: exposure (slippages) due to "replicating" the liability Greeks (eg, delta, gamma, vega, rho, etc) with Greeks of the derivative/reinsurance assets transacted. As a consequence, if the acquired asset was a complete reinsurance that resulted in 100% of the risks being transferred to the reinsurer, the hedger would no longer be exposed to any market risks.

- Rollover risks: exposure due to replacing the time-decaying assets with new ones, in the process "rolling over" from one asset to another. Like the market risks, this risk will not be present if the hedger ends up transacting in a complete reinsurance that involves a 100% risk-transfer.

- Counterparty risks: exposure to the claim-paying ability of the counterparty from whom the over-the-counter hedge was purchased. While this never used to be considered a source of concern before the 2008–9 financial crisis, it is something that hedgers nowadays think hard and fast about, sometimes so much so that they prefer to run the risks naked.

- Liquidity risks: exposure to the ability to easily unwind the derivative transactions should they prove to be inefficient or redundant since liquidity on such assets tends to typically decrease when

  * the life of the derivative is very long (ie, typically more than 15 years in the US and shorter for other countries),
  * the underlyings on which derivatives are transacted do not have an active derivatives market trading on them,
  * the derivatives transacted in have complex path-dependent features.

The reason for this stems from the fact that the number of interested and available counterparties tends to reduce when one or more of the above situations become a reality.

- Actuarial (mortality, behavioural (eg, fund switches, surrender, annuitisation) risks): in many transacted hedges, the bulk of mortality and behavioural risks end up residing with the writers of the VA even after the implemented trades. As a consequence, any deviations between expected and realised values of the mortality/behavioural patterns causes the hedger to be either under or over hedged, resulting in potentially excessive hedging costs.

- Operational (process, model, data integrity, systems risks): once a hedging programme is implemented, in addition to the operational risks exposed during the pre-hedging phase (see page 207), the hedger would be typically be exposed to the following.

  * Key-person risks: the staffing required to run a hedging programme effectively and efficiently needs to be done prudently. The reason for this arises from the fact that, to avoid any potential "rogue"-trader-type situations, an organisation needs to ensure that personnel involved with trading and/or risk-management functions are backed-up and rotated out of their positions frequently. In this way, any mis-reportings (or inconsistencies in reporting) do not go undetected for a long time – something which can quite easily happen given the long-dated nature, complexity and illiquidity associated with variable annuities. Included in this category of risks is also the instance where there is only one person performing a particular function, so that it is a black box to everyone else in the organisation (eg, a quant/programmer who is responsible for modelling/programming/maintaining the integrity of the systems without any well-documented source code).

  * Process/control risks: in running a hedging programme, it is imperative to ensure that anyone

involved in the process, regardless of whether they are collecting policyholder data, programming models, trading the risks, performing the analysis for financial reporting, or administering the payment of claims, etc, has clearly defined accountabilities. As a consequence, there needs to be a clear separation of responsibilities and reporting structure so as to ensure that the personnel responsible for compliance/controls can operate independently and not be influenced by those responsible for trading and reporting the impact of trades and risks. An example of this is the running of the overnight risks reports by the front-office and the independent validation of these results by the back-office during this time. Despite this, it is common to see that it is a struggle in many small-to-medium-sized insurance companies (and to some extent even in some larger ones) to get enough funding/budget/attention to implement such controls/processes without compromising the integrity of the implementation. The unfortunate consequence of this is that thorough documentation of process/controls becomes an afterthought on the heels of fraud, trading disasters, etc.

* Systems-related risks: given the complexity of the model used to report risks underlying a hedging programme, the daily need to communicate between different systems (eg, actuarial, asset management, financial market information, administration systems) and the length of time taken to run through the policies so as to be able to produce risk-reports in a reasonable amount of time, it is important to be able to ensure that system does not break down during the runs. The consequence of this breakdown could be drastic, especially during moments of market turbulence when the hedger needs to urgently put on transactions to prevent further bleeding of the hedging programme. Therefore, it is imperative to have "back-up" systems or to make alternative arrangements for these analyses/reports to be run so as to

ensure that the required results are available for trade execution.

- Regulatory (risk of volatility in capital, reserves or financial statements): since the calculation of the volatility in capital/reserves is typically driven by the appropriate conditional tail expectations metrics, the results of these calculations tend to change every quarter (as market conditions and in-the-moneyness of the guarantee change). As such, implementing any kind of hedging strategy would have an impact on these metrics. It is exactly these types of risks that the hedger needs to concern themselves with when running a hedging programme, making sure that appropriate credit is given for running a sound and effective programme.

In addition to the above, the nature of the VA riders can sometimes introduce an additional disincentive to do any kind of non-reinsurance-based hedging. More precisely, certain types of riders, like the accumulation and withdrawal benefits, are considered as derivatives, hence allowing for a marked-to-market type of reporting. For riders that cannot be classified as derivatives, any derivatives-based hedging strategy (no matter how sound) will only cause additional volatility in the financial statements, due to the fact that the liabilities cannot be marked-to-market, whereas the hedge assets are marked-to-market.

QUESTIONS TO ASK WHEN RUNNING A HEDGING PROGRAMME

Given the complexities associated with hedging VA exposures, it is quite easy for important explanations to senior management and board members to get lost in translation when someone close to the hedging programme is asked to explain any part of it. As a consequence, it is important for any hedging organisation to be able to answer the following questions (in no particular order).

Hedging strategy

- What is the objective of the hedging programme (ie, are you managing economic risks or managing volatility in required capital or a combination of both, etc)?

- How much (in annual basis points) are you prepared to spend on the hedging programme?

- In the event that the hedge budget is insufficient to cover the risks you want to eliminate (which happens if your product is underpriced relative to the risks assumed), what types of risk exposure would you like to keep versus transfer to the market and/or counterparty? More precisely, do you want to use your budget to hedge

  - the first dollar of the exposure and cap it at some pre-defined level, or

  - the tail component of the exposure (in the process leaving the exposure starting from the first dollar to the commencement of the tail cover), etc?

- What instruments would you like to use to mitigate the risks (eg, reinsurance, over-the-counter customised options, equity futures, interest rate swaps, etc.) or, equivalently, what kinds of risk-management programme do you want to run (eg, equity delta hedging, equity/interest rate delta hedging, quasi-static hedging)?

- What is the rationale that is used to obtain the trading limits currently used?

Risk quantification

- How well does the behavioural assumption used to price this product "compare" against 100% rational policyholder behaviour?

- How confident are you about the inputs used to quantify the risks, especially when some inputs are

  - calibrated using derivative prices that are not liquid, easily observable or tradable?

- computed using historical information and hence are a function of the amount of history, return period, weighting of the historical return data and statistical methodology used?

- When should you "upgrade" your models (or use more sophisticated ones) so as to be able to capture uncertainty in the variables more accurately?

- When should you change/update your actuarial and behavioural assumptions if you have started experiencing realised actuarial/behavioural values which undergo adverse derivations from those originally stated?

- When should you change/update your statistically computed inputs if you have started experiencing variations from those used?

- Do you have a mechanism in place to dissect the hedging programme performance so as to identify sources of slippages, especially if the sources of inefficiency are due to deviation in the actuarial/policyholder behavioural assumptions as opposed to the poor hedging practice (eg, selection of improper assets, taking an incorrect view on markets, use of poor models, etc)?

- How confident are you about your counterparties' ability to fulfil their obligations at the times when claims become due?

Controls

- What is the worst thing that can hypothetically happen in the current hedging programme (in terms of adverse movements in financial markets and irrational policyholder behaviour)?

- What is the likelihood of the hypothetical worse-case scenarios happening relative to historical and current market conditions?

- What is the impact of the hypothetical worse-case scenarios on the balance sheet?

- How do you know that your current hedging programme is working and will continue to work?

- Have all your models or processes deployed in the hedging programme been independently audited (either internally or externally)?
- If you are dealing with third-party vendors, do you have the internal expertise and resources to

    - decide which third-party vendor software/solution is technically efficient, effective and superior?

    - independently and constantly validate the third-party software and solutions you have decided on (or selected) so as to ensure you understand what is being done?

- Is there a division of responsibilities and reporting structure between the personnel trading, maintaining the software, independently validating the models and the reporting of the day-end results, etc?
- Has your risk-management programme/process been documented sufficiently well that all checks/controls/balances are in place and anyone involved in the programme can be temporarily displaced for a few months with very minimal hiccups by a new person who is technically competent?
- Is there a mechanism in place to ensure that view taking (speculation) on the hedging programme can be easily identified, quantified and controlled?
- How well-informed and up-to-speed is the board of the hedging programme regarding its efficiency, flaws, exposure, conflicts, etc?

This chapter is based on the author's 2008 unpublished working paper "What You Need To Know About Managing VA Risks?" Please contact the author for a copy.

---

1   Examples of these instruments are index futures, currency futures, bond futures, swaps, index options, swaptions, customised options.

Section 5

Accounting and Regulation

Introduction

Tigran Kalberer

KPMG

As we have seen in the preceding chapters, VAs present new challenges to the insurance industry. New risks emerge with the provision of VAs, and the valuation and risk management of the guarantees need sophisticated models. These challenges are reflected in the regulation and the accounting of VA products.

In Chapter 19 Sam Gutterman focuses on the regulation of VAs. Supervisors have of course realised that these products may harm the interests of policyholders, as it is not obvious that insurance companies can fulfill all the obligations towards policyholders they have generated by offering VA products.

Supervisors thus have to make sure that companies have a proper risk management strategy in place to ensure that the policyholder obligations can be met with an adequate level of security. These risk management measures include adequate reserves for the guarantees.

Reserving approaches vary by jurisdiction, the main approaches are:

- formula-based approaches;

- factor approaches;

- stochastic approaches, like the Canadian CALM or the US VACARVM approach, which define the reserves such that they cover the average loss in the majority of worst cases.

But reserving alone is not sufficient, as the value of the guarantees might increase very fast.

Product design issues, especially the required solvency capital requirements, are important.

In some jurisdictions these solvency requirements are based on a "conditional tail expectation" (CTE), also called "expected shortfall", such as Canada's Minimum Continuing Capital and Surplus

Requirement (MCCSR) or Switzerland's Swiss Solvency Test (SST), but in most jurisdictions the requirements are Value-at-Risk (VaR) based, as in the EU (Solvency II).

Additionally, VAs are relatively new products in some jurisdictions. Thus, the legal framework may not yet be in place to cope with such products or may imply restrictions too onerous for insurance companies offering such products. This is the case for some European jurisdictions. Therefore, it is a popular approach in Europe to produce VAs in a regulatory jurisdiction within the European Economic Area (EEA) that has a reasonable approach towards VAs and make use of the "Freedom of Services" rights, which are guaranteed in the EEA treaties. Freedom of services within the EEA allow an insurance company to produce an insurance product in one EEA country and offer it to policyholders in another EEA country.

In Chapter 20 Stefan Engeländer describes the accounting treatment of VA contracts. VAs require significantly deeper consideration than other life-insurance contracts, as they are exposed to severe financial risks and show asymmetries that are unknown in conventional contracts. Thus, existing accounting approaches do not cope well with VA contracts; accounting approaches typically show worst-case scenarios as long as there is no sufficient evidence that these can be avoided, eg, by a direct link between the guarantee features and the hedging assets.

At the time of writing in late 2009, there is no international best-practice approach for accounting VAs, as the International Accounting Standards Board (IASB) has not completed its Insurance Contract Project. Some examples of accounting treatment explored in Section 5 are US GAAP, which uses a deferral and matching approach, Irish GAAP, which uses a prospective valuation of cashflow approach in conjunction with a percentile-based security level, and German GAAP, which uses an approach originally developed for conventional life insurance and thus introduces substantial conservatism.

19

An Overview of the Regulation of Variable Annuities

Sam Gutterman
PricewaterhouseCoopers LLP

Because of their long-term nature, the fiduciary responsibility involved, the investment risks and guarantees and their complexity and similarity to investment products, the regulation of variable annuities (VAs) has played a crucial role in their development and evolution. Nevertheless, the fundamental concerns of regulators about these products are little different from their concerns regarding other products offered by life insurers, namely,

- their coverage and product features are suitable for the needs of their purchasers,
- because of their long-term nature and complexity, the communication with clients, especially through insurers' sales efforts, is clear and appropriate, and
- the assurance that promises made are kept and obligations are upheld.

In order to satisfy these concerns, regulators need adequate information to appropriately assess the performance of the applicable insurer and the contracts.

These concerns can be categorised in practical terms as follows:

- initial and ongoing acceptability of a company and distributors to operate in this area;
- approval of products, including in some cases minimum standards for product design, pricing and distribution-related compensation;
- requirements for ongoing information necessary to assess the likelihood that the company's fiduciary responsibilities are being carried out and promises made to consumers will be kept.

In some respects the role of regulators may vary depending on whether the purchaser is an individual buying these annuities or a knowledgable group purchaser. For less sophisticated purchasers and owners of these products, more intensive oversight and proper educational opportunities are needed to facilitate better decision making.

In some jurisdictions, multiple regulators may be involved. One set of regulators are involved with the offering and trading of an entity's stock (shares) in a capital market, safeguarding the interest of investors. Another group of regulators are involved with the business itself, including its authorisation to conduct such a business and to operate in a manner consistent with the public interest. Yet another area in which regulatory oversight is often called for is in the area of consumer protection, including proper sales practices and even product and pricing design, particularly for retail sales (that is, those contracts sold to individuals). In some jurisdictions, particularly where sales of VAs are not significant or where markets, product features or the regulatory framework are relatively unsophisticated, little, if any, specific legislation or regulatory reference has been directed at these products.

The key elements of effective fiduciary regulatory oversight to ensure proper assessment of the financial condition of insurance and annuity products can be illustrated by a review of the major components of Solvency II, a risk-focused set of regulatory capital required in the European Union and the European Economic Area from October 2012. There are no specific rules applicable to VAs. Its solvency assessment takes the form of three major components.

- **Pillar I:** Quantitative requirements. These address rules for determination of both liabilities for insurance products and capital requirements. Minimum capital is determined by a specified approach (a "minimum capital requirement"). This is determined as the minimum of results from a standard model, the "solvency capital requirement" (SCR), reflecting insurance, counterparty and market risks or by a reliable internal model. A rigorous methodology has been established for accepting the results of an internal model, including a "use test" that verifies whether the insurer actually uses the results of the model in managing the applicable business.

- **Pillar II:** Supervisory review. Under the supervisory review process, the supervisory authority reviews and evaluates company strategies, processes and reporting procedures in a qualitative manner. This is important because not all risks can be quantified and assessed under Pillar I.

- **Pillar III:** Supervisory reporting and public disclosure. Market discipline is added by means of information regarding the insurer's risks through transparency of risks and its capital position.

Although they are outside the scope of this chapter, in some jurisdictions non-insurers are permitted to sell VAs (eg, from 2002 banks have been permitted to sell VAs in Japan). This requires that those regulators outside the traditional insurance regulatory framework have specialist knowledge to oversee the provision and management of these products. One approach to addressing this concern is a gradual worldwide movement towards consolidated financial-services-industry regulatory oversight, where functional oversight is increasingly relied on to enable a more effective focus on risk on the part of regulators, while reducing the chance of cracks emerging in the regulatory framework, that is, by providing comprehensive and appropriate oversight to the distribution, sales practices and assessment of financial reporting and solvency.

PRODUCTS

The types of VA products available are not dealt with in this chapter, as they have been covered comprehensively elsewhere in the book. Variations that affect the regulatory approach taken include accumulation versus payout products, individuals versus group customers and the level of guarantees and options provided through various VA products.

PRODUCT DESIGN ISSUES

When the focus is on the complex features in many VAs, what can sometimes be overlooked are the underlying guarantees involved: that assets are invested in a manner consistent with the asset mix described to the annuitants or their sponsors at the time of sale and that the entitlement to and investment return from a designated set of assets be kept safe. In some cases, similar to mutual funds, there is a wide range of investment options, eg, growth stocks, real estate and money market funds. In many cases, the choice includes a share of the general funds of an insurer.

This fiduciary responsibility is accompanied by legal and contractual guarantees, sometimes dictated by law or regulation. In some jurisdictions, the designated set of assets are "bankruptcy remote", that is, the owners of the VAs have first priority in the case when an insurer becomes bankrupt. In other jurisdictions, the obligations associated with the assets underlying the promises associated with variable products are treated in a way consistent with the other obligations of the insurer, in some cases backed up by state- or industry-sponsored guarantee funds.

However, it is the guarantees provided in these contracts that usually attract the most regulatory attention and concern, such as minimum death or living benefits. Each of these benefit features involves one or more types of risk, each of which relate to the performance of the underlying assets. Although the allowable types of guarantees may depend in part on regulatory requirements, those available are usually dictated more by the level and type of competition in the market place, as well as the primary mitigation techniques available, eg, through reinsurance and hedging opportunities. These features will also depend on the market involved, eg, large pension plans purchasing these funds will typically look towards more flexibility in product design and lower compensation to the distribution channel, as well as to the value for the guarantees provided.

Often the level of regulatory involvement will be greater for retail types of products, that is, particularly relating to sales to individual purchasers. The more complicated the rules, the more complicated the features, which in turn may lead to further complexity of the rules.

LIABILITY ISSUES

Liability requirements currently differ between jurisdictions. However, with increased convergence internationally, this variation may decrease over time. In most cases relating to the liabilities which are directly related to the underlying separate account (or equivalent) liabilities, the rules for measurement are straightforward, usually exactly equal to the market value of the corresponding assets.

A potential complication arises where the applicable accounting standard does not provide for recognition of a certain type of asset that is invested in the separate account. Examples are own-company shares or company occupied property, which are not recognisable in certain countries. The greater the illiquidity of the asset, the greater the difficulty in deriving a value for this and certain other assets; the key in such situations is to ensure that the value of the liabilities is consistent with the value of the corresponding assets.

Since the reliability of estimating probabilities of transfer of funds is speculative at best, it is usually assumed that the current distribution of funds continues in the future.

Several methods have been used to derive accounting values for the guarantees involved with these products. There are basically three approaches to measuring liabilities for these products.

- A formula approach, such as the greatest present value, used in the US in the Commissioners' Annuity Reserve Valuation Method (CARVM), which involves the worst-case scenario of possible outcomes, applying the formula of the present value of expected benefits minus the present value of expected future premiums.

- A factor approach, reflecting a set of reserves using a factor selected from a table of such factors such as age, gender, investment fund class or ratio of account value to guaranteed value.

- A scenario approach, developing a set of costs associated with each of multiple scenarios and corresponding sets of probabilities. Although the scenarios and corresponding probabilities are usually derived stochastically, this third approach in some cases can be derived using a set of representative deterministically derived scenarios.

Most modern systems use the third approach; two examples are briefly described below.

- In Canada, the Canadian Asset Liability Method (CALM) has been used, requiring stochastic analysis of applicable guarantees. In general, a conditional tail expectation (CTE) at a 60–80% probability level is used. The basis usually applied is a regime-switching lognormal model (with two regimes used).

This recognises that either a stable or an unstable regime might apply in the future, with the possibility (at a certain level) of switching between these two regimes. Within each regime, the stock price (or price of another relevant asset type) is assumed to follow a lognormal probability distribution over time. The selected probability level, corresponding to the desired level of security and professional standard guidance, is then selected.

- Introduced in 2009 in the US, Actuarial Guideline (AG) 43, known as VACARVM (Variable Annuity Commissioners' Reserve Valuation Method), describes the method to be used to determine liabilities for VAs requirements. To a great extent it was modelled after the Canadian approach described above. This liability is the greater of either a "standard scenario amount", using a prescribed set of assumptions including a deterministic scenario or a liability determined according to a "conditional tail expectation amount", based on a CTE at 70% of stochastic scenario projections using prudent estimate assumptions based on company experience and expectations.

Whatever the method applied, disclosure of the significant risks involved is usually required, in some cases via an independent audit regarding a proper statement of the entire financial statement of the insurer and/or an actuarial opinion regarding the adequacy or appropriateness of the liabilities established for these contracts, either in a separate statement or in combination with the liabilities of all other insurance and annuity contracts provided by the company.

SOLVENCY AND CAPITAL ISSUES

The level of and approach to the determination of required capital for VA contracts have also varied considerably by jurisdiction, similarly to the extent of variation seen in requirements for other annuity and insurance contracts. The objective of this determination is to provide, in addition to the underlying liabilities, a financial cushion to ensure that insurers have sufficient funds to fulfill their overall obligations to all their policyholders. The amount of capital is typically determined on a company-wide basis, with different factors being separately applicable to different products, liabilities and assets held. Recently, as underlying risks have been better identified (sometimes as a result of actual adverse developments), the required formulas have increased in complexity, with the resultant levels of required capital generally increasing in size.

In some jurisdictions, multiple levels of regulatory capital are provided for. The lowest action level is the amount of capital below which a regulator is required to take over the operations of an insurer, possibly winding it up. At higher levels, usually at a multiple of the minimum required to continue to operate, other regulatory actions can be taken, such as discontinuation of new business or a "watch level" at which corporate action plans are required for regulatory review.

In the latter part of the 20th Century and beyond, more modern capital formulas included: Minimum Continuing Capital and Surplus Requirement (MCCSR), applicable in Canada, which since 2002 has required a suitable solvency margin for minimum guarantees in VAs equivalent to the CTE at a 95% level for these risks; Risk Based Capital (RBC), in the US; and Solvency II (to be introduced in the European Union in October 2012). With VAs, since most of the direct investment risk is borne by the policyholders, required capital is not needed for the direct asset risks involved. However, minimum levels of capital primarily relate to the risks associated with the various guarantees and longevity risks included in VA contracts; even though investment return risk is not borne by the insurer, the risks an insurer takes on are primarily a direct performance (or rather, lack of performance) of investments and asset valuation.

The regulation of solvency involves a number of issues, including consideration of the adequacy of the charges included in these products, the proper management and reporting of any counterparty risks, the proper valuation of any options and guarantees and the overall management of the company distributing and offering these products. To the extent, if any, to which the obligations are not perfectly matched by a separate account (or similar vehicle), insurers offer investments in a general account outside the VA separate account. In this case capital requirements would be associated with any guarantees of investment performance for those funds.

HEDGING ISSUES

Many companies have decided to hedge certain of their risks through the use of reinsurance or financial hedges purchased in the capital markets. Regarding reinsurance, the regulator may have concerns relating to the reinsurer, in particular with respect to the admissibility of the company regarding their financial condition or other aspects of their operation; overall these concerns and rules are similar to those relating reinsurers and reinsurance of insurance or other annuity products. Regarding hedging, concerns relate to the effectiveness of the hedges acquired, in relation both to the credit taken for reserving purposes and to acceptable credit for regulatory capital treatment. In either case, regulatory concerns relate to proper provision for counterparty risks or hedging credits.

OTHER ISSUES

The complexity of common product features incorporated in many VA products and the resultant regulatory requirements have raised compliance to become significant operational insurer functions. This has in some cases resulted in complicated rules, actions needed to comply and compliance resources devoted to ensuring that those rules are being followed.

20

Variable Annuities: Accounting Challenges

Stefan Engeländer

KPMG

Variable annuities (VAs) have peculiarities which are not unique; they are also found to some extent in a number of other contract types. However, the risk exposure of some of those features is predominant in the case of VAs and shapes the overall economics of the contracts. As a consequence, the accounting issues for VAs are not unique, but their solution requires a significantly deeper consideration and more care than in other cases, where those features are merely insignificant. Most important is the fact that VAs include severe financial risks, often in addition to significant biometrical risks, especially longevity. Market-consistent calculated minimum guarantees on market prices of specified assets produce an asymmetry which is unknown in conventional life-insurance contracts. These significant asymmetries are artificial and specific to the individual contract styling and therefore deviate from typical assets found in active markets. Also, since often earnings depend directly on the market prices of those assets, downward asymmetries result in a leverage of the market risk for the insurer. Matching instruments are also artificial and are individually designed for the specific risk of the VA itself. The ultimate residual risk, mainly credit risk or market volatility risk, is hardly quantifiable.

Overall, considering the peculiarities of VAs, existing accounting approaches do not cope well with the peculiarities of those contracts. The internal risk management might accept that the products are highly speculative and rely significantly on simplifying actuarial models. Conservative accounting approaches, designed to provide warning indicators regarding unclear risks, need to punish such a business attitude. Accounting rarely allows the reliance on subjective management views but prefers to show worst-case scenarios as long as there is no positive evidence by markets, or at least any other objective evidence, that significant risks are not present or at least are not larger than reported. If unquantifiable residual risks are assumed to be material, the typical accounting response is to defer income until risks become quantifiable or are assumed to be extinguished.

The fact that regulatory authorities feel satisfied with certain models applying a pragmatic viewpoint after a self-assessment does not mean that general-purpose financial reports can simply expect independent third parties in capital markets to make financial decisions on that basis. They demand adequate decision-useful information about any risk rather than opaque statements with questionable objectivity. The difference in function between solvency reporting and general-purpose financial reports becomes obvious here.

SEPARATION OF EMBEDDED DERIVATIVES

Some accounting systems require separation and fair-value measurement of specific embedded derivatives. Embedded derivatives are contract components that modify contractual cashflows otherwise payable in response to changes of market factors (like unit prices). These could be floors (like minimum guarantees), caps (like maximum charges otherwise dependent on fund values) or leverages (like some forms of ratchets). They apply mainly to surrender or withdrawal rights. No separation applies if derivatives include significant insurance risk, eg, since the modifications of cashflows in response to market factors affect only life-contingent cashflows. Consequently, embedded derivatives affecting only the payout amount of life-contingent annuities (eg, ratchets) would not qualify for separation.

REVENUE RECOGNITION

One of the main accounting concerns is the appropriate allocation of revenue to accounting periods. Revenue should not be recognised before the associated entity activities (the resulting obligations) are performed, including release from any residual risks other than immaterial risks. Consequently, many accounting systems care merely for retaining earnings than measuring obligations, eg, US Generally Accepted Accounting Principles (GAAP) determine mainly when charges are to be released to income or have to be deferred. This applies to both premiums and charges taken from the policy account. The obligation is actually only measured if the contract is assumed to be onerous.

CONSIDERATION OF MATCHING ASSETS

A basic accounting principle is the separate consideration of any individual item. Accounting does not intend to represent the value of the entire entity by considering any interrelationship of items. Consequently, even those assets held intentionally for matching specific risks from VAs are normally considered in isolation. Typically, financial instruments are reported, at least in profit or loss, at amortised cost, while obligations from VAs are often reported at current values. As a consequence, an accounting mismatch appears in the books, ie, the changes of book values of obligations and of matching assets deviate, although their market value is affected equally by changes in the financial environment.

To overcome that odd consequence, it is necessary to provide evidence of a direct link between the items, ie, that they should be seen as one for accounting purposes (unit of account). Intentionally, there is usually no contractual reference to the matching assets, since the freedom of choice whether (and to what extent) to match the obligations improves the flexibility of the insurer to cope with the risks considering entity-specific peculiarities. It might be sensible to cope with some parts of the risk itself, if the market price for matching were not affordable. But exactly that attitude will often be the main reason for treating the items separately.

However, if the matching is highly efficient, consistently applied and well documented, it might be possible to treat the matching assets and the matched obligation as a unit of account in some accounting systems. In that case, they are (although reported gross on the asset and the liability side of the balance sheet) measured consistently, ie, any change of one item is mirrored by the same change in the opposite item. Nevertheless, for the remaining inefficiencies of matching, significant cautiousness needs to be reflected in the measurement.

As a consequence, insurers need also to consider accounting consequences in determining their matching strategies.

MEASUREMENT OF OBLIGATIONS

The main issues of measurement are the consideration of

- the asymmetries introduced by the minimum guarantees,

- the relationship with matching assets, and

- the impacts of policyholders' behaviour.

The extreme sensitivity of the value of guarantees to changes in the value of underlying funds (unit prices) as a consequence of market-price asymmetries creates the need to use sophisticated capital market models, resulting in stochastic modelling of future cashflows in order to cover appropriately all possible future developments in measurement. There are two typical approaches: one attempts to be market-consistent as far as possible; the other reflects merely the expectations of the management regarding future developments of the specific investments of the entity under its investment policy.

In the first case, assumptions are based on observed risk-free market returns for the respective durations, assuming that those reflect best the time value of money and that any additional income is actually offset by acceptance of an equivalent compensation for inherent risk. Here, future development of unit prices is modelled based on overall scenario weights reflecting the current risk-free market conditions and determining the effect of asymmetries accordingly. However, using current market conditions as a basis for the weights of scenarios provides guidance only for the symmetric average, not for the actual width of the distribution, as needed for measuring asymmetries. The tail of the distribution is not clearly identifiable from the source data. Special care is needed, in doubt by implementing additional conservatism, to cope properly with that issue.

In the second case, the issue is solved by moving directly to a merely subjective measurement basis, based only on past experience. It is assumed that the unquantifiable residual risk resulting from the entity's investment policy is suitably covered by implicit cautiousness in measurement. However, the subjectivity of this approach causes more and more doubts that it is suitable for general-purpose reporting.

Even more complex issues arise if covering matching assets are considered in cashflow projections. Since these assets would not normally match the obligations entirely (at least the counter-party's default risk remains), additional asymmetries occur. Different aspects of deviation risk, often referred to as "Greeks", might, for simplification or cost-effectiveness, be ignored in matching. Markets charge especially for excessive volatility prices due to the lacking quantifiability of that risk. The measurement of these individual risks will accordingly turn out to be most complex. The product cannot be reported "cheaper" than the cost occurring by fully matching it in the market. Matching is ultimately a tool of solvency issues in order to avoid capital requirements, since the solvency of the counterparty, usually also a regulated financial institution, can be utilised. For general-purpose reporting, residual risks cause significant issues.

VAs are often lapse sensitive, if benefits from minimum guarantees apply only to ordinary completion of the contract, ie, at death or maturity. Consequently, occurrence of premature cancellations or partial withdrawal of funds releases the insurer to some extent from the burden of those minimum guarantees. Counterparty behaviour is a controversial issue in accounting. Some believe that counterparties should be assumed to act rationally. Since it is not determinable what is "rational" from the counterparty's viewpoint, it is assumed as a proxy that the counterparty's worst-case decision for the insurer is rational. This is often simplified to a "minimum-deposit floor", ie, a requirement that the liability must not be lower than the amount which the counterparty can withdraw on demand. This is embodied, for example, in European regulations for solvency measurement and in IAS 39.[1] Others follow the ideas of behavioural economics, assuming that it is possible to make money from counterparty's behaviour. Consequently, current expectations regarding policyholders' behaviour may be introduced in measuring VAs, including significant margins for uncertainty. There is no appropriate theory for how to determine such margins in an objective manner.

AUDITABILITY AND VERIFIABILITY

Financial risks, which are not traded in active markets and are in addition highly artificial (eg, floors on fund values or ratchets for annuities) cause significant issues of reliability of measurement, especially fair-value measurement. Values of such asymmetries cannot be derived directly from observable market prices. In particular, stochastic modelling includes subjective assumptions to such an extent that there are significant concerns about auditability and verifiability. The reliance of market participants on (audited) general-purpose financial reports is based on the assumption that the information provided represents a general consensus regarding the result of the calculation. While regulatory reports are directly under the control of and subject to decisions of the regulator, the main recipient of the general-purpose financial reports, the general public, requires a higher level of reliability. It is therefore necessary to ensure that, in particular, valuations based on stochastic models make use of robust and verifiable assumptions, although that might cause an additional burden in processing and, more importantly, result in additional conservatism. Deferral of income until it is positively proven to be earned is the typical accounting response.

EXAMPLES OF MEASUREMENT OF VARIABLE ANNUITIES IN DIFFERENT ACCOUNTING SYSTEMS

Until the International Accounting Standards Board (IASB)[2] completes its Insurance Contracts Project 2011 according to its current timetable, there is no internationally widespread applied approach to account for insurance contracts and VAs in particular. To provide an overview, we have chosen three examples of accounting approaches. US GAAP is the most widespread approach, as in addition it is applied by several large insurance groups outside the US as continued accounting policy for insurance contracts under International Financial Reporting Standards (IFRS). Irish GAAP was chosen since Ireland attracted some subsidiaries of European insurance groups in order to sell VAs all over Europe, utilising the merely liberal Irish regulatory requirements. German GAAP includes a conventional accounting approach in compliance with traditional views of EU-regulation.

US GAAP

US GAAP guidance for insurance contracts is significantly based on a deferral-and matching approach. Insofar as contract components are embedded derivatives not to be separated and consequently measured at fair value, normal accounting guidance (FAS 60, FAS 97 and SOP 03-01) for insurance contracts, specifically for universal-life contracts, applies (Herget 2006). Accordingly, the stated policy account balance is reported as the policy benefit liability amount, acquisition costs are deferred and amortised in proportion to "estimated gross profits", charges are recognised when due except if they need to be deferred to avoid future losses and premiums are not reported as revenue but credited directly to the policy account. Within the US and few other countries, investments are held in separate accounts, requiring special legal recognition and separation in bankruptcy cases. The separate accounts are measured at fair value, resulting in a general consistency between policy accounts and matching assets. Consistency may not be achievable in countries where separated accounts cannot be introduced in the absence of the required legal recognition. Consistency in measurement between assets (which match minimum guarantees but are not held in the separated account) and the matched obligation cannot always be achieved. In addition to requirements to defer income to avoid future losses, there is a mandatory loss-recognition test to be applied on each reporting date, requiring that the liability minus the deferred acquisition cost is never lower than the current estimate of cashflows. The loss-recognition test ensures that guarantees in-the-money are recognised at least at the expected value of cashflows.

Irish GAAP

Reports in compliance with Irish GAAP are, for practical reasons, often based on reports prepared for the Irish Financial Services Regulatory Authority (IFSRA). Regarding VAs, Irish GAAP is less restrictive than the IFSRA regulations.[3] The measurement is based on a prospective valuation of future cashflows, applying a specific margin, which might be lower than that required for regulatory purposes; eg, achieving a 50% percentile security level might be sufficient for Irish GAAP purposes. The measurement can be based on stochastic modelling and may consider available matching assets. A further difference from regulatory reports is that it is permitted to defer the acquisition cost and there is no need for a close-down, resilience or expense overrun reserve, although it might sometimes be necessary to provide for otherwise uncovered expected future administration costs. Although the appointed actuary does not have an official role in the case of general-purpose financial reports, the measures taken for regulatory reports are often accepted here. Investments covering VAs are mostly measured at fair value.

German GAAP

German GAAP[4] assumes that any guarantee is entirely covered by a portfolio of widespread and well-diversified investments and consequently permits discounting for future guaranteed cashflows, including minimum guarantees, not exceeding the general interest rate as provided for by the EU, ie, currently 2.25%. As a consequence, the minimum amount of the liability for the contract (especially in the early stage) significantly exceeds the aggregated fund value. Since the guarantees are usually calculated with significantly higher discount rates, the liability cannot usually be financed by contractually charged premiums. The resulting initial loss affecting the overall financial report might question the entire business. In addition, some regulatory requirements increase the applied conservatism even more. The excess liability on top of the fund value needs to be covered by widespread and well-diversified investments. Most assets typically used to match the minimum guarantees would not comply with this requirement. The capital requirements for guaranteed interest benefits apply to the entire minimum guarantee, not just for the excess on top of the fund value. German GAAP permits to some extent the capitalisation of future premiums reported as an asset, as far as needed to cover acquisition costs. In any other case, future earnings must not be capitalised if that results in an anticipation of gains before realised. Typically, any balance sheet item is considered separately, but, in the case of a demonstrable link between items (as in an effective and systematic matching), the items might be measured consistently as a unit of account. This applies equally to investments, which otherwise need to be measured at the amortised cost. Units directly linked to the contracts are generally measured at fair value.

---

1 http://www.iasb.org.

2 See note 1.

3 Further guidance can be found in the Association of British Insurers' "Statement of Recommended Practice (SORP)", November 2003 (http://www.abi.org.uk/) or from the Society of Actuaries in Ireland (http://web.actuaries.ie).

4 German GAAP is based on non-codified generally accepted accounting principles, on legal guidance found in HGB, RechVersV, VAG and DeckRV.

REFERENCES

Herget, R. T., 2006, *US GAAP for Life Insurers*, Second Edition (Society of Actuaries).

Section 6

Other Related Topics

Introduction

Tigran Kalberer
KPMG

The preceding chapters presented a comprehensive overview of VAs: the products, the markets, the risks and risk management approaches. Nearly all aspects of these products have been addressed. We have seen, however, that there are some specific topics which are relevant for VAs and deserve more attention; this is exactly the purpose of Section 6. In this section we have gathered contributions regarding the following specific topics:

- Which approaches exist to manage basis risk?

- How do we use replication-portfolio approaches for hedging?

- How do equity analysts look at VAs?

- How do rating agencies look at VAs?

- How has the 2008–9 financial crisis affected liquidity in derivatives markets and thus VAs?

Basis risk was one reason (but not the only one) for the losses incurred by some VA writers in the 2008–9 financial crisis. VA writers typically offer a substantial number of different actively managed funds to policyholders and guarantees on top of these. How can they expect to be able to quantify and manage the resulting risks? The answer lies in the fact that they use the strong assumption that these funds can be approximated by "surrogate portfolios", consisting of financial instruments which are measurable and hedgable, eg, equity indexes. The process of determining these "surrogate portfolios" and measuring their adequacy is far from trivial. And it is important to bear in mind that the goodness of fit of these approximating portfolios is dependent, for example, on correlation assumptions, which can break down in a financial crisis and typically do so.

In Chapter 21 Pin Chung describes the typical determination of surrogate portfolios and, perhaps even more importantly, the underlying assumptions and thus model risks. It ends with suggestions on how to manage basis risks better in the future.

As we have seen, managing the risks of VAs requires constant and fast determination of key risk statistics, eg, sensitivities of the VA portfolio towards small changes in the underlying fund value, also called "Greeks". These quantities are necessary to perform a dynamic-hedging programme and have to be determined on a daily basis over the whole portfolio of contracts. This is a challenging task, as this typically requires applying stochastic simulation, which is a very time-consuming task. The replication-portfolio approach can dramatically decrease the time required to perform this task and reduce the calibration error substantially. The replication-portfolio approach also allows a thorough hedge efficiency analysis. Such an analysis builds upon a large number of "real-world" scenarios that reflect all relevant risk factors, eg, equity prices, interest rates, volatility, basis risk, policyholder behaviour, etc. Then the hedging process will be simulated along each projected scenario, resulting in a distribution of the hedge slippages and typically revealing the high impact of non-hedged risks on the slippages. The realisation of the shortcomings of a planned hedging approach is of utmost importance. Chapter 22 by Tigran Kalberer elaborates on these replication-portfolio techniques.

In creating and distributing VAs, life-insurance companies should enhance their value to shareholders, but they introduce new risks for the shareholders too. Therefore, it is important that the value creation potential and the risks of VAs are communicated transparently to the financial community. Chapter 23 is written by Darin Arita from the perspective of an equity analyst and describes which type of disclosure is required to maintain the trust of investors in a company offering VA products.

Rating agencies also face the problem of analysing the risks in companies which offer VAs. The level of detail required is high and only after proper consideration of all risk drivers (distribution, products, capital adequacy, profitability, liquidity, risk management, including hedging approaches and financial flexibility) is it possible to assess the risks inherent in offering VAs. Diversity in distribution channels is better than dependence on just one channel, and more tightly controlled distribution channels allow better control of policyholder behaviour risks. The products are important too: some products offer guarantees that are just too rich to be profitable. A sufficient level of capital is key in being able to produce VAs. Even if economic capital is sufficient, regulatory capital requirements might be higher and it is important to fulfill these requirements. VAs typically do not show high margins and it is important that these margins are based on solid assumptions and should not erode if results deviate only slightly from the pricing assumptions. An understanding of the behaviour of VAs in extreme scenarios is crucial in assessing the rating of a life-insurance company, but looking at such scenarios should indeed be a crucial part of the overall risk management. In Chapter 24 Scott Robinson describes how a life insurance company issuing VAs is assessed from the perspective of a rating agency.

The recent developments on the financial markets have highlighted an issue which is crucial for VA products: the shortage in liquidity for long-term volatility. VA products are obviously exposed to long-term volatility as they are offering very long-term equity guarantees.

The supply-and-demand side for long-term volatility changed in the financial crisis and Naveed Choudri, Edward Tom and James Masserio argue in Chapter 25 that this change is here to stay. Interestingly enough, this change can be explained with supply-and-demand-side arguments.

21

Quantifying and Managing Basis Risk

Pin Chung
Allianz Investment Management

Variable annuity (VA) writers on average offer 20–60 different funds to contract holders. The available range of funds typically covers a wide variety of investment styles. The funds consist of different types of assets and most funds are actively managed, ie, their asset allocation is adjusted frequently, reflecting the views of the funds manager. In most jurisdictions, it is not possible to short-sell these funds, which implies that they are not directly hedgable. In order to solve this problem, funds are related to more liquid indexes using a set of linear relationships; this is called "fund mapping". This procedure is used to determine a portfolio of hedgable assets, usually equity indexes, which replicates the funds as closely as possible. This portfolio is called a "surrogate portfolio" or "replicating portfolio". Actually, the surrogate portfolio is then hedged instead of the funds themselves. Usually, but not always, fund mapping is performed by means of an ordinary-least-squares linear (OLS) regression using historical data for the fund and the indexes of its surrogate portfolio. As the returns of the funds can deviate from the returns of their surrogate portfolio, a new risk enters the scene: the so-called basis risk.

Basis risk attracted substantial attention among variable annuity (VA) writers during the financial crisis in 2008 because rapid market movements changed the composition of both VA funds and their replicating portfolios. During this crisis some sector indexes (eg, financials, real estate) lost significantly more value than other sectors, changing the composition of many funds. This caused a considerable basis mismatch. Another cause of basis mismatch is the increased correlation of indexes in a falling market (correlations approaching 1).

The relationship between the funds and their benchmark portfolio might break down during extreme market movements, such as those observed in the second half of 2008. The financial crisis of 2008 caused VA writers to review their fund mapping procedures and philosophies, which eventually led VA writers to make some strategic changes in their product pricing, hedge designs and hedge executions.

SOURCES OF BASIS RISK

Basis risk is the deviation between expected and actual fund performance due to

- a fund manager's under- or overperformance relative to their benchmark portfolio,
- correlation risk.

In the case of VAs, since it is impossible to use underlying funds as hedging instruments, this leads to intrinsic basis risk with most hedge designs. This is usually because either there are no hedging instruments or the combination of hedging instruments does not match the fund closely enough. Most funds have more than 20 constituents and are actively managed by professional portfolio managers. These portfolio managers have to follow their mandates to maintain certain investment styles (equity focus, fixed-income focus or specialty focus) and subject to a range of limits (leeway); ie, they should not deviate too much from their benchmark for too long; short-term deviations are allowed as opportunities come along.

Sometimes the "tracking error" is used to measure the severity of deviation. Tracking error is defined as the annualised volatility of the difference between the return of the fund and the benchmark. It is common to allow for up to 5% tracking error for actively managed funds, so the fund managers might deviate substantially from the benchmark to pursue perceived opportunities.

While the benchmark of a fund is disclosed, fund managers typically do not share their trading strategy (treated as "proprietary information") with VA writers; hence, most VA writers might not have direct access to up-to-date fund constituents, which would be very valuable information for hedging purposes.

Several possible sources of basis risks are summarised below:

- changes of the fund manager's style, ie, deviation from their benchmark;

- deviation between the benchmark and the surrogate portfolio;

- unanticipated fund expenses or unanticipated tax expenses could lead to a greater than expected drag on the fund performance;

- changes of funds' return profiles, ie, prices drop or rise drastically, which causes a change in the funds' composition;

- changes of the correlation relationship between indexes (in particular, it is even more difficult to judge if the change in correlation is permanent or just a temporary phenomenon).

HOW DOES A TYPICAL US VA WRITER PERFORM THE FUND MAPPING PROCEDURE

Most VA writers provide 20–60 funds to policyholders in order to offer different investment vehicles for both domestic and international opportunities. Some VA writers allow policyholders to set their asset allocation process, which means the policyholders can assign different percentage weights to a set of different funds when they purchase their policies. Typically, VA writers rebalance policy account values on every anniversary date (or every quarterly anniversary date) to their when-issued asset allocation weights. Some VA writers take a different approach: the so-called "forced asset allocation" approach. This approach offers a set of different investment styles (eg, aggressive, moderate and conservative for different risk appetites) by assigning pre-defined asset allocations to policyholders. In this case, the policy prospectus would specify all the details of how frequently the accounts would be rebalanced, how the accounts would be rebalanced and the types of different asset allocations.

There are several ways to conduct the fund mapping procedure. The overall goal of fund mapping is to properly reflect the systematic components (beta coefficients) of the underlying funds across selected indexes for hedging. Two popular methods will be demonstrated below. Method 1 is usually referred to as fund mapping performed at fund level or "seriatim-on-seriatim fund mapping"; method 2 is referred to as fund mapping performed at investment style level, or "forced asset allocation fund mapping". Most of the time, fund mapping process is carried out through OLS regression.

Review of the OLS Method

The general linear model is expressed as

$$y_i = \beta_0 + \beta_1 x_{i,1} + \beta_2 x_{i,2} + \cdots + \beta_{p-1} x_{i,p-1} + \varepsilon_i$$

where y_i is the ith value of the dependent variable, $\beta_0, \beta_1, \ldots, \beta_{p-1}$ are the regression parameters, $x_{i,1}, x_{i,2}, \ldots, x_{i,p-1}$ are known values of the independent variables, and ε_i is the ith independent random error, typically assumed to be distributed as $N(0, \sigma^2)$. In matrix notation the general linear model as can be expressed as $y = X\beta + \varepsilon$, where y is an $n \times 1$-vector of dependent values (where n represents the number of total observations), X is an $n \times p$-matrix of known constants, β is a $p \times 1$-vector of regression parameters and ε is an $n \times 1$-vector of identically distributed random errors, assume to be distributed as $N(0, \sigma^2)$.

For the estimation of the vector β, we minimise the total sum of squares S, where

$$S = \sum_{i=1}^{n} \varepsilon_i^2 = \sum_{i=1}^{n} (y_i - \beta_0 - \beta_1 x_{i,1} - \beta_2 x_{i,2} - \cdots - \beta_{p-1} x_{i,p-1})^2$$

By simultaneously solving the following p first-order (or normal) equations

$$\frac{\partial S}{\partial \beta} = 0 = \left[\frac{\partial S}{\partial \beta_0} = 0, \frac{\partial S}{\partial \beta_1} = 0, \ldots, \frac{\partial S}{\partial \beta_{p-1}} = 0 \right]'$$

In matrix form, we minimise $S = (y - X\beta)'(y - X\beta)$ by solving

$$\frac{\partial}{\partial \beta} [(y - X\beta)'(y - X\beta)] = 0$$

with the resulting estimator for β expressed as $b = (X'X)^{-1}X'y$.

Let $\bar{y}$ be the mean of the observed values, $\hat{y}$ be the vector of modelled values and let $\bar{\hat{y}}$ be the mean of the predicted values. Let e denote the vector of residuals from the model fit: $e_{(n \times 1)} = y - Xb = y - \hat{y}$. We can derive $SS_{total} = SS_{err} + SS_{reg}$, where the total sum of the squares, $SS_{total} = (y - \bar{y})'(y - \bar{y})$, the regression sum of the squares, $SS_{reg} = (\hat{y} - \bar{\hat{y}})'(\hat{y} - \bar{\hat{y}})$ and the sum of the squared errors (also known as the residual sum of squares), $SS_{err} = (y - \hat{y})'(y - \hat{y})$. The coefficient of determination is defined as

$$R^2 = \frac{SS_{reg}}{SS_{total}}$$

R^2 compares the explained variance with the total variance: it is a statistical measure of how well the regression line fits the real data. A model with higher R^2 indicates that regression line fits the data better.

In order to capture the breadth, depth and consistency of the relationship between underlying funds and hedged indexes, the following aspects are considered.

- Using too few indexes may not cover the breadth of exposures presented in the funds. However, using too many indexes may make the fund mapping procedure more complex, may not be cost effective in day-to-day hedging execution and may introduce additional operational risk.

- Using too short a period of funds data (eg, less than three years of monthly data) may not give enough credible data for OLS regression. Using too long a time-span (longer than 10 years of daily data) may risk regression against outdated historical funds returns.

For a typical US-based VA writer, some available hedging indexes may include: S&P 500 Total Return (SPTR), Barclay's Aggregate Bond Index (AGG), Russell 2000 (RUT), MSCI EAFE (EAFE) and S&P 400 Mid-Capital (MID). Typically, daily or weekly return data of each fund and index return profiles for a period of three to seven years are used for OLS regressions. Furthermore, if VA writers have a higher concentration of international separate accounts that would be hedged with international indexes, these writers must pay attention to incorporating the "one-day delay" or other time-delay effects. This effect is due to the fact that closing times of the stock exchanges around the globe are different and thus, for a funds valuation, outdated (last days) information might be used. This effect may result in spurious beta coefficients and may cause significant basis risk if this effect is not reflected properly.

MORE ON THE FUND MAPPING PROCEDURE
Method 1: fund mapping performed at fund level

(i) Construct daily or weekly returns data of each fund and candidate hedging index return profile for a three- to seven-year period.

(ii) Perform OLS regression on each fund to get beta coefficients for each index.

(iii) If necessary, apply different weighting schemes to return data; eg, equally weighted returns or exponential decay coefficients on observations.

Method 2: forced asset allocation fund mapping

(i) Construct historical return profiles of different forced asset allocations by applying either daily or weekly returns data for a three- to seven-year period and following pre-defined rebalancing policy weights.

(ii) Perform OLS regressions on each asset allocations to get beta coefficients for each index.

(iii) If necessary, apply different weighting schemes to the return data.

Under method 1, we first collect historical return profiles of each individual fund. Next, by regressing fund return data to the selected historical return data of hedged indexes, we could obtain beta components of this particular fund. Method 1 provides direct fitting results; some of the fund regressions might have reasonable or good fit (eg, judged by higher R^2); some of the fits might not be too good (eg, a real-estate fund or emerging market bond fund regressed on SPTR and AGG). VA writers may conduct this procedure one fund at a time to complete the whole process.

After obtaining the estimated beta coefficients through the fund mapping procedure, VA writers could first calculate each policyholder's dollar amounts allocated to different funds. Next, after proper beta adjustments, we could aggregate all betas to calculate corresponding hedge deltas of different hedged indexes. It is time-consuming to conduct this procedure since the fund mapping regression must be conducted one step at a time. However, the beauty of this procedure is that we may easily identify which fund has values better fitted to hedged indexes (and which fund has not). Hence, this approach allows us to perform a fund selection with the aim of reducing basis risk.

Method 2 is to perform fund mapping at the forced asset allocation level. There are more assumptions to be made in this approach, which include a well-defined policy weight and a pre-determined frequency of rebalancing to policy weights. The benefit of this approach is that it is relatively easy to conduct regression analysis, since there are fewer regressions to perform. The main drawback of this approach is that it is difficult to identify which funds cause deviations from the benchmark and may thus break the fund mapping process.

AN EXAMPLE OF THE FORCED ASSET ALLOCATION FUND MAPPING PROCESS

Consider a VA writer that offers three asset allocations to its policyholders with different investment styles, namely, aggressive, moderate and conservative asset allocations. Assume there are four underlying funds to constitute the above three different investment styles: an equity fund, a balance fund, a bond fund and a real-estate fund. Assume that each fund has more than 20 constituents and is actively managed by professional portfolio managers. Using the equity fund as an illustration, we can express the expected returns as follows

$$\text{Exp Return(Equity Fund)} = \sum_{i=1}^{n} w_i \cdot \text{Exp Return(Name}_i)$$

where Name_i is one constituent of the fund and w_i is the relative weight of Name_i in the fund.

We can use the following system to express the linear relationship between different investment styles and underlying funds (EF denotes equity fund, BaF denotes balance fund, BoF denotes bond fund and REF denotes real-estate fund)

Aggressive $= 0.8 \times \text{EF} + 0.1 \times \text{BaF} + 0.07 \times \text{BoF} + 0.03 \times \text{REF};$

Moderate $= 0.15 \times \text{EF} + 0.7 \times \text{BaF} + 0.1 \times \text{BoF} + 0.05 \times \text{REF};$

Conservative $= 0.05 \times \text{EF} + 0.15 \times \text{BaF} + 0.7 \times \text{BoF} + 0.1 \times \text{REF}.$

Let $A = B \cdot C$, where A is representative of the policyholder's investment style, B represents the asset allocation of each investment style and C represents the underlying funds. In matrix form,

$$A = [\text{Aggressive}, \text{Moderate}, \text{Conservative}]',$$

$$C = [\text{EF}, \text{BaF}, \text{BoF}, \text{REF}]',$$

$$B = \begin{bmatrix} 0.8 & 0.1 & 0.07 & 0.03 \\ 0.15 & 0.7 & 0.1 & 0.05 \\ 0.05 & 0.15 & 0.7 & 0.1 \end{bmatrix}$$

Furthermore, we can map investment styles into hedgable indexes by first obtaining linear OLS relationships between different funds (equity fund, balance fund, bond fund and real-estate fund) with hedgable indexes and then collecting and sorting out similar terms. For example, the following fund mapping exercise is conducted by regressing the return of matrix A to the returns of three liquid and tradable indexes, SPTR, AGG, and EAFE

$$\text{Aggr.} = 0.72\,\text{SPTR} + 0.13\,\text{AGG} + 0.15\,\text{EAFE} + \varepsilon_1, \quad R^2 = 0.83,$$

$$\text{Moder.} = 0.55\,\text{SPTR} + 0.12\,\text{AGG} + 0.33\,\text{EAFE} + \varepsilon_2, \quad R^2 = 0.76,$$

$$\text{Conserv.} = 0.14\,\text{SPTR} + 0.75\,\text{AGG} + 0.11\,\text{EAFE} + \varepsilon_3, \quad R^2 = 0.82$$

Sometimes we can regress the return matrix into four potential hedged indexes, namely, SPTR, AGG, EAFE and RUT, to obtain the following results

$$\text{Aggr.} = 0.63\,\text{SPTR} + 0.08\,\text{AGG}$$
$$+ 0.15\,\text{EAFE} + 0.14\,\text{RUT} + \varepsilon_4, \quad R^2 = 0.87,$$
$$\text{Moder.} = 0.45\,\text{SPTR} + 0.22\,\text{AGG}$$
$$+ 0.13\,\text{EAFE} + 0.2\,\text{RUT} + \varepsilon_5, \quad R^2 = 0.79,$$
$$\text{Conserv.} = 0.08\,\text{SPTR} + 0.72\,\text{AGG}$$
$$+ 0.05\,\text{EAFE} + 0.15\,\text{RUT} + \varepsilon_6, \quad R^2 = 0.84$$

It is observed that with more indexes as regressors on the right-hand side of the equation, in general, the R^2 may improve. However, bear in mind that, with more regressors, VA writers may need to hedge more indexes. Hence, it might increase operational risk as well as the cost of hedging, and also this better R^2 might just be the consequence of over-fitting.

We can also calculate the historical correlation relationship of hedgable indexes; eg, $\Sigma_{3\times3}$ represents the correlation matrix of SPTR, AGG and EAFE. This information is most often used when pricing new products or for financial-reporting purposes. However, we must bear in mind that, since the correlation matrix was based on historical data, regular monitoring and updating the correlation matrix would be very important, especially during financial crises.

During the 2008–9 financial crisis, VA writers observed the following deficiencies of the fund mapping procedure:

- due to fast movements on securities pricing, it was relatively difficult to have quick access to the true compositions of individual funds which deviated from the expected return profile at the fund level;
- individual funds deviated from their policy mandate substantially, which also contributed in some degree to the basis risk;
- policyholders exercised their leeway of changing the mix of their funds, which increased basis risk;
- the linear regression relationships between funds and indexes may no longer have been valid;
- the most severe impact may have been on the diversification effect, due to the fact that the variance–covariance relationship between indexes also breaks down, the correlation between indexes increases and, hence, the diversification effect, which would otherwise have reduced the basis risk of a portfolio of funds, was lost.

All of the above items created and exacerbated the impacts on the basis risk.

HOW TO MANAGE BASIS RISK NOW AND IN THE FUTURE

Due to the hedge breakage seen by VA writers in the second half of 2008, companies are looking for different approaches to developing fund mapping procedures. The following are a few approaches which depend on individual VA writers' strategic thinking and philosophy.

From the fund manager's end:

- limit fund choice to narrow the tracking error;
- establish direct relationships with VA writers;
- provide more "real-time" estimates of allocations to VA writers.

From the VA writers' end:

- start by incorporating basis risk measures into the product design and pricing for new product design;
- review performance of actively managed funds and possibly revisit offering them;
- consider reducing the number of funds offered to reduce volatility and improve performance;
- aim to redesign products to utilise more index funds and exchange-traded funds, or to use more passively managed funds;
- improve the fund mapping approach by monitoring and repeating the fund mapping process with a higher frequency, eg, from an annual update to a semi-annual or quarterly update (but note that the operational risk could increase as a consequence);
- update fund mapping coefficients on a more frequent basis, exercising with direct contact with fund managers;
- overlay coefficients derived from OLS regression with some qualitative considerations;
- consider hedging additional indexes or currencies if necessary;
- consider setting aside some capital to offset basis risk, possibly including the cost of capital in the product pricing process;
- develop a contingency plan to cover extreme market conditions.

CONCLUSIONS

Basis risk is one area that some VA writers had neglected until the financial crisis started in 2008. It is a risk with great potential to cause severe financial loss to VA writers. Several VA writers are now reducing the severity of basis risk inherited in their product offering by moving away from actively managed funds into market tradable liquid indexes or exchange-traded funds, simplifying the products and possibly price in the basis risk component, increasing the frequency of monitoring the fund mapping procedure and having a back-up plan in order to react appropriately.

22

Replication Portfolios and Hedging

Tigran Kalberer

KPMG

As we have seen in the preceding chapters, one of the main problems of managing the risks generated by a portfolio of VAs is determining the exposure associated with such a portfolio in a language that a financial expert (or the typical IT systems managing financial risk) can understand. The problem lies in the fact that the exposure is buried deeply in the features of a typically large amount of highly complex insurance contracts, and cannot be determined directly using the data stored in an insurance contract administration system.

Thus, determining the exposure, which is the basis of all risk management, requires three steps:

- extracting the exposure from each insurance contract by translating the administration system data into exposure data, eg, statements like "if the S&P is at 1000 on December 31, 2010, then the value of the guarantee will be US$2,000";
- aggregating all these exposures for all contracts;
- determining the required parameters for hedging, eg, delta.

Typically, there are many dimensions (or dependencies) to consider, as the shortfall might be sensitive to a wide variety of indexes, interest rates, foreign exchange rates, etc.

This situation results in several numerical problems associated with performing the above-mentioned tasks.

As we have seen, the typical valuation approaches, which are also used to determine the hedge parameters, are based either on exact knowledge and analytical tractability of the exposure or on stochastic simulation.

In most observed cases there is no analytical tractability such that stochastic simulation is used.

- A financial model allows the projection of the shortfall for each capital market (and actually each insurance risk) scenario and each contract; this is onerous even for one scenario and one contract.

- A number of capital-market scenarios (and sometimes also insurance-risk scenarios) are produced such that

    - these scenarios reflect the possible variations as completely as possible,

    - these scenarios allow capital-market consistent valuation,

    - the number of necessary scenarios is typically large (1,000 or more),

    - the scenarios are then evaluated for each contract (typically we observe millions of such contracts),

    - the evaluation procedure has to be repeated for each sensitivity required for hedging purposes,

    - the evaluation procedure has to be performed on a daily basis.

This approach has some obvious disadvantages, as it can be very time consuming and relies on the quality of the scenarios used. The scenarios used for this purpose have to be calibrated so that they are market consistent, ie, they reflect the market prices of financial instruments, which are liquidly traded and where prices are available. The asset models used for generating such scenarios typically do not allow for an adequate reflection of all features of the market prices of financial instruments. Features like the dependency of volatility on time and moneyness (smile) are difficult to reflect in the calibration of the scenarios used for valuation.

A POTENTIAL SOLUTION: THE REPLICATION-PORTFOLIO APPROACH

Both problems could be solved by using a replication-portfolio approach for valuation and risk management of VA products.

The underlying idea is very simple and the accuracy of this approach can be quantified. The approach gives in most cases very accurate approximations for the required calculation results.

The replication portfolio

The replication portfolio of a portfolio of liabilities is defined as a portfolio consisting of (potentially fictitious) assets (candidate assets) with certain properties which generate similar cashflows at all points in time under all possible investment scenarios.

For some purposes it is only necessary to replicate the market value and its dynamics at a certain point in time and not the cashflows.

These replicating assets should posses the following properties.

- Their value should be easy to determine, preferably using closed-form solutions. This allows the determination of the value of the guarantees with less numerical error, but it does preserve the potential calibration error.

- If possible, there should be market prices (in contrast to just model prices) for these assets. If this is possible, the calibration error can also be minimised.

The idea of replicating complex and possibly large portfolios of liabilities using replication portfolios is an old one, but only lately has there been widespread application in the insurance industry.

An introduction to this approach, focusing on traditional life business, is given by Oechslin *et al* (2007), while an introduction focusing on VA business is given in the SST-methodology documentation of SCOR (2008).

The approach is based on a list of candidate assets, which have the properties described above, and finding the linear combination of these assets that replicates the given liability cashflows in an optimal way, eg, minimising the average deviation between the cashflows of the liabilities and the replication portfolio measured using a convenient metric, eg, least squares.

In most cases the weights of the optimal portfolio can be determined using linear algebra.

Replication portfolios for VA products

Figure 22.1 examines a large portfolio of VA contracts which mature in a certain point in time (t), where the maturity payment depends on the same underlying funds' value at t only. This implies that there is no dependency on either the path or any other financial instruments (aside from the underlying ones). The overall payout generated by

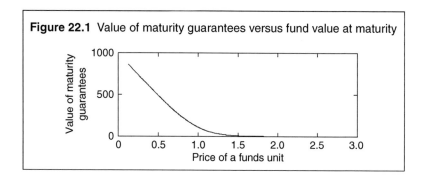

Figure 22.1 Value of maturity guarantees versus fund value at maturity

Table 22.1 Optimal linear combination of the candidate assets

Strike	Notional
0.2	0.00000
0.4	39.20392
0.6	133.0466
0.8	218.4072
1.0	282.6702
1.2	204.7578
1.4	82.24168
1.6	34.89139
1.8	10.96966
2.0	−0.60765

the guarantees of the contracts will be a decreasing function of the funds' value. As the figure illustrates, this looks surprisingly smooth. The reason for this is that we consider a large portfolio with different guarantees and, more importantly, different accrued asset values.

Figure 22.1 contains all the information necessary to describe the payout of the guarantee over the whole liability portfolio.

If this graph is successfully approximated by a linear combination of simple functions, dependent on the same underlying, it is possible to represent this potentially large portfolio of contracts by a small set of functions.

An obvious set of candidates to approximate the graph is a set of plain vanilla put options on the underlying with term 10 years and different strikes.

This example chooses strike prices 0.2, 0.4, etc, up to 2. The strike prices are chosen so that they cover the area where the payout function needs to be approximated (here in the range 0–2). The optimal

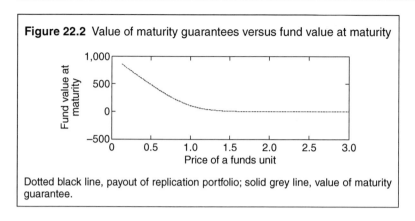

Figure 22.2 Value of maturity guarantees versus fund value at maturity

Dotted black line, payout of replication portfolio; solid grey line, value of maturity guarantee.

linear combination of these candidate assets is given in Table 22.1. The approximation given by these instruments can be visualised as in Figure 22.2.

The optimal replication portfolio for our purposes is defined as the linear combination of the candidate assets minimising the squared deviations between the payout function and the approximating replication portfolio for a sufficiently large number of scenarios.

Depending on the purpose it may be necessary to choose another metric for this optimisation.

It is important to note that this approach uses the results produced for the purpose of pricing (ie, the scenarios used for pricing), building on these results in a natural way.

If the liability cashflows are path dependent, then there would be multidimensional dependencies between the different risk factors at different points in time and the cashflows. This would be a little bit harder to visualise but the same principles would apply. In these cases path-dependent candidate assets would have to be chosen.

Note also that the candidate assets chosen here need to have the right asymptotic behaviour. The value vanishes for high asset values (as does the value of the guarantees) and has the correct combined slope for vanishing asset values (ie, the same as the liabilities do: the sum of all guarantees). The replication-portfolio approach uses only the information provided by the scenarios used. If these do not contain enough information about extreme situations (which can be the case for high-dimensional problems), then it the optimisation routine may end up with a replication portfolio showing weird behaviour in these extreme cases, as there is no cashflow to match against. And this can result in failing to produce the right sensitivities using the replication portfolio. Using knowledge about the products replicated is essential in avoiding such issues.

The choice of candidate assets

Determining the candidate assets is the real challenge of applying the replication-portfolio approach and requires high levels of skill and experience.

The example used here is a very simple one and in reality the features of the guarantees would be much more complex, eg, they would include path dependency. This does not imply that the approach no longer works; it merely implies that the candidate assets, used in determining the replication portfolio as a linear combination of these candidate assets, may also be more complex, eg, may also include path dependency.

There are several approaches to determining these candidate assets:

- by analysing the relative importance of each potential candidate asset from a large list of potential assets in a first step and focusing on the most important ones only in a second step (as over-fitting should be avoided);
- by using *a priori* knowledge of the liabilities to choose appropriate candidate assets, eg, floating strike look-back options to reflect certain advanced features of VA products.

The control-variate approach

The difference between the liability portfolio and the replication portfolio can be considered as a new asset, the "difference asset". The payouts of this asset have a considerably lower volatility than the payout of the liability portfolio itself. Thus, the estimation of the value of this "difference asset" using stochastic scenarios has a considerably higher degree of accuracy than direct estimation of the value of the payouts.

Therefore, the value of the liability portfolio can be determined with very low stochastic error as the value of the replication portfolio (the closed-form solution or even the available market price, thus no stochastic error) plus the value of the "difference asset" (low stochastic error due to low variance of payouts). This approach is called a "control-variate" approach and is widely used in determining the value of contingent payments using stochastic simulation.

If the replication-portfolio approach was used solely as a control variate, this alone would justify its determination.

Using the replication portfolio as a control variate requires considerably fewer scenarios for estimating the value of the guarantees, while preserving the level of accuracy. Alternatively, the level of accuracy can be considerably increased while using the same number of scenarios as under the naive approach.

If it is possible to determine direct market values for the assets of the replication portfolio, then the calibration problem can also be addressed. In fact, the potential model error introduced by inadequate calibration impacts only on the stochastic valuation of the difference asset, which, by construction, is small. The valuation of the replication portfolio is usually exposed to much lower model error, as the assets in the replication portfolio can be valued directly in the market.

Thus, the impact of both the above-mentioned problems is substantially reduced.

Determining sensitivities (Greeks)

The replication-portfolio approach can also be used to determine the sensitivities of the value of the liabilities to changes in the underlying economic variables, the so-called "Greeks".

The most popular method of determining these sensitivities is the so-called "bumping the model" approach. In this approach, the value of the liabilities is determined for the current value of the variable and a shocked value.

This approach has severe disadvantages:

- the sensitivities estimated this way usually have a large estimation error;
- determination of the sensitivities is time-consuming, as the stochastic simulation has to be performed repeatedly for each sensitivity and for each model point.

Using the replication-portfolio approach to produce sensitivities

It is relatively straightforward to use a replication-portfolio approach in order to determine the sensitivities.

After the replication portfolio has been determined, the sensitivity of the replication portfolio can easily be determined, as the replication portfolio is based on instruments which have closed-form solutions for their value and usually also for their sensitivities.

Error bounds for the replication-portfolio approach

In order to be able to use this method in a reliable manner, the error bounds need to be established for the sensitivities determined using the replication-portfolio approach.

We now discuss two possible approaches to estimating the error potentially introduced by this approach.

Error bounds for estimating sensitivities using the likelihood-ratio approach

The likelihood-ratio (LHR) uses re-weighting of the scenarios in order to determine the value of a cashflow under changed assumptions.

Let Q denote the probability measure based on the current calibration and let Q' denote the probability measure for a calibration where the economic variable has been changed by a small amount. Let dQ and dQ' denote the associated probability densities and assume all necessary requirements on dQ, dQ' are fulfilled such that

$$E^{Q'}\left(\frac{Z}{N}\right) = E^{Q}\left(\frac{Z}{N}\frac{dQ'}{dQ}\right)$$

where Z denotes the cashflows and N the chosen numeraire.

This result can be used to estimate the error produced by determining the sensitivities using the replication-portfolio approach compared with the exact sensitivity

Exact sensitivity − estimated sensitivity (via replication-portfolio)

$$= \left(E^{Q}\left(\frac{Z}{N}\right) - E^{Q'}\left(\frac{Z}{N}\right)\right) - \left(E^{Q}\left(\frac{Z^R}{N}\right) - E^{Q'}\left(\frac{Z^R}{N}\right)\right)$$

$$= E^{Q}\left(\frac{Z}{N}\left(\frac{dQ'}{dQ} - 1\right)\right) - E^{Q}\left(\frac{Z^R}{N}\left(\frac{dQ'}{dQ} - 1\right)\right)$$

$$= E^{Q}\left(\frac{(Z - Z^R)}{N}\left(\frac{dQ'}{dQ} - 1\right)\right)$$

where Z^R is the cashflow as generated by the replication portfolio.

This error term is now estimated by using the empirical estimator for this error term, using the previously generated results for the stochastic scenarios

$$E^Q\left(\frac{(Z - Z^R)}{N}\left(\frac{dQ'}{dQ} - 1\right)\right)$$

$$\approx \frac{1}{M}\sum_{i=1}^{M}\frac{(Z(X_i) - Z^R(X_i))}{N(X_i)}\left(\frac{dQ'(X_i)}{dQ((X_i))} - 1\right)$$

The variance of this estimator can also be approximated. This allows error bounds for any required level of security to be estimated using the law of large numbers.

If the replication portfolio is not determined using the scenarios to determine the error bound, the estimator for the error is unbiased.

The likelihood ratios dQ'/dQ should be determined using the analytical formulas for the distributions, if available. The economic scenario generator producing the asset scenarios for the stochastic valuation is typically based on stochastic differential equations which can be used to determine the likelihood ratios.

However, caution must be exercised, as the random variables could be multivariate distributed, meaning that the payout could depend on more than one economic variable.

It could be argued that this chapter could finish here as this approach seems to work so nicely. The trick is that, so far, the law of large numbers has been used to estimate error bounds. At this point it is not known beforehand, when the convergence of the approximation of the expected value by stochastic simulation to the real expected value is sufficient such that we can assume that the error is really normally distributed with the empirical volatility as standard deviation.

Large movements in the risk factors, such as the funds price in our example, generate too few scenarios to guarantee that the results of the Central Limit Theorem or law of large numbers apply.

One indication for this is that

$$\frac{1}{n}\sum_{i=1}^{n}\left(\frac{dQ'(X_i)}{dQ((X_i))}\right)$$

is considerably smaller than 1 in such situations. The approach described above for estimating error bounds is not applicable in these situations. The effect of this is important for one of the potential applications mentioned later in the chapter.

However, the approach is perfect for just estimating sensitivities from a given set of scenarios, as very small shocks are required; this is exactly the case when our approach to estimating error bounds works well.

Do we need error bounds?

A more robust approach is to estimate the impact of the potential error on the overall hedging process. In the end, this is what matters, and this approach can be used easily for path-dependent options and options dependent on several economic variables.

A so-called "hedge assessment" is performed for this approach. This is a task that would have to be prepared anyhow in order to assess the quality of the dynamic hedge process.

For this purpose, a sufficiently large set of scenarios is generated under the physical measure (ie, using the best-estimate "real-world" probabilities including risk premiums) with sufficient granularity, which in most cases means on a daily basis, and we simulate the effect of the hedge operations along these scenarios, measuring the shortfall at maturity. The shortfall is defined as the difference between the amount necessary to fill up the funds value to a potentially higher guarantee level and the value of the hedge portfolio at maturity.

Due to the fact that the hedging instruments used are typically linear instruments and the change in value of the liabilities is non-linear, a hedge slippage can be observed.

The sum of all these hedge slippages at maturity is the total hedge slippage for each scenario. The hedge slippages for all scenarios can be used to derive an empirical distribution of the hedge slippages.

If an initially fitted replication portfolio is used to determine the sensitivities or Greeks at each future point in time for each scenario, instead of "properly" calculated sensitivities, then the error produced by this approach can be estimated very easily. In fact, it can be assumed that the exposure of the replication portfolio is hedged and the difference between the payout of the hedge portfolio and the payout implied by the guarantee is exactly the error introduced by using the replication portfolio. This error can be determined for the scenarios considered, which in turn can be regarded as an empirical estimate of the error.

In addition to this error, the hedging process will not work perfectly and produce losses and gains, mainly because of hedge slippages and basis risk: typically the underlying funds are actively

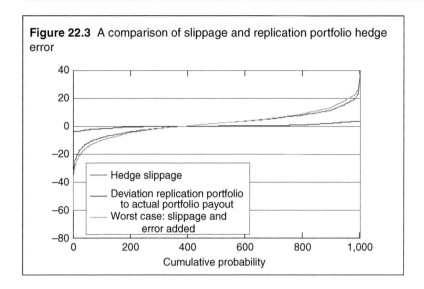

Figure 22.3 A comparison of slippage and replication portfolio hedge error

managed and cannot be short sold; for hedging purposes they have to be replicated using market indexes. This approach gives rise to basis risk.

The author's experience shows that the error introduced by hedging the replication portfolio will be negligibly small compared with the hedge slippage itself.

If a hedge-assessment is performed for a sample portfolio, assuming a weekly Delta hedge, the result in Figure 22.3 is produced. The graph shows profit and loss from the hedging operations and the error implied by using the replication-portfolio per scenario. The biggest losses are to the left.

The fact that the replication portfolio was hedged rather than the actual portfolio does not add a significant amount of risk. The hedge slippage itself has a far bigger magnitude than the error introduced by the replication-portfolio approach. Owing to tracking error, in most cases the basis risk alone is far bigger than the deviation caused by using the replication portfolio. This justifies the use of the replication portfolio approach for assessing the hedging strategy.

Of course, in this example, the hedge strategy is simplified in that we assume a weekly delta-hedge only. In reality a more frequent hedge, potentially using non-linear hedging instruments, would be used, decreasing the hedge slippage considerably. On the other hand, the hedge slippage in this example was calculated without taking any volatility risk into account, which would increase the hedge slippage.

The advantage is that the replication-portfolio approach is much simpler for handling the sensitivities, ie, Greeks can be determined based on closed-form solutions within mere fractions of a second in comparison with the full stochastic approach, "bumping the model", which needs hours, if not days, of computation time to determine the Greeks.

This approach to determining the error of the replication portfolio method has the following advantages:

- it measures the impact of a potential deviation in terms of risk and not the sensitivity itself;
- it compares the replication approach error to other sources of risk, which are usually much bigger, and thus prevents overly complex approaches delivering spurious accuracy;
- it allows a proper hedge assessment without the need for nested stochastic calculations, saving an immense amount of computation time.

Appropriate experience with this approach is required to determine the candidate assets and prevent nasty surprises concerning approximation errors. But, as demonstrated above, this approach is worthwhile considering, as the actual hedging application can be simplified and significantly accelerated, allowing for additional checks and risk measurements on a daily basis.

Applications of the replication-portfolio approach

As we have seen, the approach can be used for at least three different purposes.

(i) Determination of the sensitivities/Greeks based on one stochastic base run by

- performing a base run for liabilities and all candidate assets,
- determining the replication portfolio,
- determining sensitivities based on the replication portfolio,
- increasing the accuracy of the base run using the control-variate approach.

(ii) Performance of stochastic base runs only if necessary and use of the replication portfolio in the meantime.

- The daily hedging routine will be based on the replication portfolio as long as the risk factors do not move too far away from the base case used for determining the stochastic simulation.

- Large deviations to the base case can lead to unreliable estimations of the error bonds and convergence problems.

- The stochastic simulation and the determination of the replication portfolio has to be repeated if

  - the risk-factors move too far away from the base case,
  - the liability portfolio has changed (typically monthly).

(iii) Hedge-assessment calculations.

- Performing a hedge assessment based on a full stochastic approach is not always feasible, as discussed above. The main problem is that this is a nested stochastic approach and needs considerable run-time.

- Performing the hedge-assessment based on the replication portfolio is a very efficient alternative and sufficient to discuss the main issues arising from the planned hedging programme.

Whether any of these approaches are applicable depends on the nature of the VA products. There is no general rule that will give advance indication on whether the approach works reliably. However, using the techniques presented in this chapter, it should be possible to decide whether the approaches work and how accurate they are once they have been applied.

CONCLUSION

Implementing a dynamic-hedging approach for VA products presents large technical challenges. In particular, the determination of the sensitivities/Greeks can be very time consuming and can involve considerable estimation error. To perform the tasks implied by a dynamic-hedging scheme it is suggested that a replication-portfolio approach is used. This not only increases the speed and reliability of the computations but also increases accuracy and removes calibration error.

REFERENCES

Hull, J., 2000, *Options, Futures, and Other Derivatives* (Englewood Cliffs, NJ: Prentice Hall).

Kalberer, T., 2006, "Market Consistent Valuation of Insurance Liabilities: Basic Approaches and Tool-Box", *Der Aktuar* 12(1).

Kalberer, T., 2007, "Guaranteed Links to the Life Market", *Life & Pensions*, December.

Oechslin, J., O. Aubry, M. Aellig, A. Kappeli, D. Bronnimann, A. Tandonnet and G. Valois, 2007, "Replicating Embedded Options", *Life & Pensions*, February.

SCOR, 2008, "From Principle Based Risk Management to Solvency Requirements", URL: http://www.scor.com/www/index.php?id=433&L=2.

23

Variable Annuities: An Equity Analyst's Perspective

Darin Arita

Deutsche Bank Securities Inc

Strong sales of variable annuities (VAs) driven by the attractiveness of living benefits and coupled with a rising equity market were helpful contributors to positive life-insurance stock performance from 2003 to 2007. During that time, life-insurance stocks increased by 87% on average, compared with a 67% increase by the S&P 500 Index. In 2008, however, life-insurance stocks declined dramatically, falling by 44% and underperforming the S&P 500 by six percentage points. The complexity of VA risks has been one of the reasons why life-insurance stocks have come under pressure.

VA LIVING BENEFITS WERE A STEP IN THE RIGHT DIRECTION

The strong popularity of VA living benefits in the period 2003–7 was a welcome sign that the life-insurance industry was moving from helping consumers to accumulate assets to creating lifetime streams of income for consumers. The living-benefit features were becoming popular at the right time, as the US population of 80 million baby boomers was nearing retirement. In addition, the living benefits also addressed liquidity concerns and provided upside potential with equity returns. By helping consumers manage the risk of outliving their assets, the life-insurance industry would once again be able to differentiate itself from other asset-gathering financial institutions, such as asset managers and banks.

EQUITY MARKET GUARANTEES INTRODUCED NEW RISKS

Some of the life insurers made great efforts to explain to investors the risks of these new living-benefit features, and how the companies would manage these risks to protect shareholders. Discussions about reinsurance and derivative hedging seemed thoughtful and logical, but they raised an important question for VAs. Was the life-insurance industry doing something outside of its core competency by providing equity market guarantees through these living benefits? The robustness of the risk management systems for these products was based on stochastic models, untested by a severe down equity market. Most investors, however, seemed to shrug off that risk as the equity market continued to rise each year and operating income and return on equity increased. Meanwhile, the life-insurance industry continued to roll out products with more valuable benefits, as companies tried to outdo each other and grow sales. The sky seemed to be the limit, with roll-up features going from 5% to 7% to 10%, and the frequency of resets changing from every few years to every year, every quarter and to every day. The risks in these living-benefit features have long tails, meaning that the insurers will carry these risks for many years without knowing the true costs.

THE MARKET CRASH MADE THE PROBLEMS EVIDENT

The decline in the equity market in 2008–9 has introduced significant volatility to statutory earnings, statutory capital and risk-based capital ratios. The life-insurance managers are having difficulty quantifying the effect of the equity market decline in real time. Rating agencies are downgrading the life insurers, partly because the liabilities for these living benefits are growing rapidly. It is unclear at the time of writing, in October 2009, whether the hedges and risk management have worked, and investors are now unwilling to use blind faith to buy the equity and debt of life insurers that have large exposures to VAs.

IMPROVING DISCLOSURE IS IMPERATIVE

The life-insurance industry has responded to the equity market decline by increasing prices and reducing benefits for VAs with living benefits. These actions make sense, but the changes primarily affect new sales. The original liabilities remain with the life insurers, and will weigh on the minds of investors. The problem with the living-benefit exposures is that there is insufficient disclosure for investors to analyse the liabilities and draw their own conclusions on the risks.

START WITH THE BASICS

What disclosure makes the most sense? The companies should disclose to investors the key metrics that senior management and the board of directors have been looking at as a starting point. Also, it would be helpful to see what the companies present to the rating agencies to give them comfort.

DETAILED DISCLOSURE OF THE EXPOSURES SHOULD BE NEXT

Additional disclosure should be focused on helping investors break down the exposure for a particular guarantee by vintage and, within those vintages, to see the average age of the policyholder, the account value, a scale of guaranteed amounts[1], the lapse rate to date and the investment mix. With this information, an investor can model the exposures using their own assumptions and compare them with the value of the hedge assets. Clearly, the investor models would simplify a complex equation, but at least the investors would be able to start to measure the economic risk of these liabilities rather than rely on the assurances of management.

DISCLOSURE OF THE ASSUMPTIONS UNDERLYING THE LIABILITIES

A popular disclosure by life insurers has been the hedge breakage, which is the amount by which the hedge assets have moved relative to the hedged liabilities on a Generally Accepted Accounting Principles (GAAP) basis. The companies, however, do not disclose the assumptions underlying the calculation of those liabilities; disclosure of the key assumptions that make the biggest difference in the liability calculation for living and death benefits would be helpful, but at the least we would like to see the assumptions for market appreciation, interest rates (for GMIBs), lapse rates and expected benefit utilisation. Some insurers have broken out the effect of FASB 157 non-performance risk,[2] and we hope that all insurers could provide this data.

A RACE TO SIMPLICITY

In addition to improving disclosure, we expect the life-insurance industry to move to simpler product designs and hedging techniques. How do we invest in these companies if we could relive periods of significant equity market declines? Such periods are not unusual, as the equity market declined by 34% over 2001–2 and 42% over 1973–4. If the industry can make these changes and still have products that are attractive to consumers, it will restore confidence among investors, distributors and consumers, lower the cost of capital and lead to higher share prices. The industry can then go "back to basics" by competing on distribution, brand and cost effectiveness and by using its understanding of mortality to differentiate itself from other financial service industries. This should lead to a more tranquil period of long-term, profitable growth.

1   That is, the points where the living benefit goes in-the-money for 20%, 40%, 60%, 80% and 100% of the policyholders; VA companies that offer guaranteed minimum income benefits (GMIBs) should also expand this table with sensitivity to varying interest rate levels.

2   See http://www.fasb.org/summary/stsum157.shtml.

24

What Does Moody's Look for when Evaluating Companies that Write Variable Annuities?

Scott Robinson
Moody's Investors Service

For a substantial number of life-insurance groups, variable annuities (VAs) can have a significant impact on insurance financial strength ratings,[1] so a proper consideration of these products is a crucial step in our deliberations. At Moody's Investors Service, the rating process for all life insurers is driven by a global rating methodology, which incorporates various business and financial profile factors (Moody's Investors Service 2006a). In this chapter, we discuss how our analysts[2] view and analyse VAs in the context of the rating methodology, and we review the additional disclosure that facilitates their analysis.

MARKET PRESENCE

Market position, brand and franchise strength are key rating considerations that represent a company's ability to develop and sustain competitive advantages in its chosen markets. In a commodity product line such as VAs, an insurer's absolute and relative size in the market tend to be highly correlated with its success. All else being equal, a company featuring a well-managed block of annuities of significant size has advantages over smaller competitors. Scale advantages can be present in operating cost-effective hedging programmes and in managing expenses, for both administration and distribution.

Of course, there are exceptions. Size is not a panacea for managing risk, especially if companies are highly leveraged in the VA business (eg, if they have a substantial block of VAs relative to their capital base). A company rapidly accumulating a large block of VAs may quickly lose any size advantage if the business is mispriced or poorly managed. In some cases, much faster growth than the rest of the industry may be the result of offering more generous, potentially mispriced guarantees.

In order to evaluate market presence in the VA market, we find it beneficial to look at the assets under management, as well as net flows. Net flows are a key element, which should be disclosed readily by companies.

DISTRIBUTION

The more control and influence management has over a distribution channel, whether a captive/controlled or an independent third-party channel, the better it is able to achieve its objectives of business production, persistency and profitability.

In general, VAs sold through wirehouses and/or independent broker–dealer channels tend to have lower and less predictable persistency (a measure of business retention) than VAs purveyed through captive agents. Overall, we believe that these distribution channels are subject to the most intense pricing competition. These may have higher upfront expenses; they are also more likely to have "hot" money, and contract holders, guided by their brokers, may be more likely to take advantage of guarantees that come into the money.

The diversity in a company's distribution channels can mitigate its dependence on specific channels and on its vulnerability to sales disruption. We also consider concentration of sales through a particular distribution partner and the potential impact of losing that partner.

Sales per distribution channel is an important piece of information that most public companies are comfortable sharing with investors.

PRODUCT FOCUS AND DIVERSIFICATION

We view VAs with guarantees as being at the higher end of the risk spectrum of life-insurance-company products. VAs often come with embedded options and guarantees and, as markets fluctuate, the fees derived from assets under management follow suit because few, if any, insurers hedge fee income. Also, notwithstanding a robust product-development process, the extent of a VA risk may not be fully known and understood at the time the product is first introduced and marketed, especially in the light of the uncertainty related to long-term policyholder efficiency in terms of exercise or election of their various contractual features.

As experienced in 2008, volatile equity markets can upend both the earnings and capital adequacy of a company with a material block of VAs. In response to the financial impact of the extreme capital market conditions in the second half of 2008 and into 2009, many life-insurance companies suspended sales of old VA products and introduced new VAs with increased prices and less generous guarantees. Many of the changes related to guaranteed living benefits (GLBs)[3], features that serve to protect the annuity contract holders during their lifetimes, providing some form of equity participation with downside protection.

Guaranteed living benefits include guaranteed minimum withdrawal benefits (GMWBs) and guaranteed minimum income benefits (GMIBs). Features of these guarantees became increasingly generous in the years leading up to 2008 as enhanced guarantees became the market standard and a virtual requirement to participate in certain distribution channels. For example, GMWBs offering guaranteed lifetime income of 6–7% of a guaranteed income base became increasingly common; the typical guarantee dropped to around 5% in 2009. To compete with the income feature of GMWBs, many GMIBs featured, and continue to feature (although with less generous terms than in the past), dollar-for-dollar withdrawals with 5–7% roll-ups[4] that provide steady income to a client up until the point of annuitisation, after which income can increase.

Guarantees on newer business may have become less generous and/or more expensive, but they can still represent material risks to companies if not managed properly. The risks can be mitigated or exacerbated by risk management practices, as well as by market position, distribution, underwriting and pricing. Along these lines, it is worth noting that a company selling VAs could get significant earnings-diversification benefit by successfully diversifying into non-equity-market-sensitive products.

In order that outsiders can fully understand the risks of a company's VA business, we believe that transparency related to product risk should be improved. For example, to evaluate the impact of policyholder behaviour on a specific VA company, it is beneficial to see the exposure to different guarantees, how much the guarantees are in-the-money and the historical efficiency of policyholders, as well as the potential impact of their behaviour on profitability and capital.

ASSET QUALITY

Some fixed income options in VA products may be backed by assets in the general account, in which case the insurance company assumes the risk of providing a minimum guarantee. Credit losses and low reinvestment rates can place pressures on spreads, hurting profitability.

Another potentially significant asset of uncertain value on the balance sheets of insurers selling VAs is the goodwill or value of business acquired (VOBA) associated with acquisitions and deferred acquisition costs (DACs) (Moody's Investors Service 2003). Goodwill is generally considered as being of lesser quality than VOBA and DACs, but any of these assets could be vulnerable to write-downs if equity markets decline. The adverse effect of a write-down is mitigated by the fact that it is a Generally Accepted Accounting Principles (GAAP) accounting event; thus, it does not influence cash-flow, and it does not have a direct impact on liquidity. Nevertheless, the resulting abrupt decline in shareholders' equity can boost financial leverage and could thin the cushion that a company needs to meet financial covenants, including permissible leverage ratios in bank lending and other agreements.

CAPITAL ADEQUACY

At the heart of Moody's assessment of an insurer's creditworthiness is its opinion about the insurer's economic capital and capital adequacy (eg, solvency) or operational leverage. Given the decline in the equity markets during 2008 and into 2009, capital requirements for companies selling VAs spiked. The increase in regulatory capital requirements has been especially noticeable.

Since the end of 2005, life insurers selling VAs have been subject to capital requirements under C3 Phase II.[5] Both the impact of C3 Phase II and the sensitivity of a company's capital needs under different market scenarios are major parts of Moody's analysis for companies with material exposure to VAs. A new statutory reserving standard for VA products with GLBs and GMDBs, VA

Commissioners' Annuity Reserve Valuation Methods (VACARVM), becomes effective on December 31, 2009. Although management may argue that the reserve requirement under VACARVM or the capital required under C3 Phase II is not theoretically correct, the regulatory requirements can still have a material effect on a company's regulatory financials and capital position, which in turn can influence the market's perception of the company and its financial flexibility.

Moody's recognises that regulatory capital levels are, in most cases, conservative compared with the economic capital required. Additionally, many companies cede the risk associated with guarantees on VAs to affiliates in jurisdictions that are not subject to C3 Phase II. As a result, Moody's finds it essential to look through the regulatory capital levels and considers how companies' "economic" capital levels compare with actual capital that may be needed to fund VA guarantees under stress scenarios. Hence, Moody's ratings incorporate regulatory capital requirements and reserves and their impact on financial flexibility, as well as the "economic" capitalisation of a company.

(See Appendix III for a description of how Moody's may adjust the National Association of Insurance Commissioners (NAIC) risk-based capital (RBC) for companies with large blocks of VAs.)

PROFITABILITY

Variable annuities are thin-margined commodity products that can produce potentially high returns on equity simply because companies have allocated modest amounts of "required" capital to the product line, yet absolute earnings can be low relative to the size of the product reserves. In evaluating profitability of VAs, it is important to look at an entire block of VAs. This may be better able to withstand a market downturn than a newly originated block of business because most of the upfront expenses have already been recovered on older VA contracts.

Consequently, long-term-oriented, pricing-disciplined companies with the ability to withstand market volatility should eventually realise acceptable returns for a diversified block of VA business. Of course, not every company issues the same product, so understanding its specifics and its pricing assumptions are essential to the analysis.

As fortunes in the VA market rise and fall with equity markets, the benefits of diversification cannot be overstated. A company solely dependent upon equity-oriented products will have a much more volatile income stream than one marketing a more diversified portfolio. Increased volatility in earnings will lead to a less creditworthy business.

Accurately measuring profitability for VAs is not as straightforward as it might seem, especially in the short term. On a statutory basis, acquisition costs are expensed upfront, leading to statutory strain for companies growing rapidly.

Theoretically, GAAP is a better profit measure, which amortises VA DACs in line with expected future gross profits. However, caution is warranted when interpreting GAAP profits as, when markets fall, we have found that some managements are overly optimistic about expected future gross profits; hence, they remain more susceptible to future DAC adjustments, because these assumptions deflate when exposed to reality.

In order to facilitate comparison between all issuers and their products on a consistent basis, Moody's believes that it is helpful to have companies calculate and publicly disclose the present value of their VAs' future profits by using a constant, realistic gross-investment return projection, such as 8% for all equity investments. Similar standard assumptions can be developed for other asset classes and other capital market assumptions, such as volatility and interest rates. Disclosures regarding policyholder behaviour and their potential impact on capital and income would also be extremely helpful in comparing companies.

LIQUIDITY AND ASSET LIABILITY MANAGEMENT

There is no question that the industry has come a long way in quantifying and managing the risk of VA secondary guarantees. Given their increasing exposure to complex VA secondary guarantees, however, many companies still need to improve their risk management practices if they are to handle their increased exposures more effectively. Moody's believes that insufficient attention is being paid by some insurers to certain specific financial results that are unlikely but possible, at least in extreme tail scenarios, often when equity markets perform very poorly, equity market volatility increases, interest rates decline and policyholders become more efficient. Importantly, the definition of a "tail scenario" will differ depending on the VA features prevalent in a company's block of business. These scenarios can constrain economic, GAAP accounting and regulatory results, and we note that insurers have found it difficult to simultaneously manage all of these different ways of measuring risks and profits.

Overall, managements use three main tools to handle VA risk: product design, reinsurance and hedging (Moody's Investors Service 2005, 2006b, 2008). Companies can most effectively control the risks to which they are exposed by defining them through product design. Given the increased costs of hedging and the limited availability of reinsurance, product design may currently be the most desirable and cost-effective solution.

With the guarantees on mainstream VAs, prudent product design alone does not eliminate the need for reinsurance or hedging programmes. Faced with a lack of affordable reinsurance and the recognition of counterparty risk associated with reinsurers, many companies selling VAs have implemented hedging programmes over the past five years. This is a plus from a credit perspective, although the verdict on the true effectiveness of hedging programmes is yet to be fully determined. Given the sizeable reported hedge-breakage costs for the second half of 2008, it is clear that basis and execution risks are both significant.

Moreover, we believe that, for many hedging programmes, true economic effectiveness cannot be tested in the short term but, rather, can only be tested after there are more statistically credible observations related to policyholder behaviour. If policyholders behave much more efficiently than anticipated in tail scenarios, some insurers could possibly suffer material losses.

Many of the US publicly traded companies have historically focused on hedging GAAP earnings. After the severe equity market declines and high volatility in 2008 pressured companies' regulatory capital levels, managements increasingly added "macro hedges." These hedges are often designed to help mitigate the volatility associated with regulatory capital. It is vital to understand what companies are hedging and, just as importantly, what they are not hedging. In the longer term, it is essential that a company hedges economic exposure.

To help analyse VA risk and how companies are managing it, detailed information on the products themselves, as well as on the reinsurance and hedging programmes, is essential. Details are important because capital market and actuarial assumptions will drive the results. Understanding stress scenarios is especially crucial and valuable for analysts. Although management may not want to give away proprietary pricing information, providing stress tests under generic assumptions to quantify the risk is beneficial for analysts. For example, if the S&P 500 dropped by 20%, 30% and 40%, what would the impact be on earnings and capital levels?

The stress tests need to be carefully considered and may need to be customised for a company's product features. For example, for a company with material GMIB exposure, the worst scenario may be declining equity markets with a prolonged low interest rate scenario. Or, a worst-case scenario may be less intuitive: rising equity markets (at which time the benefit base may reset) followed by a severe market decline and low interest rates.

FINANCIAL FLEXIBILITY

Financial flexibility, as dictated by financial leverage/double leverage, earnings coverage, cashflow coverage and access to capital markets, is a key determinant of the insurer's credit profile. In general, higher-rated insurers tend to have less financial leverage, broader coverage and greater access to capital markets than their lower-rated peers.

For an insurance company with a material block of VAs, declining stock markets pushing down shareholders' equity can have an adverse impact on financial leverage and on earnings and/or cashflow coverage. The latter refers to the ability of management to move cash to the holding company to cover its cash needs. In the US the payout of dividends from the insurer to the holding company is generally limited by the greater of 10% of policyholder surplus or statutory operating earnings in the previous year. In some states, it is the lesser of the two.

Material declines in equity markets can also have an exaggerated impact on regulatory capital and earnings, placing pressure on financial flexibility. For example, if risk-based capital declines substantially, management may have less ability to move funds to the holding company.

PUTTING IT ALL TOGETHER

Ultimately, all of these factors are weighed together in order to come up with an insurance financial strength rating for the company. The resulting stand-alone credit profile (excluding support from a parent/affiliate) may also incorporate the management, governance and risk-handling characteristics of an insurer. For VA companies with guarantees, an assessment of risk management is an area of analytical focus. Significantly, the "stand-alone" profile may be different from the published rating. The published rating may reflect explicit guarantees or ownership by a larger organisation.

APPENDIX I: VARIABLE ANNUITY "BELLS AND WHISTLES"

- **Guaranteed Living Benefits (GLBs):** these serve to protect the annuity contract holders during their lifetimes, providing some form of equity participation with downside protection. GLBs come in various forms, including GMIBs, GMABs and GMWBs (see below).

- **Guaranteed Minimum Accumulation Benefits (GMABs):** a GMAB gives a floor on guaranteed account value return over a given time horizon. Recent designs have combined GMABs with GMWBs (see below).

- **Guaranteed Minimum Death Benefits (GMDBs):** these provide a guaranteed minimum death benefit to the beneficiary of a VA independent of the contract's actual cash value. The modest return of premium guarantee pays the beneficiary a minimum death benefit of the initial premium paid. Other guarantees provide for some additional degree of appreciation.

- **Guaranteed Minimum Income Benefits (GMIBs):** a GMIB gives the contract owner the right to annuitise a prescribed accumulated account value (benefit base), at a guaranteed annuitisation rate, after a contractually stated waiting period (typically seven or more years). Often, the right to annuitise is limited to a time window on each anniversary. Dollar-for-dollar withdrawals provide income as a percentage of the benefit base prior to annuitisation, without reducing the benefit base.

- **Guaranteed Minimum Withdrawal Benefits (GMWBs):** these allow the contract holder to take periodic withdrawals, such as 5–7% per year, of a prescribed base amount, which can be equal to the total deposits or, in the case of a VA with a step-up, the deposits plus market returns as of a specified date. At the time of writing in late 2009, it is the most popular GLB. Recent designs have allowed GMWB withdrawals for life.

- **Variable annuity secondary guarantees:** these are additional features added to the base VA product. They include GLBs and GMDBs.

APPENDIX II: BACKGROUND ON US REGULATORY CAPITAL REQUIREMENTS FOR VARIABLE ANNUITIES

Since the end of 2005, life-insurance companies selling VAs have been subject to capital requirements under C3 Phase II. This standard, which the NAIC developed in response to new guarantees offered in variable insurance products, represented one step towards incorporating the results of stochastic modelling into the determination of regulatory capital requirements.

To determine the additional asset requirement – the excess of the total amount of assets required to fund the guarantees over the statutory reserves held – the projected surplus, which is modelled over a range of stochastic scenarios for the life of the VA, is discounted to the start of the projection period. Once all scenarios have been run, the surplus required (shortfall in assets) in the worst 10% of the scenarios are averaged to determine the 90th percentile conditional tail expectation (CTE).

The overall minimum level of capital to be held is subject to a floor, as determined by a prescribed "standard scenario". Companies are able to incorporate hedging programmes into the analysis; however, no hedge rebalancing is recognised under the standard scenario. Both the lack of hedge rebalancing and severe market assumptions make the standard scenario the limiting scenario for a number of companies that have not reinsured business offshore to an affiliate.

For certain firms that have elected to "smooth" their C3 Phase II, the capital requirement is determined by weighting the calculation results from the previous year and the current year. In 2008, the "smoothing" effect mitigated the impact of C3 Phase II for a number of companies. In 2009, the smoothing effect will work against these insurers if equity markets improve.

APPENDIX III: THE C3 PHASE II SURVEY

Moody's annually collects proprietary information from the largest VA writers in order to accomplish two main goals. Firstly, we want to quantify the impact of a 30% drop in the equity markets on a statutory entity's RBC ratios.

Secondly, we can calculate "adjusted RBC" ratios to take into account the impact of "tail" or stress scenarios on companies' financial resources. Specifically, we can perform the following calculation

$$\text{Adjusted RBC ratio} = \frac{\text{TAC} - \text{CTE 98}}{\text{RBC} - \text{C3 Phase II RBC related charge}}$$

where TAC denotes the total adjusted capital. This ratio will be a supplemental part of our analysis of a company's capital adequacy; in other words, it is not the primary ratio that Moody's analysts use to evaluate capital, but it is another input for the analyst to consider in evaluating capital adequacy. The primary benefit of the adjusted RBC ratio is that it directly incorporates the "tail" risk of VA guarantees and removes the multiplicative impact of holding an arbitrary multiple (eg, 350%) of the regulatory capital requirement, as defined by C3 Phase II.

The impact of the adjustment on the RBC ratio will depend on the relationship of the CTE 98/CTE 90 ratio to the company's RBC level. Consider two companies with RBC ratios of 300%, with TAC equal to US$300 and RBC equal to US$100. If, for the first company, the capital requirement associated with CTE 98 is US$50 and that associated with CTE 90 is US$10, then the adjusted RBC ratio is

$$\frac{300 - 50}{100 - 10} = 278\%$$

Hence, because of the steep slope of the tail risk, the adjusted RBC ratio is less than the reported RBC ratio.

For the other company, if CTE 98[6] is US$20 and CTE 90 is US$10, then the adjusted RBC ratio is

$$\frac{300 - 20}{100 - 10} = 311\%$$

In this case, because there is less tail risk, the adjusted RBC ratio is greater than the reported RBC ratio.

1   Insurance financial strength ratings are assigned to life-insurance operating companies and are Moody's opinions of the ability of insurance companies to pay punctually senior policyholder claims and obligations.

2   Rating agencies may have different views about VAs as well as different rating processes and procedures; this chapter presents how one rating agency (Moody's Investors Service) incorporates VAs into its rating methodology for life insurers.

3   See Appendix I for definitions.

4   See the definition of GMIB in Appendix I for a description.

5   See Appendix II for a discussion of regulatory capital requirements for VAs and Appendix III for a discussion of the Moody's C3 Phase II survey.

6   The surplus required (shortfall in assets) in the worst 2% of the scenarios is averaged to determine the 98th percentile CTE.

REFERENCES

Moody's Investors Service, 2002, "Ghost of Bubbles Past: Equity Markets Haunt Variable Annuities", Report 76146, October.

Moody's Investors Service, 2003, "Big DAC Attack: Variable Annuity Writers Remain Vulnerable", Report 77304, February.

Moody's Investors Service, 2005, "Hedging the Bet: Variable Annuity 'Bells and Whistles'", Report 94553, October.

Moody's Investors Service, 2006a, "Moody's Global Rating Methodology for Life Insurers", Special Report 98207, September.

Moody's Investors Service, 2006b, "Variable Annuity Writers Improve Hedging For Embedded Options: Moody's Releases Results of Variable Annuity Hedging Survey", Report 96761.

Moody's Investors Service, 2008, "Variable Annuity Writer's Hedging Programs Tested by Market Turmoil", Report 110355, August.

Moody's Investors Service, 2009, "Variable Annuity Guarantees Test US Life Insurers' Regulatory Capital", Report 113860, January.

25

Liquidity in Global Derivatives Markets

Edward K. Tom, Naveed Choudri and James Masserio
Credit Suisse

As we have seen in the preceding chapters, derivatives can play a crucial role in managing the risks of variable annuity (VA) products. They may be used for hedging long-term volatility but the real question is whether the market for such derivatives is really liquid. In this chapter, we focus on this question, which is of special relevance for the risk management of VA products.

BACKGROUND

Historical examination of the markets reveals that legislative and regulatory actions often precipitate abrupt shifts in supply and demand for financial products. Accordingly, with respect to the market for long-dated (5–10 year) volatilities, C3 Phase II regulations, coupled with a host of other economic and accounting motivations, played a pivotal role in catalysing the transformation (beginning in 2005) of a sleepy and thinly traded market to a robust one which, by early 2008, traded upwards of US$500 million vega notional per annum: an amount roughly equivalent to the total vega commanded at the height of the entire convertibles market.

Since the Lehman Brothers' bankruptcy in September 2008, however, the market for long-dated volatility products has entered into a bit of a stalemate, whereby buyers of long-dated volatility are seemingly hesitant to transact sizeable volumes at offered price levels. Although the 30–50 basis point (bp) widening in long-dated bid–ask spreads may account for some loss of liquidity, it cannot fully explain the 70% decline in average weekly transactions in long-dated volatilities. This prompts the following questions:

- What has caused this implicit loss of liquidity?

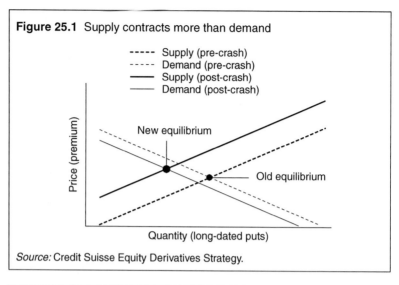

Figure 25.1 Supply contracts more than demand

- - - - Supply (pre-crash)
- - - - Demand (pre-crash)
───── Supply (post-crash)
───── Demand (post-crash)

New equilibrium

Old equilibrium

Price (premium)

Quantity (long-dated puts)

Source: Credit Suisse Equity Derivatives Strategy.

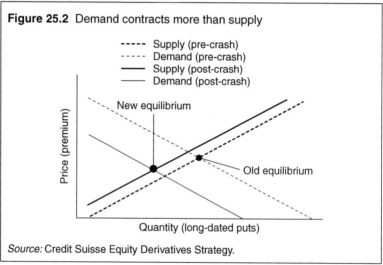

Figure 25.2 Demand contracts more than supply

- - - - Supply (pre-crash)
- - - - Demand (pre-crash)
───── Supply (post-crash)
───── Demand (post-crash)

New equilibrium

Old equilibrium

Price (premium)

Quantity (long-dated puts)

Source: Credit Suisse Equity Derivatives Strategy.

- Is this dissipation a temporary phenomenon or is it indicative of a permanent shift in the supply and demand relationship for long-dated volatility products?

Our analysis of trading flows indicates that the extraordinary level of market volatility experienced in the last quarter of 2008 is the primary culprit. Moreover, we also posit that the impact of last autumn's market turbulence may have been magnified by pre-existing structural trends within the VA industry itself. Together, these events have resulted in a situation in which consumers have decreased their appetite for long-dated premium while, at the same time, suppliers have decreased their proclivity to provide it. As illustrated in Figure 25.1, this has caused a supply–demand shift such that, regardless of the relative net changes in supply and demand, each and every equilibrium price point is associated with a lower quantity traded (ie, lowered liquidity).

In this chapter, we thus examine the structural and market dynamics responsible for the contraction in both demand-side and supply-side liquidity.

DEMAND-SIDE FACTORS

On the whole, insurers have traditionally been, and continue to be, the primary consumers of long-dated volatility, typically in the form of index puts. The degree of their appetite is contingent, in turn, upon two factors: the amount of long-dated exposure generated and, more importantly, the extent to which they desire to statically hedge this exposure. Interestingly, the extraordinary level of market volatility experienced over the financial year 2008–9 has served to depress both.

DEMAND POTENTIAL

At the onset of the long-dated market in 2005, the primary goal of insurers was to hedge existing exposures. As a result, the demand for long-dated volatility at that time was proportionate to the total US dollar assets under management of equity-linked VAs. However, as these "legacy" exposures were hedged, the ongoing demand for long-dated volatility became, and continues to be, largely a function of new sales.

Demand-side liquidity for long-dated puts, therefore, remained robust leading up to the Lehman Brothers' bankruptcy, as VAs until that point garnered an average growth rate of 10% per annum. The 2008 market crash, however, became a turning point that precipitated an investor aversion towards equity instruments, including the equity-linked VAs that drove the demand for long-dated hedges. As the demand for VAs waned, the bid for long-dated volatility weakened as well.

Despite the material significance of investor risk aversion, it is our belief that waning interest for VAs does not fully explain the growing illiquidity of long-dated volatilities. For 2009, the Life Insurance and Market Research Association (LIMRA) estimates that Guaranteed Minimum Benefits sales trend at US$154.8 billion per annum (compared with 2008 sales of US$182 billion). Assuming that 10-year at-the-money S&P 500 puts are used as the primary hedge for 100% of the exposure, this implies a healthy demand for approximately US$200 million of vega per annum. We hypothesise that it was the combined effects of a number of other factors instigated by the 2008 market volatility, including

- the demand for alternative hedges,
- term-structure roll-downs, and
- cheapening structures,

that also increased the price elasticity of long-dated volatilities and pared the actual demand for long-dated volatilities.

THE ELASTICITY OF DEMAND

In general, the demand for long-dated volatility had always been subject to varying degrees of price elasticity, as insurers not only controlled the proportion of assets they wished to hedge but also the type of hedging used. A 2007 survey conducted by the Society of Actuaries (Gilbert *et al* 2007) notes that only 42% of VA exposures were actually hedged using one of the four major types of hedges: delta hedging, static hedging, capital markets reinsurance and traditional reinsurance. Of the four, static hedges most directly affect the demand for long-dated volatility.

The popularity of static hedges, in turn, is a function of implied volatility levels. As 10-year implied volatility levels increased from an average of 23% in 2007 to nearly 38% in October 2008 (see Figure 25.3), the cost of buying premiums became much more expensive.

In response, insurers responded by rolling a portion of their static hedges "down the term structure". "Rolling down the term structure" refers to a situation in which the implied volatility term structure is upward sloping. In such a case, long-dated options are considerably more expensive than shorter-dated options. As an example,

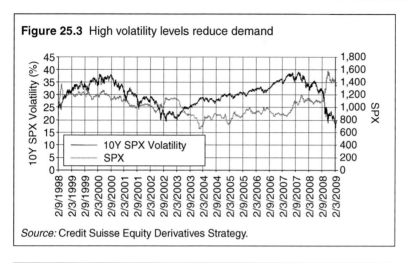

Figure 25.3 High volatility levels reduce demand

Source: Credit Suisse Equity Derivatives Strategy.

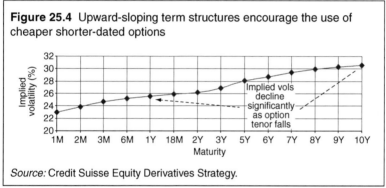

Figure 25.4 Upward-sloping term structures encourage the use of cheaper shorter-dated options

Source: Credit Suisse Equity Derivatives Strategy.

Figure 25.4 shows the S&P 500 implied volatility term structure as of August 13, 2009. In this instance, one-year implied volatilities are seven volatility points lower than 10-year implied volatilities. Using current market levels, this translates into savings of 32% per option.

Obviously, VA hedgers would be hesitant to use shorter-dated structures to hedge longer-dated exposures if the resulting substitution was very poor. However, a principal-components analysis of the term structure of volatility reveals that that is not the case. In fact, our analysis indicates that a large proportion (approximately four-fifths) of the daily change in the implied volatility term structure is attributable to parallel shifts. In other words, the use of shorter-dated volatilities can be quite effective in hedging longer dated exposures. (Of course, additional factors, eg, exposure to roll risk, would need to be taken into account when considering shorter-date hedging.)

This migration away from 10-year static hedges towards shorter-dated options has thereby increased the liquidity of shorter-dated tenures at the expense of longer-dated liquidity. Moreover, the roll-down effect has also been compounded by recent structural adaptations to address capital requirement issues. Thus, as a consequence of lowered demand for VA products and greater price elasticity for long-dated structures, demand-side liquidity has, by our estimates, curtailed the demand for long-dated volatilities to approximately US$80 million vega per annum, down from around US$500 million in 2008.

SUPPLY-SIDE FACTORS

Despite the pull-back in demand-side hedges, the long-dated volatility market would still provide a high degree of liquidity if the suppliers of long-dated volatility were willing to offer implied volatilities at lower levels. However, as the turbulent market conditions have suppressed insurer demand for long-dated hedges, so too has it constrained supply-side appetite to provide long-dated products.

Over the last four years, a number of entities including investment banks, pension funds and, most recently, hedge funds, have stepped in to offer long-dated volatility products. The ability (and desire) of these entities to sell what is, in essence, long-dated insurance on the market was based upon risk–reward assumptions generated by historical observations of the markets. Accordingly, the events brought forth by the credit crisis forced the suppliers of long-dated volatility to re-evaluate these assumptions as well as their appetite for warehousing risk.

INCREASED FOCUS ON CAPITAL

The typical products offered by the above-mentioned entities can be described as over-the-counter (OTC) puts and variance swaps with maturities ranging from five to ten years.

A major consequence of the credit crisis, though, has been an increased focus on the efficient use of capital as well as a general lessening of risk appetite; of course, both of these factors are inextricably linked. As a result, volatility traders at banks, pension funds and hedge funds have gravitated away from OTC products and towards listed instruments and shortened the duration of their desired exposures in favour of products with maturities of three years or less.

RISK MEASUREMENT

In addition to a declining risk appetite for issuing long-dated products, a paradigm shift in how the risk of these products are assessed has also contributed to the curtailment of supply-side liquidity.

In most banks, the amount of exposure a trader is allowed to carry on their books is a function of its value-at-risk (VaR). The total amount of VaR-adjusted exposure any given trader may take is referred to as their "risk budget". Prior to the credit crisis, VaR calculations for long-dated exposures reflected the extremely low-volatility regime from 2002 to 2007 and therefore consumed very little of a trader's risk budget.

After the Lehman Brothers' bankruptcy, however, long-dated instruments began to consume substantially more risk capital as VaR calculations began to incorporate levels of volatility that were double and triple those used by prior VaR historics. As a result, volatility traders had less VaR to work with; at the same time, long-dated instruments consumed more VaR. These risk budget allocation issues coupled with increasingly adverse mark-to-market valuations thereby resulted in a dissipation in supply-side liquidity for long-dated volatility.

OUTLOOK AND CONCLUDING REMARKS

Recent surveys of economic forecasts, investor sentiment and trading flows all seem to indicate that the equity markets have finally begun to recover from the market turbulence that catalysed the pullback of liquidity in long-dated volatilities. However, the turmoil itself precipitated what we believe to be a structural paradigm shift for both consumers and suppliers that is likely to result in a persistent if not permanent stagnation in long-dated liquidity.

On the demand side, insurers have introduced a series of adaptations and financial innovations that removes some of the path dependency inherent in their previous offerings. As a consequence, their overall need for long-dated hedges has lessened, as these "simplified" products can be more easily hedged using comparatively more liquid short-dated options.

On the supply side, following the severity and rapidness of autumn 2008's market decline, banks, pension funds and hedge funds have reassessed their assumptions of diversification and tail risk. As a result, these entities have simultaneously reduced their tolerance for long-dated risk and increased the premium required for taking on such exposures.

The combination of these two reinforcing effects forces us to conclude that a return of long-dated volatility to pre-crisis levels is unlikely in the foreseeable future.

Please read the Credit Suisse disclaimer at http://www.csfb.com/legal_terms/market_commentary_disclaimer.shtml

REFERENCES

Gilbert, C. L., K. Ravindran and R. R. Reitano, 2007, "Results of the Survey on Variable Annuity Hedging Programs for Life Insurance Companies", Report, Society of Actuaries.

Index

(page numbers in italic type relate to tables or figures)